BEYOND

ANIMAL

WELFARE

BEYOND ANIMAL WELFARE

The Art and Science of Wellness

TERRY L. MAPLE, PH.D.

Palmetto Publishing Group
Charleston, SC

Beyond Animal Welfare
Copyright © 2019 by Terry L. Maple, Ph.D.

ISBN-13: 978-1-64111-447-9
ISBN-10: 1-64111-447-9

Dedication

This book is dedicated to my mother, Evelyn May Maple, who taught me to be kind to animals, and to my dear wife, Addie, who spent the last fifty years being kind to me.

Front cover: Red-capped mangabey (*Cercocebus torquatus*) in the Zoo360 tunnel at the Philadelphia Zoo. Courtesy of Andy Baker and the Philadelphia Zoo.

CONTENTS

Foreword ix

Preface: A Life Worth Living xiii

Acknowledgments xix

Chapter 1   Beyond Animal Welfare · 1

Chapter 2   Evolution of a Construct · 24

Chapter 3   Efficacy of the Wellness Brand · 49

Chapter 4   Wild Animals and Wellness · 74

Chapter 5   Wellness-Inspired Zoo Design · 98

Chapter 6   Institutional Wellness Centers · · · · · · · · · · · · · · · · · · · 122

Chapter 7   Teaching the World About Wellness· · · · · · · · · · · · · · · · 144

Chapter 8   Reconciling Wellness and Welfare · · · · · · · · · · · · · · · · 160

Chapter 9   The Case for WELL Building Certification · · · · · · · · · · · · 175

Bibliography. 187

Index 210

FOREWORD

D r Terry Maple's been on a roll for a while now, and I'm rolling right with him on his zoo and aquarium animal wellness strategy. First introduced in his 1993 book *Zoo Man,* the concept of moving beyond animals coping to animals thriving in an optimal state of welfare is expanded in his 2013 book with Bonnie Perdue, *Zoo Animal Welfare.* This idea was further concentrated and integrated in his 2016 *Professor at the Zoo,* along with essential supporting concepts such as the "empirical zoo". Now the multi-layered wellness concept has evolved as the focus of *Beyond Animal Welfare,* as Terry writes:

I've written this book to help others understand the broad scope of the wellness construct and why it is so useful in unifying our messages about conservation and wellness and for applications to both animal populations, captive and wild, and human communities throughout the world.

In typical Maple style, this edition wanders frequently along the back roads of personal discovery. These journeys add authenticity as well as interest, celebrating earlier innovators, less well known, but not less valued students and co-workers and connecting the dots in a complex and often confounding field to reveal patterns of real possibilities. For less patient readers like myself, the good stuff, the specific strategies, successful examples and recommended actions, are clearly presented, often with highly quotable quotes, one of Terry's particular strengths.

One of the appealing notions presented is that welfare is graded from bad to good, while wellness has no upper limit. This statement is a challenge that our best still isn't as good as it could be, that improvement, adaption and innovation will always be needed. I also strongly support a concept interwoven through *Beyond Welfare*, but worthy of stronger declaration, that welfare and wellbeing must apply not only to the animals in our care, but to all stakeholders affected by our actions using win-win strategies.

I first met Terry at a zoo conference at Lincoln Park Zoo in 1983. Soon after I was delighted to receive his invitation to lecture his environmental psychology class for architecture students at Georgia Tech in Atlanta. Terry describes the fruitful outcome of the meeting in Chapter 5, Wellness-Inspired Zoo Design. Later collaboration resulted in two additional major turning points in my career: 1) The 1985 publication of my foundation paper "Design and Perception", the theory behind the design of immersion exhibits based upon fundamentals of human behavior. Terry was then founding Editor of the new scientific journal *Zoo Biology*, saw merit in the paper, published it and it has become widely cited in discussions of naturalistic zoo exhibits. 2) As the new Director of the Atlanta Zoo, Terry hired me, my partner Gary Lee, Nevin Lash and our firm CLR Design in 1985 to develop his zoo master plan and thereafter collaborate with him on the design and implementation of most of their major new exhibits and visitor facilities for the next eighteen years.

Through these and many subsequent discussions and collaborations, I've found Terry Maple to be that most unique of leaders, both knowledgeable specialist and cross cutting collaborator, careful evaluator and risk-taking innovator, combining warrior commitment and action with empathy and life-long support, especially for his students, past and present. I've long maintained that innovation isn't found in the mainstream, but in the often-chaotic collision of widely different philosophies, perspectives, technologies and politics. This seems to be Terry Maple's natural habitat. Innovation carries risk, but stagnation in last year's best practice and proven low risk approaches carries the danger of obsolescence, and in the context of this book, the certain danger of losing public support, the social license, essential for institutional survival. That path leads to extinction, and properly so. Put another way, the twin principals of ecology, be it wildlife or urban life, are that everything is connected and everything changes.

Purposeful change, guided by science, art and empathy, in support for the sustained wellness of the animals, plants, staffs, volunteers, visitors and businesses in our care; what could possibly be better?

I'll conclude with this admonition from *Beyond Animal Welfare*:

> *"To simply survive, zoo and aquarium visionaries must design and build an entire planet of credible zoos and aquariums".*

Jon Charles Coe, Landscape Architect, Environmental Planner & Zoo Designer.

A LIFE WORTH LIVING

A few years ago, Bonnie Perdue and I wrote *Zoo Animal Welfare*, summarizing what we knew about animal welfare science at the time of its publication in 2013. Based on data collected by Springer/Verlag, the book has been very well received. Although growth in the science of animal welfare is impressive, I've taken the opportunity to think bigger about the subject and expand our expectations for animals in captivity. *Beyond Animal Welfare* introduces the wellness construct, a bold step beyond traditional models of animal welfare. The book is written as a personal account of how I discovered the wellness construct in my journey through the zoo world, and began to see its value as an approach to managing wildlife. My dual career as a university professor and a zoo executive has been replete with challenges along the way; in short, a life worth living. All of the books I've written were meant to be readable by a general audience; I hope I've succeeded in the present case.

In 1970 I entered the doctoral program in psychobiology at the University of California (UC), Davis. I began to study rhesus monkey social attachment in the spring of 1971 in the laboratory of Professor Gary D. Mitchell, an academic disciple of the iconic Harry F. Harlow. My opportunity to work with a population of rhesus monkeys (*Macaca mulatta*) at the California National Primate Research Center was a good fit with my interests and my experience.

After he joined the Davis faculty in 1966, Professor Mitchell received a group of male rhesus monkeys that had grown up in Harlow's lab. While I had no problem studying these psychologically damaged animals, on another level I felt sorry for them. I knew that I was not constitutionally capable of separating young monkeys from their mothers to create the conditions of isolation that were required in Harlow's standard research protocols. There were enough isolates to study, I reasoned; surely, we didn't need to create any others. Further, I made a pledge to myself that I would try to find a way to repair the psychological damage resulting from the experimental conditions of isolation and social deprivation imposed on monkeys and apes in research centers. My growing understanding of psychopathology led me to focus on primates in zoo collections as I knew that they too could also be victims of social deprivation. In those days, zoos throughout the nation were populated by primates disabled by serious socioemotional disorders induced by shortcomings in living conditions.

Although animal rights groups vilified Harlow for his primate studies (Blum, 2011), I appreciated the fact that his exhaustive demonstration of the effects of separation, deprivation, and isolation in the laboratory were all the evidence I needed to advocate for normalized living conditions in zoos. This advocacy was revealed in my later publications; my presentations at regional, national, and international meetings; in sessions in the nation's capital where I argued for reform, and in my federal agency consulting engagements. I took the first bold step with *Captivity and Behavior: Primates in Breeding Colonies, Laboratories, and Zoos* (1979), edited with my mentor Gary Mitchell and my colleague Joe Erwin. As we prepared this book, I was careful not to be too critical of the institutions where I conducted my research, but one chapter I wrote required candor, not diplomacy. "Great Apes in Captivity: The Good, the Bad, and the Ugly" was an unusual insider account of what was wrong with zoos and primate research labs in the late seventies. It formed the foundation of a career of constructive criticism, which became an academic specialty of mine. My ideas and opinions were encouraged by architecture and design colleagues and collaborators who were eagerly taking down hard buildings and replacing them with habitable, soft landscapes throughout the country (Jones, Coe, & Paulson, 1976; Coe, 1985; Wineman & Choi, 1991). The 1980s were a truly transformative period in the history of zoo design, and I was a foot soldier happily immersed in it. Atlanta's old zoo was a veritable *tabula rasa*, and we were preparing to dramatically change it.

Harlow consciously borrowed from the human literature when he was formulating and testing monkey models of behavior (Harlow & Mears, 1971). His insight is instructive as I have also discovered many useful applications to animal welfare derived from the research history of human wellness (Dunn, 1961) and the human potential movement known as humanistic psychology (Maslow, 1962). Coincidentally, Abraham Maslow was Harlow's first graduate student at the University of Wisconsin. Harlow's research approach prepared me to advocate for changes in the way zoo and laboratory primates were managed and exhibited. This became my highest research priority for the students and collaborators in my graduate group at Emory University and Georgia Tech for the next thirty years. In 1970, one of my mentors at Davis, environmental psychologist Robert Sommer, introduced me to the published work of the Swiss ethologist Heini Hediger, a professor at the University of Zurich and the director respectively of the Bern, Basel, and Zurich Zoos. Hediger's abundance of publications were focused on the psychology of captive wildlife, but his books and papers also influenced a generation of psychologists who studied mental hospitals and prisons and other institutionalized human populations (Sommer, 2008). Building on Hediger's findings, Sommer's classic book *Tight Spaces* (1974) included a chapter on the hard architecture of zoos. The contrast between hard and soft architecture defines the difference between traditional and naturalistic zoological parks.

In the formative years of my career at the academy, I was largely a theoretician, but fate intervened, and I was given the opportunity to implement and test my ideas as the reform director of Zoo Atlanta. When I entered academia as a young professor, deficiencies in the physical and social environment were factors in the etiology of animal psychopathology. I saw clearly that superior facilities were needed to deliver a high quality of life for laboratory and zoo animals. What we called revitalization was in fact nothing short of revolutionary change. Because my students and I have been able to study the worst and the best conditions in zoological facilities continuously for a long period of time, I have a deep understanding of what constitutes high standards and best practices in exhibition and management. Modern zoos reflect institutional and organizational commitments to a global vision of animal welfare based on decades of research and practice by animal welfare scientists. A rich history of institutional change, reform, and revitalization inspired me to write this first book on the art and science of wellness. I chose the title *Beyond Animal Welfare* with considerable thought. I did not mean "instead of" animal welfare. I was not suggesting "better" than animal welfare. In fact, I intended the word to convey the meaning "to be more than or not limited by" animal welfare.

My perspective on wellness is somewhat unique in the universe of animal welfare scientists. I was twice a chief executive, and my ideas have had to be balanced according to the needs of a complex organization with a bottom line. For this reason, I was at first cautious in promoting the significance of the wellness construct. I still believe it is not fully tested by enough institutions to know that it is the holy grail of welfare. For one thing, to fully implement a wellness regime, the leaders of any institution must be prepared to invest the necessary funding to build truly visionary exhibits and facilities. Institutions that are not strong financially will struggle to meet elevated wellness standards. On the other hand, failure to reach these standards will eventually lead to public dissatisfaction with the status quo. If animals are perceived to be suffering, or just barely coping, the future of the zoo may be at risk. The best way to achieve wellness is to create a long-term plan, commit to a vision of change, and step by step, bring each exhibit into compliance with the new norms. I recommend starting with the exhibits and facilities that are in greatest need of reform. I hasten to add that *Beyond Animal Welfare* is not a comprehensive textbook on the science of animal welfare; it is a primer on wellness provided to demonstrate how wellness can be deployed to advance and extend animal welfare standards and practices. Needless to say, wellness is not a threat to the primacy of animal welfare. It is simply a platform that runs parallel to the mainstream. The rich history of animal welfare science leads inevitably to a construct like wellness.

My interest in wellness for wildlife has led me to examine my own health and wellness, and this is one of the most unique and promising features of the construct. Wellness applies to all living things. Although humanity long ago accepted the utility of wellness, it is a new idea for zoo and aquarium professionals. In the pages that follow, I will fully define and explore wellness and demonstrate how it can be applied to design and to operate humane and ethical zoos that bring out the best in each and every individual. Through the creative fusion of wellness and conservation, we will lift and extend the priorities for all of us to equitably share the natural resources of our planet with all other forms of life. It is our duty to identify the key variables that ensure the high standard of a life worth living is achievable. Life in the zoo should not be too easy. Effort in overcoming a challenge builds a healthy resiliency. We must find a way to deliver these opportunities to thrive in a world of constraints and limitations.

After the publication of the Portuguese edition of *Professor in the Zoo*, I decided that my next book should be released simultaneously in Portuguese and Spanish, so I approached Palmetto Publishing in Charleston, South Carolina, to coordinate three editions for marketing and sale through Kindle Direct Publishing/Amazon. Now is the time for the wellness strategy to be widely distributed to zoo professionals and students beyond the English-speaking world. It is an unfortunate fact that there are many zoos and aquariums that are in serious trouble. I believe that *Beyond Animal Welfare* will be a helpful resource for reform-minded zoo leaders who need encouragement and support to dramatically improve substandard institutions. Together we can build a better world for animals and people where wellness is the new normal.

ACKNOWLEDGMENTS

This book would not have been possible without the continuing support of an anonymous philanthropist who has supported my work for the past five years. These have been among the most productive and satisfying years of my life and I am deeply grateful for her confidence in me. I am also indebted to my many colleagues and friends at the Jacksonville Zoo and Gardens who have created an institution that is not afraid of new ideas. I am happy to say that wellness is not just a theory at the Jacksonville Zoo, it is a roadmap that we are implementing together day by day. As an operating philosophy, wellness has prospered in Jacksonville because of the strong leadership of zoo director, Tony Vecchio and the continuing support and encouragement of our board of directors. We are also fortunate for the close partnership we enjoy with the University of North Florida. I thank Dean of the College of Sciences, George Rainbolt and the members of his administrative team, Lev Gasparov and Anne-Marie Campbell; and colleagues in the biology and psychology departments who have enthusiastically supported the elevation of Jacksonville Zoo and Gardens to its special position as an emerging empirical zoo. Finally, I thank the many former students and current collaborators who read portions of the manuscript and offered valuable suggestions and direction. The critical comments of Jon Coe and Chris Kuhar were especially helpful as I shaped the contents of this book. I am indebted to Professors Richard K. Davenport, Martin T. Gipson, Harry F. Harlow, Heini Hediger, Gary D. Mitchell, and Robert Sommer, mentors during my career who influenced my thinking and encouraged me to mentor others. My zoo career would have been very brief were it not for the continuing encouragement of Ron Forman, Carolyn Boyd Hatcher, E.H. Loveland, Robert C. Petty, Clare Richardson, Deen

Day Sanders family, Anderson D. Smith, Lessie Smithgall, and Mayor Andrew Young. Many thanks. I was able to experiment with the wellness construct in Palm Beach, Florida thanks to the generous support of Melvin and Claire Levine. I am also indebted to the wellness team in Jacksonville; Dan Maloney, Valerie Segura and Megan Morris who enthusiastically led our transition to a zoo where thriving was our goal. Fatima Ramis was diligent in helping me with technical issues including the bibliography. My editors at Palmetto skillfully prepared the manuscript to meet my specifications. They are true professionals. Finally, in dedicating this book to my mother and my wife, Addie, I acknowledge the importance of family to all who seek out solitude to think and to write. Unconditional love drives creativity and confidence, the fuel necessary for serious scholarship to advance. Needless to say, I am solely responsibility for any errors or omissions in this book.

Terry L. Maple, Ph.D.
Fernandina Beach, Florida

Chapter 1

BEYOND ANIMAL WELFARE

To properly understand the limits of animal welfare and the promise of wellness, we must examine the positions taken by associations responsible for the welfare of animals in managed human care. For example, the Association of Zoos and Aquariums (AZA), headquartered in Silver Spring, Maryland, is concerned with the animal's collective physical, mental and emotional states over a period of time, measured on a continuum from good to poor. Lincoln Park Zoo uses the same definition, but they substitute the word *great* for *good*. Similarly, the American Veterinary Medical Association considers welfare as an indication of overall mental and physical health. By this standard, assessments of animal welfare require institutions exhibiting animals to meet their mental and physical needs. The approach advocated by these organizations is not yet aspirational, but it is recognized as a reasonably good starting point. Poor welfare must be avoided; good welfare must prevail. Great welfare is a synonym for wellness. In fact, institutions that do not use the term *wellness* are actually moving in the direction of wellness. AZA accreditation standards now reflect optimal standards of welfare. In a discussion about AZA standards, an interview distributed by Zoo Advisors consultants, Jill Mellen (2019) recently stated that "our charge is to create a situation where animals thrive under human care." It is quite possible for welfare, wellness, and well-being to coexist as labels with slightly different meanings while reflecting a comparable commitment to higher standards and better practices. Some colleagues have told me they prefer to stay with welfare, but they appreciate the distinction I am making between welfare and wellness.

On the other hand, the World Organization for Animal Health focuses on how animals cope with their living conditions. An animal is thought to be in a good state of welfare if it is healthy, comfortable, well-nourished, safe, and able to express innate behavior patterns while not suffering from unpleasant states such as pain, fear, and distress. Suffering is not tolerated in accredited zoos and aquariums, but coping can sometimes drift into suffering. I believe most of the animals living in modern zoological facilities are coping well with the conditions of life in captivity, but thriving is the preferred alternative to coping. In the published overview of animal welfare in *Fowler's Zoo and Wild Animal Medicine* (Volume 9) edited by Miller, Lamberski, and Calle (2018), Paul-Murphy and Molter provide a table of guiding principles for assessing animal welfare. The last category in the list is labeled "opportunities to thrive." Included in this category are the following requirements: (a) a well-balanced, species-specific diet; (b) species-specific substrates that enable animals to self-maintain; (c) supportive environments that increase the likelihood of optimal health; (d) quality spaces and appropriate social groupings that encourage the expression of species-specific behavior; and (e) living conditions that permit the animal to exercise choice and control. Zoo animals that can do these things are no longer coping; they are thriving. Animal welfare scientists have warmed up to the term *thriving* whether they embrace wellness or not. The historic shift from suffering to coping to thriving is depicted in Figure 1.1 from our publication in *Zoo Biology* (Maple & Bocian, 2013). Thriving is becoming the goal of every zoo that is seeking upgrades to their facilities. With thriving as our goal, it is essential that we learn to recognize thriving when we see it. Soon after the *Blackfish* controversy erupted, SeaWorld Entertainment produced television commercials asserting that their killer whales were thriving. Although SeaWorld doubled the space for orcas, it is not nearly enough. Orcas cannot thrive in sea parks as they are currently configured.

When I began to examine the wellness construct as director of the Palm Beach Zoo in 2005, the zoo profession was just beginning to prioritize animal welfare in its accreditation and membership standards. Animal care standards and practices in zoos and aquariums throughout the world are advancing rapidly, setting a pace for quality improvement that requires new funding, new policies, and new ideas. Without adopting wellness as the natural alternative to welfare, zoos and aquariums are behaving as if they have in fact moved beyond welfare, hence the title of this book. It is no longer enough to simply provide acceptable surroundings for captive wildlife; we have to do better than that. Although traditional ideas about animal welfare have driven progress for animals in agriculture, biomedicine, aquariums, and zoos, the focus on minimal regulatory standards has served as a cap on reform. To this end, zoo visionaries from within and without the zoo profession have created new ways of presenting animals and new ways of activating them. The trend today is to reform our exhibit standards and management practices so that welfare is optimized. Accreditation standards at AZA are now driving this trend. Whether you call it optimal or great welfare or wellness or the triumph of an institutional commitment to psychological well-being, we are no longer satisfied with mediocre performance. Welfare must be elevated to its highest form to meet public expectations while driving our own high standards of husbandry and managed care. I've never met a zoo director, curator, keeper, consulting architect, or veterinarian who didn't want the best for the animals in their care. It is very gratifying to acknowledge this trend to optimal standards and practices is real, robust, and resilient. In the history of AZA, there has never been a time when zoo leaders were more unified in their pursuit of excellence in animal care. There are specialists in every zoo and aquarium dedicated to meeting or exceeding the current standards. The steady advance of standards supported by the AZA accreditation process requires that every zoo and aquarium commit to a process that is thoughtful and inclusive. Although the expression of such high standards will not be uniform, they are in reach of any zoo whose leaders have prepared to achieve them.

LAUNCHING THE JACKSONVILLE WELLNESS PROGRAM

The chief executive of the Jacksonville Zoo and Gardens, Tony Vecchio, once worked for me as Zoo Atlanta's curator of mammals. During the time we worked together, we were engaged in the transformation of a substandard zoo that had become an industry pariah. Tony's commitment to reform helped launch Zoo Atlanta as an innovator in exhibition and animal management. As he rose through the ranks to become a successful zoo director in Rhode Island and Portland, Oregon, he earned his reputation as an educator and thought leader. Once retired from my own executive career, I jumped at the chance to join him in Jacksonville, Florida, as a consultant in 2014. I had just completed a three-year engagement at the San Francisco Zoo where I successfully installed the first wellness program in a zoological setting. In recruiting me to become a member of the Jacksonville zoo team, his exact words were "I want you to do for us what you did for the San Francisco Zoo." He was aware that wellness was different from welfare, and he wanted to explore its potential in a zoo that was already a leader and an innovator among AZA zoos and aquariums. By this time I had examined the wellness construct for more than a decade, but I was cautious in promoting it to others. I wanted my colleagues to investigate and test the construct, kick its tires to see how it worked for them, but it took time for the idea to germinate. I knew that what we did in Jacksonville would be a formidable challenge. For this reason, I worked with Tony Vecchio and Deputy Zoo Director Dan Maloney to build a wellness team comprised of academic partners, talented students, and a few key staff. Since there was only one other wellness operating unit in North America, we knew we were conducting an experiment that would be widely emulated if we were successful. Tony's approach is to manage a small paid staff and reach out to the entire staff to build an institutional culture that embraces conservation and wellness. We are doing just that.

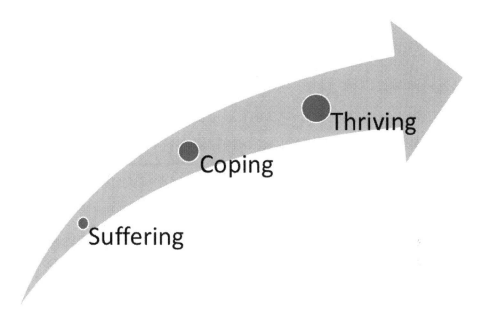

FIGURE 1.1. TRANSITION TO WELLNESS (THRIVING). AFTER MAPLE AND BOCIAN, 2013.

During my West Coast engagement to introduce the wellness construct, the San Francisco Zoo team made the transition to wellness fairly quickly. Leadership made sure the zoo staff understood that wellness was a significant upgrade to traditional animal welfare. They also knew that some reforms could be made easily, while others would await the construction of new exhibits. I used the phrase "wellness-inspired design" to describe the process of converting exhibits to facilitate the outcome we were seeking. A few of their exhibits already reflected wellness ideas, but the word was not in use when these innovative exhibits opened. For example, the Hearst Grizzly Gulch exhibit for grizzly bears (*Ursus arctos*) at the San Francisco Zoo provided a shallow, riverine setting, seeded regularly with living fish. The natural behavior patterns elicited by these exhibit features fit the definition of thriving. Once the zoo started to market wellness as its brand, it was possible to aggressively promote naturalistic design as a new approach to exhibition (see Chapter 5). The next task for me was to suggest that the zoological society hire a full-time leader in wellness who would be responsible for implementing a comprehensive menu of change. A national search attracted many qualified candidates. I thought the job would attract a lot of younger colleagues, but I was surprised when a number of highly qualified zoo biologists entered the competition. Dr. Jason Watters relocated from the Brookfield (Chicago) Zoo to become San Francisco's first "Vice President for Wellness and Animal Behavior." No zoo professional in North America had ever been appointed with this unique job title. Once Jason settled in the West, my temporary assignment was complete. An added benefit with Jason's recruitment was his stature as the current editor of the journal *Zoo Biology*. With his hire, San Francisco, California, became the new headquarters of this prestigious journal and a major disseminator of publications in animal welfare science. Since his arrival at the helm of the new wellness unit, Dr. Watters has equated "optimal animal welfare" to "wellness." This is the same definition my research collaborators offered in a recent special issue of the journal *Behavioural Processes* (Maple & Bloomsmith, 2018).

My three-year engagement in San Francisco was supported by a donation from the Stanton Family Fund. This generous gift reflected the concerns of Board Chair Dave Stanton, who wanted better facilities and improved welfare for the zoo's entire collection. His support was essential as I began to tutor zoo staff and board members on the opportunities for significant reform. I never expected to duplicate this funding scenario in my next consulting engagement, but the San Francisco experience opened doors for me in Florida. Once Tony and I began to discuss how I might work in Jacksonville, I offered to find funding from philanthropists who had supported my work in the past. In 2014 an anonymous donor who was familiar with my work history agreed to make a generous gift to launch the wellness project at the Jacksonville Zoo and Gardens. I promised that I would write a new book as my first contribution to an emerging global wellness strategy. *Professor in the Zoo* was published in 2016. It is interesting how this book is shaping zoo policies around the world. A Portuguese edition was initiated after I spoke in Brasilia, Brazil, in 2018 thanks to the efforts of my colleague Igor Oliveira Braga de Morais, who translated the book. Published in 2019, the Portuguese-language edition (*O Professor Ni Zoologico*) is now available on demand at Amazon.

Building on my collaborations in San Francisco, I began to think about how we could build a model wellness program at the Jacksonville Zoo. The zoo was getting my services at no cost since my compensation was provided by a donor, but I needed an assistant who could help me on the ground. Tony agreed to provide start-up funds for this purpose, so I contacted a young professional whom I had met while I was working in California. Valerie Segura was about to graduate from a master's program in behavior analysis at the University of the Pacific. Because I had a need for students to help me observe animals at the nearby San Francisco Zoo, I asked her if she had the time to drive to the zoo a few times each week. She proved to be a valuable employee. When I returned to Florida, I thought of Valerie and invited her to join the wellness team in Jacksonville. As a native Californian who reluctantly left the state to work at Emory University in Atlanta, Georgia, in 1975, I knew it wouldn't be simple or easy for Valerie to relocate to Florida, but I am happy she did. She formed the backbone of our wellness program and proved to be a prodigious worker. Because of her background in applied behavior analysis, I assigned her the title "Applied Animal Behavior Analyst." It was our intent to make behavior analysis the initial focus of our wellness program.

I've consistently championed applied behavior analysis for its potential as a zoo management tool. Behavior analysts have worked in zoos and aquatic parks for many years, resulting in some important publications such as *Don't Shoot the Dog: The New Art of Teaching and Training by* Karen Pryor (2006). In recent years, however, Skinnerian animal labs have fallen out of fashion in academia, a victim to the rise of cognitive psychology and relentless pressure from animal rights activists. Without the guiding lights of imbedded operant conditioning experts, zoos and aquariums have relied on trainers tutored by other trainers. Elephant "handling" is the training tradition most distant from behavior analysis given the handlers' history of working with elephants in carnivals and circuses before they were hired by zoos. You had to respect the best of these elephant handlers as they risked their lives to train these powerful creatures, including fierce bull elephants. The fundamental difference between circus trainers and behavior analysts is the former's reliance on aversive training techniques. The man who trained Zoo Atlanta's first African elephants, Alan Campbell, a native of Jacksonville, was killed in 1994 by a berserk elephant he was hired to calm and control in Honolulu, Hawaii. At the time of his death, he was widely regarded as the best elephant trainer in the world. It seemed to me that zoos employing former circus personnel would benefit from connecting trainers from an entertainment background with the more advanced expertise of academic behavior analysts. Valerie and I made this case in a paper we wrote for *The Behavior Analyst* (Maple & Segura, 2014). We advocated returning to an earlier time when there were many applied behavior analysts working with marine mammals and other species with support from aquariums, zoos, and the federal government. In those days, many serious scientists were studying bottlenose dolphins (*Tursiops truncatus*) with funding from the United States Navy, the National Institute of Mental Health, and the National Aeronautics and Space Administration. With funding so scarce today, the need to use operant methods to enhance psychological well-being will likely be sustained by individual donors and private foundations. Another wellspring for applied scientists is the Animal Behavior Society's Certified Applied Animal Behaviorists program. The field of applied animal behavior specializes in the behavior of companion animals through behavior modification; animal welfare and enrichment tactics; the behavior of farm, zoo, and lab animals; and some applied field studies. People with Animal Behavior Society certification are also qualified to work in zoos and aquariums.

The blending of animal behavior and behavior analysis was purpose driven. When Valerie arrived in Jacksonville in 2015, we understood that our wellness program would operate from a foundation of research with a special interest in practice and the delivery of psychological services. These synergistic interests were illuminated once we connected the dots between comparative and clinical psychology (e.g., Maple & Marston, 2016; Maple & Segura, 2017). Thus, from the beginning, wellness at the Jacksonville Zoo was both basic and applied. Valerie was so successful in balancing these perspectives that she was recently promoted to curator of wellness and animal behavior. We anticipated that more applied behavior positions in the zoo and aquarium profession would emerge as our unique program and Valerie's notable achievements become better known, and indeed, this is beginning to happen. An example of this promising trend is the decision by Fresno Chafee Zoo to hire a "wellness supervisor" to serve in their newly formed animal welfare department. They honored our work in Jacksonville by reaching out to recruit our own Megan Morris. With so many new exhibits at Fresno Zoo, it is a zoo that is poised to experience significant improvements in quality of life for zoo animals. Megan will have the opportunity to help Fresno become a wellness leader on the West Coast.

FIGURE 1.2. FATIMA RAMIS STUDIES GIRAFFE SOCIAL ORGANIZATION IN JACKSONVILLE. (JENNIFER GRISSOM).

An axiom in animal welfare circles suggests that many species exhibited in zoos are poorly understood by the caregivers who manage them.
This is not the fault of the caregivers; the science of zoo biology is just getting started. Superior care requires that we learn about the specific needs of
each and every species. Therefore, the first priority of our wellness program
had to be a discovery process. If there was an adequate body of literature
on the species, we were obligated to read that literature. For animals where
there was no paper trail or history of research, it was necessary to plan
studies to learn what we needed to know. Without a basic understanding
of a species' behavior, social organization, activity, food preferences, and
basic needs, we cannot arrange its living conditions to encourage thriving.
Successful wellness outcomes require detailed information on behavior and
natural history. Welfare standards and practices are advancing so rapidly
that many zoos are attempting to gather data on every animal in their collection to calculate its welfare, but data without an understanding of how
the animal behaves in the wild is a shot in the dark. I discovered this when
I began to study zoo orangutans in 1978. After the birth of a male, I observed its mother repeatedly mounting and thrusting her genitalia against
the infant. Thinking like a clinical psychologist, I immediately concluded
it was an abnormal behavior. When I reported this to my senior colleague,
Professor Richard K. Davenport, who had studied orangutan behavior in
the wild, he asked me how I knew it was abnormal. Of course, I didn't
really know the origin of this odd behavior; I jumped to this conclusion
without sufficient information. In the years my students and I studied
mother-infant relationships, we observed many cases of newborns inexpli-
cably mounted by captive chimpanzee, gorilla, and orangutan mothers. I
still don't completely understand it, but I might have interpreted the phenomenon as "poor welfare" if we had operated with the same zeal in 1978
as we do today. Behavior data cannot be an indication of welfare if we don't
know what is regarded as the norm for a given species. Primate psychologist, Frans de Waal, made a similar point when he asked the question "Are
we smart enough to understand how smart animals are?" De Waal's best-
selling book (de Waal, 2017) demonstrates that he is one scientist who does
understand the continuity of intelligence from animals to humankind and

the biases of our own species when it comes to objectively describing the abilities of all other animals. So how can we know if we are actually enhancing mental well-being with any of our actions as their caregivers? Our science is imperfect, but we do them an injustice if we don't accept the idea that they think a lot like we do. If we continue to study the animals we exhibit in zoos and those who reside in nature, we will soon be able to provide them with the opportunities they need to thrive in managed human care.

THE VALUE OF DEDICATED STUDENTS

During the 50 years I have been supervising graduate students, they have made many key discoveries that have helped us to achieve higher standards and better practices in animal care. When we began our studies of giant pandas in 1995, pandas in zoos were not reproducing. Observations of social development and parenting by Rebecca Snyder in our panda research lab and by scientists at the San Diego Zoo generated new information on maternal norms (Snyder et al., 2003). It continues to be our belief that pandas are taken from their mothers too early, producing a deprivation effect similar to the effects of premature separation on rhesus monkeys (Harlow, 1971; Snyder et al., 2006). The tradition of loaning pairs of pandas for exhibition by other zoos was also a factor in their dismal record of reproduction. Pandas don't live in pairs in the wild. We also learned more about how giant pandas literally see the world. In an experiment using operant methods, Kelling et al. (2006) discovered color vision in Zoo Atlanta's giant pandas, an ability that had not been previously revealed. Another new finding by scientists from the University of Vienna (Baotic, Sicks, & Stoeger, 2015) is the discovery that giraffes are not silent after all as they have been found to emit a low frequency humming vocalization audible at 92 Hz. This discovery was reported after 947 hours of audio recordings in three European zoos. We are discovering new things about animals every day in zoos with our dedicated scientific programs.

Because we know so little about even common zoo animals, wellness research must begin with basic studies including comprehensive ethograms of each species represented in the collection. To widely share knowledge with zookeepers, curators, educators, and veterinarians, we will need to invite outside experts in universities to form scientific partnerships. Animal welfare priorities do not permit exemptions for little-known species; all zoo animals must be evaluated and understood to provide the best care possible. Academic entomologists, for example, know insects much better than most of us in the zoo. At Zoo Atlanta I was able to recruit the services of Professor Duane Jackson, an academic psychologist at Morehouse College who specialized in stick insects, to serve as the zoo's part-time curator of insects. When he wasn't teaching at the university, he was helping us develop this unique section of our collection. Working with students, he also wrote and published papers on visitor behavior. I had the pleasure of taking him to Africa when we made a film about Kenya wildlife. His interpretation of dung beetle behavior was illuminating. Professor Jackson became so valuable to the zoo that he eventually ascended to a position on the Zoo Atlanta board of directors.

TIES WITH ACADEMIA

In previous publications my colleagues and I have reviewed the importance of zoos and aquariums partnering with colleges and universities (Finlay & Maple, 1986; Maple, 1999; Anderson et al., 2008; Maple & Lindburg, 2008; Maple & Bashaw, 2010; Maple & Perdue, 2013; Maple, 2016; Maple & Sherwen, 2019). Starting at Emory University and continuing with colleagues at Georgia Tech, we were innovators in the use of applied behavior analysis. We applied operant methods to stop aggressive behavior and overcome fear, we practiced reliable techniques to change negative behavior patterns to positive ones in primates and other species, and we taught undergraduates how to use behavioral methods in training sessions (Bloomsmith et al.; Lukas, Marr, & Maple, 1998; Bloomsmith, Marr, & Maple, 2007; Clay, Bloomsmith, Marr, & Maple, 2009; Martin, Bloomsmith, Kelley, Marr, & Maple, 2011). Over the years such partnerships spontaneously emerged when an entrepreneurial scientist made an offer that could not be refused. In almost every case, the scientist filled a need that was not being addressed in the zoo's organizational structure. My experience working in zoos and primate research centers has convinced me that the principles of behavior analysis are essential tools in the management and husbandry of animals. Using these techniques, refined years ago with rats and pigeons in animal psychology laboratories, we can now easily train the largest and most difficult animals to submit to noninvasive physical exams, draw blood, and measure blood pressure with their compliance. We ask lions to open their mouths to check their teeth, and we touch their bellies to obtain ultrasound images of developing offspring. Despite this great progress, there are only a few zoos and aquariums that employ qualified, credentialed behavior analysts. If I were a director today, the first hire I would make in establishing a research department would be a certified behavior analyst with an advanced degree. Short of full-time investments in core staff, any zoo can reach out to behavior analysts in clinics and institutes that specialize in human behavior intervention. Consulting with such skilled professionals can save a lot of time and do a lot of good. Thankfully, there are several qualified consulting groups that work in the zoo and aquarium field. Precision Behavior, founded by Thad Lacinak, is an excellent option and Active Environments is another company that I have employed for training work at Zoo Atlanta. Lacinak and his associates are now working within the Palm Beach Zoo wellness program. Both consulting groups are active globally. Disney's Animal Kingdom (DAK) has effectively deployed key operant personnel throughout their park. It is a proven approach to achieving better welfare, so it is surprising that there are not more institutions where certified behavior analysts are welcome.

A HISTORY OF COLLABORATION

As a newly minted PhD from Stanford in 1930, Harry F. Harlow began his monkey studies at the Vilas Park Zoo, a tiny facility in Madison, when his new employer, the University of Wisconsin, could not immediately deliver a dedicated campus laboratory (Harlow & Mears, 1971). When Yale

University's Robert Yerkes needed a gorilla to study its mental capacity, he located the young female Congo in a private collection and later followed the animal when it was sold to the Ringling Brothers Circus (Yerkes, 1927; Maple, 1979). Similarly, in the 1950s, Duane Rumbaugh, a new assistant professor on the psychology faculty at San Diego State College, arranged to study behavior in the abundant rodent and primate collection at the nearby San Diego Zoo (Maple, 2018). Rumbaugh carried his knowledge of zoo research to Atlanta when he joined the faculty at Georgia State University and affiliated with the Yerkes Primate Research Center. With Yerkes director Geoffrey Bourne and attorney Richard Reynolds, Rumbaugh coauthored the bylaws of the newly formed Atlanta Zoological Society, the basis of changes ultimately made to transform the zoo in the 1980s.

I too negotiated partnerships to study animals at the Sacramento Zoo, the Audubon Zoo, Kingdom's Three theme park (formerly Lion Country Safari), the Atlanta Zoo, the Palm Beach Zoo, and the San Francisco Zoo from 1970 until the present. I developed these venues while I was a graduate student, member of the faculty, zoo executive, and paid or pro bono consultant. In the latter role, I also advised other scientists who were starting programs in Alabama, Arizona, Florida, and North Carolina. For 40 years I have been on call by telephone and online to deliver input and encouragement to hundreds of students, faculty, and caregivers contemplating research in the zoo. Other psychologists and ethologists in academia are currently observing zoo animals in Birmingham, Alabama; Chicago, Illinois; Los Angeles, California; Miami, Florida; Orlando, Florida; Portland, Oregon; San Diego, California; and Seattle, Washington, to name a few of the more active institutions. Most of the zoos and aquariums in North America do not employ dedicated scientists, but there are many other promising opportunities to carry out zoo and aquarium research as formal and informal collaborators. Even the smallest zoos and aquariums have collections that can be used in studies by nearby faculty and their students. A surprising number of smaller colleges and universities are assigning students to use their local zoos as living laboratories for teaching about animal behavior. Many of these ongoing programs are described in the new book *Scientific Foundations of Zoos and Aquariums* (Kaufman, Bashaw, & Maple, 2019) recently published by Cambridge University Press. The surprising depth, breadth, and global reach of zoo and aquarium conservation and research is described in this comprehensive collection of 23 chapters comprising 663 pages of text. If we dig deep enough, we will also discover that scientists such as Frans de Waal started their research careers in a zoo. De Waal's mentor, J. A. R. A. M. van Hooff, introduced him to captive primates at the Burgers Zoo in Arnhem, Netherlands, a zoo operated by van Hooff's family. I first met Frans in Arnhem in the 1980s when he was finishing his doctoral research on chimpanzee behavior. Other prominent primatologists such as Hans Kummer carried out research on hamadryas baboons at the Zurich Zoo under the supervision of Heini Hediger. Professor Kummer thoroughly studied this species in captivity and in nature, providing contemporary zoo managers the basic knowledge to exhibit baboons and other primates successfully (Kummer, 1971). A tribute to professor Kummer was recently published in the *American Journal of Primatology* (Anzenberger and Falk, 2013). The advantages of these partnerships for both zoos and universities are reviewed in a chapter written for the Cambridge volume (Maple & Sherwen, 2019).

THE JACKSONVILLE/UNF SCIENTIFIC PARTNERSHIP

A comprehensive wellness program (or animal welfare program for that matter) is a good fit for zoo and aquarium professionals, but wellness is a broad concept that offers enrichment for people as well as animals. Although committed staff are essential, most of them do not have sufficient time to devote to engineering better welfare standards and practices. To meet the highest standards as they are now outlined, dedicated personnel must be put in place to supplement the efforts of caregivers. The traditional view that veterinarians are the highest-ranking animal welfare advocates/practitioners in an organization is also a limitation since the daily work of veterinary medicine is a full-time job. Ideally veterinarians will be fully committed to leadership on wellness, but their medical training must be supplemented by professionals with psychological training. We elected to insert a wellness operating unit in the animal care division and began to network with keepers and curators. However, it is almost impossible for a small staff to meet the aspirations of the entire zoo staff. Buy-in to wellness/welfare is almost immediate and completely universal as staff request attention from the dedicated wellness personnel. To manage the anticipated pace of change, the only cost-effective solution is a partnership with faculty and students who share our interests. Once partnership opportunities are sufficiently promoted on campus, it is not difficult to find many students who want to be part of the program. The other key to meeting demand is to invite caregivers to participate in the delivery of wellness services and the process of discovery.

In Jacksonville, we started with the recruitment of master's level students with tuition fully funded by the zoo. Once they were accepted for enrollment in the biology and/or psychology programs at the University of North Florida (UNF), we assigned them projects at the zoo that advanced our wellness objectives. Working with their faculty research advisors, they also planned thesis projects with a basic or applied emphasis. The first two students received their master's degrees in 2016. Kaylin Tennant wrote a thesis on lowland gorillas for the biology department, and upon graduation she accepted a research assistantship at Case Western Reserve University in Cleveland, Ohio. This doctoral program is closely aligned with the Cleveland Metroparks Zoo and is directed by my former graduate student at Georgia Tech, Dr. Kristen Lukas, coordinator of the AZA gorilla Species Survival Plan committee and an internationally known expert on both wild and captive gorilla behavior. The MetroParks affiliated scientific program at Case is one of the most important scientific centers for zoo biology, conservation and animal welfare in the world. Kaylin could not be in a better place to advance her career. A second student, Megan Morris, wrote her thesis for the psychology department, and she joined our wellness team at the zoo after graduating from UNF with her master's degree. Megan is a former zookeeper, so she has been extremely helpful in working with care staff responsible for a diverse variety of zoo animals. Megan was very involved with our Wellness for Elephants workshop in 2016, and she subsequently served as the primary editor of the finished proceedings (Morris, Segura, Forthman, & Maple, 2019). With the graduation of our first zoo-supported UNF students, we demonstrated the power of the program as a transition from the master's to the doctoral degree and as preparation for a career in the zoo profession. The current model calls for the recruitment of one new student annually from the biology and psychology departments, respectively. Our second two students are now enrolled, but there are enough opportunities to recruit additional students once additional funding is obtained. In the five years since we started this program, I believe we have demonstrated that master's level research can be positioned to contribute to the discovery and application of wellness. However, doctoral-level students can stay with a project longer and dig deeper into factors that control wellness.

Another unique feature of our partnership is the outstanding faculty contributors to our program. We have appointed two young professors to serve as visiting professors at the zoo: one in biology and the other in psychology. Dr. Adam Rosenblatt, a field biologist, is a specialist in alligators, and we have assigned one of our newest students, Marisa Spain, to work directly with Adam. In August a new comparative psychologist, Dr. Gregory Kohn, joined the psychology department faculty, and he too will be working with one of our zoo-sponsored graduate students. Both Dr. Rosenblatt and Dr. Kohn will receive summer stipends from the zoo to supplement their university nine-month teaching contracts. The expertise of these professors and their students requires far less funding than if we attempted to recruit scientists to work full time in the zoo. They also bring the academic tradition of publishing, grant writing, and presentations to professional meetings, and this will only enhance the reputation and the standing of the Jacksonville Zoo and Gardens among its peer institutions. We have also established a reciprocal lecture series with UNF where staff from the zoo deliver talks to UNF faculty and students one semester and the next semester a faculty member or student delivers a talk to our zoo staff and volunteers. The world's elite zoos are smart zoos, and we believe Jacksonville is rapidly becoming a global center for intellectual zoo biologists. Our model should work in any zoo that is located close to a major university or a small college with an animal behaviorist on the faculty. The partnership should have a long life if it is cost effective for the zoo to continue its financial commitment. As we did in Atlanta, the long-term commitment in scholarship and higher education can be protected and sustained with a dedicated endowment of sufficient size. An endowment of U.S. $3.5M is a good place to start, but I recommend at least $5M if it can be achieved. Endowments create stability, longevity and codified standards, necessary conditions to reach the high standard and best practices of optimal animal welfare and superior productivity. If we don't publish our findings, we cannot benchmark our impact on the profession.

Our young program in Jacksonville has continued the tradition of training future contributors to zoo biology from its first iteration with doctoral students at Emory University in Atlanta in 1975. At its zenith, after the partnership had relocated to Georgia Tech, the program was powered by U.S. $2.5 million in endowment funding that supported graduate students in the School of Psychology thanks to the generosity of the Charles Smithgall family in Gainesville, Georgia. All of my students carried out research at Zoo Atlanta and the Yerkes National Primate Research Center. We also emigrated our students to carry out doctoral projects at the Michale E. Keeling Center for Comparative Medicine and Research associated with the University of Texas System Cancer Center, the San Diego Zoo and Wild Animal Park, and Disney's Animal Kingdom (DAK). They were also encouraged to conduct fieldwork in Africa, Asia, the Caribbean, and South America. Once graduated, our students have been hired by universities (Agnes Scott College, Dalton State College, Franklin & Marshall College, Georgia State University, Kennesaw State University, Loyola University New Orleans, and the Yerkes Primate Research Center of Emory University), zoos (the Audubon Zoo; the Apenheul, Netherlands; the Birmingham Zoo; Cleveland Metroparks Zoo; the Detroit Zoo; DAK; the Lincoln Park Zoo; the Oklahoma City Zoo; the Santa Barbara Zoo; and the Singapore Zoo), and nonprofit nongovernmental organizations (American Humane, Center for Disease Control (CDC), the Gorilla Foundation, and the Dian Fossey Gorilla Fund International). There is clearly a market for psychologists who specialize in animal behavior, conservation education, animal welfare and management.

In Jacksonville our graduate student support program is tied to a memorandum of understanding signed by Jacksonville Zoo and Gardens director Tony Vecchio and the president of UNF. Eventually, we hope we can add four-year doctoral students to the mix, anticipating another agreement with a PhD-granting institution such as the University of Florida. In 2020 we expect to hire a postdoctoral associate who will be focused on our cognitive workstations with a diversity of species at work throughout the zoo. In addition, with time there will be projects conducted with the assistance of undergraduate students. This year Valerie Segura is coteaching a lab with UNF faculty on the experimental analysis of behavior, with undergraduates spending one day each week at the zoo. A similar course existed for many years at Georgia Tech under the supervision of my colleague Jack Marr, a distinguished behavior analyst. Several of my graduate students supervised the lab, which was one of the most popular courses at Tech (e.g., Lukas et al., 1998). Professor Marr is an example of how much a creative professor can contribute to scholarship at the zoo. He coauthored twelve publications with students in my lab over the years we worked together, and he inspired and influenced many more.

Collaboration with scientists, professors, and zoo professionals at nearby and distant institutions has resulted in several hundred publications because we were open to sharing the data and the research venues. We have successfully completed projects with Kim Bard (Clay et al., 2015), Benjamin Beck (Beck et al., 1995), Fred Berkovitch (Bashaw et al., 2007), David Bocian (Maple & Bocian, 2013), Nancy Czekala (Stoinski et al., 2002), William Dunlap (Brown et al., 1982), A. J. Figueredo (Burks et al., 2004), Larry James (Finlay et al., 1988), Duane Jackson (Jackson et al., 1989), Alison Kaufman (Kaufman et al., 2019), Donald G. Lindburg (Maple & Lindburg, 2008), Dan Marston (Marston & Maple, 2016), Ron Nadler (Hoff et al., 1982; Hoff et al., 1993), Bryan Norton (Norton, Hutchins, Stevens, & Maple, 1995), Sally Sherwen (Maple & Sherwen, 2019), Jean Wineman (Wineman et al., 1996), Zhang Zhihe, and Zhang Anju (Bexell et al., 2004). These collaborators were located at eighteen institutions in seven states, the District of Columbia, and four nations. The ease of communication globally makes worldwide collaboration feasible for almost any zoo or aquarium. Currently I am working on a special issue of the journal *Frontiers in Psychology* with an American and an Australian colleague. We communicate by e-mail and by Skype telephone calls when we need to discuss the content of this issue and make timely decisions. The addition of colleagues outside North America ensures we will produce a volume that is more inclusive.

COMMITTING TO WELLNESS

Directors and curators who are advancing the wellness construct have told me that they find it easier to explain wellness to visitors, board members, donors, and friends. Wellness is appealing because there is no limit to how well we can be and therefore no limit to how well an animal can be when we apply the same standards as we do to ourselves. In general this means an approach to zoo and aquarium design and development that liberates animals to live as they would in the natural world; they need plenty of complex spaces; an appropriate number of conspecifics; the opportunity to select mates, reproduce, and raise their young; and an abundance of food and clean water available at variable times and in unpredictable locations—essentially a challenging but safe habitat that makes life worth living. A synonym for this kind of living is thriving. No species lives forever, but every species in a managed zoo or aquarium should live well and long. A conversation with anyone who questions the value and purpose of a zoo is always comforted when they discover that we are all in on the practice of wellness. A wellness protocol demands that we activate the animals that live in our zoos and aquariums. The best way to activate them is to design a simulated ecosystem that offers a challenge at all levels. Monkeys have to climb high to find their food. Big cats have to enter the water to obtain playthings. Apes must use a joystick or touchscreen to earn delectable food rewards. The best exhibits offer choice and change. Animals might be able to choose their food, dim lights, or activate familiar sounds and smells.

Enrichment can be under the control of the animals themselves as they request browse or Boomer Balls. Some species perceive video images as real, and they ought to be able to watch their caregivers as they prepare their food, to choose the food that they prefer, and to ask for food at any time of the day (Hopper, Lambeth, & Schapiro, 2012). If we are clever enough, we can also build technology that allows the animals to tease the visitors by activating waterspouts or puffs of air. The "Think Tank" exhibit at the National Zoo recently added such features for their orangutan exhibit. Long ago, Hal Markowitz designed a pioneering interactive landscape when he built a tic-tac-toe device that pitted mandrills against zoo visitors. The mandrills almost always won. He also installed a modified car wash at the Portland (now Oregon) Zoo that enabled the elephants to pull a chain to take a shower. Others have copied his ideas but no one has yet reached his level of creativity. Hal Markowitz was a genius when it came to challenging animals with technology designed just for them. The degree of wellness we can achieve is limited only by our creativity and our commitment to creating appropriate and effective technology. By introducing mental and physical challenges to zoo animals, we are shaping the characteristic of resilience, one of the key ingredients in thriving. Resilient animals will always do better when faced with new challenges.

CALL OF THE WILD

Although we didn't have the word *wellness* in our zoo dictionary in 1988, we understood that our elephants were deprived by the traditional practice of keeping them confined and, for safety, chained in a building at night. In the wild, elephants are active day and night, so we reasoned that we should give them access to their outdoor habitat as much as possible (Brockett, Stoinski, Black, Markowitz, & Maple, 1999; Wilson et al., 2006). Today this innovation of caregiver-supervised nocturnal travel and exploration is a standard procedure in most accredited zoos. We were also one of the first zoos to stop the cruel practice of chaining. Giving animals greater freedom and autonomy and access to a natural life is what wellness is all about. During the 18 years of my reform administration at Zoo Atlanta, we worked on the cutting edge of design. Our goal was to revisit confinement and create environments where the animals could be liberated to thrive. To do this properly, we had to have a good idea of the way wild animals live, so we visited the natural habitats of many of the species exhibited in our revitalized zoological park. We took architects and key staff to East Africa to study elephants, giraffes, and other savanna wildlife. We also took them to Rwanda, Zaire (now Congo), and Cameroon to study gorillas and their habitat requirements, and we took them to the island of Bioko to study the life of mandrills and drills. The Bioko study was led by our general curator, Dietrich Schaff, who introduced us to Tom Butynski; he later joined our team as a consulting field biologist in Kenya. We never visited field sites with designers unless we were accompanied by experienced field scientists familiar with the ecosystems and the animals within them. This is no longer an unusual practice for zoo professionals who spend a lot of quality time in the bush.

After we began to implement our new ideas for revitalized zoo habitats in the African section, we started to plan facilities and landscapes for Asian animals. To understand Asia we traveled to Indonesia, including the islands of Java, Komodo, and Sumatra. Wonderfully innovative exhibits for Sumatran tigers, orangutans, and Komodo dragons followed. Our work was honored by AZA with exhibit awards from our peers for the Ford African Rain Forest, the African Savanna, and the Monkeys of Makoku. These exhibits were also successful with our visitors, our sponsors, and our donors. The new Zoo Atlanta's attendance soared in the 1990s, reaching a peak of more than one million visitors with the opening of a giant panda exhibit in 1999. An understanding of animal behavior was the driver behind each and every one of the new animal exhibits that made our reputation as innovators. My academic training formed the foundation of our approach to design, but my teaching partnership with architectural faculty at Georgia Tech provided important background in scientific programming. Because we employed landscape architects at the firm of Coe and Lee (now CLR Design), our exhibits were examples of landscape immersion in its finest form. My work with creative architects has given me great pleasure over the years. Currently I am collaborating with Nevin Lash at Ursa International and his partner Pete Choquette. Nevin and Pete designed the innovative elephant exhibit that will open at Zoo Atlanta in 2020. Nevin was previously employed by our original partners, CLR Design. Working from an excellent master plan by CLR, the creative collaboration with Nevin's Ursa International and the Atlanta-based Epsten Group has been instrumental in helping us visualize future wellness-inspired exhibits in Jacksonville. I have learned that good things happen when psychologists and architects work together.

It is worth noting that the subtitle of this book suggests that both art and science are required to advance wellness. Certainly, there is art and aesthetics when it comes to designing simulated rain forest exhibits in zoos, but it is also the case that experienced animal caregivers recognize that working with animals is a delicate process. The most skillful among them practice the art of caregiving as an extension of their personality. We know that some people are uniquely gifted, and they are accepted by animals in ways that are not completely understood. Needless to say, the best practices are always a blend of art and science. The artistic caregiver, curator, or veterinarian is able to call on a wellspring of perceptive abilities that cannot be easily quantified or measured. It is also the case that scientists are unequal in their abilities to observe and draw inferences in a research setting in the zoo, laboratory, or field. There are times when the best prepared scientists must trust their intuitive skills to find the answer to a challenging research question. When it comes to intervention, improvement often defies analysis as in the case of hospital patients that get better merely because they have rooms with a window to the outdoors (Ullrich, 1984). Still, experiments can be conducted to determine cause and effect, so with allowances to some degree of artistic interpretation, evidence-based studies should be the norm for zoo and aquarium professionals who want to understand the variables that truly control behavior, health, and wellness. The great Hediger once stated that "research is always last in the zoological garden," but in fact, the very existence of animal welfare and wellness descends from our successful history of research.

Chapter 2

EVOLUTION OF A CONSTRUCT

Wellness is an example of a "hypothetical construct" just as motivation, intelligence, and personality are considered constructs. In each of these cases, the construct is inferred from objective measurements rather than internal states. Psychologists infer intelligence from intelligence surveys. Thus, intelligence is what the intelligence tests measure. Similarly, personality is scaled according to categories. The five-factor model of personality (Fiske, 1949) is comprised of the following categories: openness, conscientiousness, extraversion, agreeableness, and neuroticism. Each of these factors represents a range between extreme personality traits. The average person lies somewhere between the two extremes in each trait. An interesting new development in personality research is the finding that many nonhuman species exhibit personality traits similar to those of human beings (Gold & Maple, 1994; King & Figueredo, 1997; Gosling & John, 1999;). However, because animals cannot respond to test questions in the way humans do, personality ratings are left to the caregivers or scientific observers who objectively rate them. Comparative studies of personality are proliferating as new species are subjected to rigorous testing. Although many monkeys and apes exhibit evidence of personality, the expanding list now includes domestic dogs, cats, donkeys, elephants, hyenas, guppies, leopards, lions, pigs, octopuses, and rats. In time, other species with personality traits will likely be identified.

Wellness is also comprised of factors hypothesized in the early work of Halbert Dunn (1959, 1961), who is considered as the father of wellness. A model of animal wellness appears below. In this model I have reduced

Dunn's original eight factors to five as human wellness is more complex than animal wellness. The uniquely human wellness factors are spiritual, occupational, and financial. Dunn's idea morphed into different forms by practitioners who sought to improve human health. Dr. John Travis opened a Wellness Resource Center in Mill Valley, California, that was branded as "alternative medicine." In the 1980s Bill Hetler organized an annual conference on wellness, while Tom Dickey established the Berkeley Wellness Letter bearing the tagline "Science-based, expert-vetted health and wellness advice" (newsletters@berkeleywellness.com). Associated with the UC Berkeley School of Public Health, this lively periodical delivers reliable reading material to subscribers. The Berkeley letter is a very accessible source for teaching about wellness. In a recent issue, colorful produce was

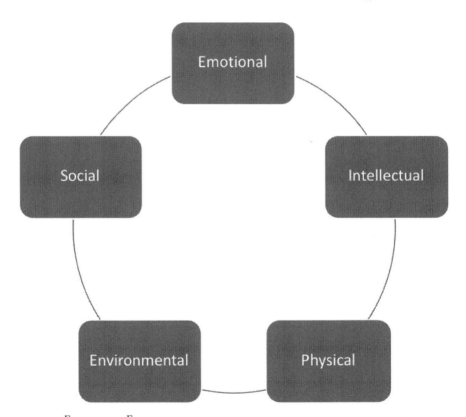

FIGURE 2.1. FIVE DIMENSIONS OF WELLNESS ADAPTED FOR ANIMALS

discussed. For example, there are 2,000 known natural pigments with specific phytonutrients responsible for color in plants, including more than 800 known flavonoids, 450 carotenoids, and 150 anthocyanins. Color makes produce appealing and indicates ripeness and flavor. Nonhuman primates follow seasonal indicators of color to decide when fruit is ripe enough to eat. One of the most important responsibilities of any education unit in a zoo is the obligation to teach people, especially young people, healthy eating habits. Animal models can be used for this purpose. There are many other online connecting points to the wellness movement. One prominent source, based in Miami is the Global Wellness Institute (globalwellnessinstitute.org). This institute provides up-to-date information on wellness events and networking opportunities worldwide. All of these authorities regularly supply assets for storytelling. For humans the eight-factor model of wellness is interconnected. Breakdowns in financial wellness, for example, are likely to affect emotional and even physical wellness. In their review of wellness and its determinants, Foster and Keller (2007) observed that wellness appeared during a parallel transformation of health to a more holistic perspective that is interrelational, positive, and focused on healthy human functioning. This transformation led to an expanded concept of health to include all aspects of the mind, body, and spirit. This multidimensional approach has been abandoned by Western culture but embraced by indigenous societies. The beliefs of indigenous people are important in fields such as wildlife ecology. A recent report in *Science* (Kutz & Tomaselli, 2019) suggests that bridging indigenous and scientific knowledge leads to improvements in wildlife surveillance and promotes reconciliations between communities that must work together to promote wildlife health. Adams (2003) identified four principles of wellness: (a) it is multidimensional, (b) wellness research and practice should be focused on causes of wellness rather than causes of illness, (c) wellness is about balance, and (d) wellness is relative, subjective, and perceptual.

THE THIRD FORCE IN PSYCHOLOGY

During my graduate school years, I attended the 1968 convention of the American Psychological Association in San Francisco. As a student volunteer, I arrived a day early to help set up tables and chairs, just in time to observe a caravan of hirsute, new-wave psychologists and their devoted students who were participating in the annual convention of the American Association of Humanistic Psychology (AAHP). I can be forgiven for the observation that these were gurus of a uniquely different kind. The American Association of Humanistic Psychology was founded at Brandeis University in 1961 and held its first convention in 1963. I was fascinated by what I learned that weekend in San Francisco as my graduate training in experimental psychology had not prepared me for this new approach to human behavior. Although the new field of humanistic psychology was just gaining traction in the late sixties, it had been germinating in the published works of its charismatic founders including A. H. Maslow, Rollo May, Carl Rogers, and Victor Frankl. Professor Maslow was the association's intellectual leader as demonstrated by his literary productivity and his reputation as a first-rate scholar (Maslow, 1954, 1962, 1971). A former elected president of the mainstream American Psychological Association (APA), Maslow characterized humanistic psychology as the "third force" with a vision vastly different than its predecessors: behaviorism and psychoanalysis. Among his peers in the new field, Maslow was the most empirical, a function of his own experience as Harry F. Harlow's first graduate student at the University of Wisconsin. Maslow made important contributions to the field of comparative psychology as he helped Harlow demonstrate the utility of nonhuman primate models of human social behavior (e.g., Harlow, Uehling, & Maslow, 1932; Maslow, 1936).

While some species, notably great apes and cetaceans, approach humans in their socioemotional and cognitive abilities, attributes of human wellness do not perfectly apply to the universe of animals managed in zoos and aquariums. However, Maslow (1962) proposed a list of attributes that can be applied to animals. I modified his original chart for a talk that I delivered at a conference in New Orleans, Louisiana, which was later presented in journal and book form (Maple, 1996; Maple & Perdue, 2013). I have generalized Maslow's findings to propose that all organisms express a biologically based and species-specific inner nature, and this inner nature is neutral, pre-moral, or good. Further, this inner nature can be studied and discovered, and we should encourage its expression. Maslow observed that this inner nature was always pressing for actualization and that its suppression leads to sickness. Finally, he argued that overcoming obstacles results in a healthy self-esteem. This latter point is particularly relevant to optimal animal welfare as we have learned that captive animals prefer to work for rewards (Washburn, 2015). By solving problems, mental or physical, animals will achieve greater resiliency, a far better outcome than dependency on caregivers. Organisms, human or nonhuman, do not thrive unless they are challenged. Of course, we must manufacture challenges in the zoo that are not too risky, unlike the life-threatening risks wild animals face from predators and other dangerous situations.

There is a long history of wellness as "alternative medicine". From this historical perspective we can see that the history of wellness is more intuitive than empirical. For example, the science behind chiropractic medicine has been questioned, but those who suffer from joint discomfort swear by its methods. Chiropractors often work alongside medical doctors as part of an athlete's physical therapy team. In the continuum from art to science, I would argue that chiropractic is a healing art and not a science. There is plenty of evidence that chiropractic procedures work, but the theory supporting its use defies scientific explanation. Chiropractic was developed in the belief that manipulating the spine affects the flow of a supernatural vital energy and thereby affects health and disease. So-called "vertebral subluxation" is widely considered a pseudoscientific concept.

THE ENTRY OF POSITIVE PSYCHOLOGY

Humanistic psychology shares its focus on human potential with the new field of positive psychology as advocated by Martin Seligman (Seligman & Csikszentmihalyi, 2014). Maslow was the first psychologist to investigate positive psychology, but Seligman extended its meaning. In their book on positive psychology, Seligman and Csikszentmihalyi equated the terminology to thriving. In a recent publication, Seligman also used the term *flourishing*. Both Maslow and Seligman advocated a science of psychology that focused on individuals who were well rather than those who were ill. The animal welfare equivalent of this approach is to focus on positive indicators of welfare rather than negative indicators. As Christopher Peterson (2006) explained in his book *A Primer on Positive Psychology*,

> Positive psychology…is a call for psychological science and practice to be as concerned with strength as with weakness; as interested in building the best things in life as in repairing the worst; and as concerned with making the lives of normal people fulfilling as with healing pathology. (p. 5)

Dr. Pauleen Bennett, a psychologist working at La Trobe University in Australia, combines her academic duties with community projects designed to improve human-companion animal relationships. She has recently begun to use principles of positive psychology in her research. She organized the second Australian Conference on Positive Psychology and Well-Being in 2010. Positive psychology has always been concerned with assisting normally adjusted people to elevate their expectations about their lives. Dr. Bennett suggests that spending time with your pets is a good way to improve your life, and she teaches people to share their lives with animals. Her team investigates human-companion relationships with standard research techniques: questionnaires, interviews, and sometimes invasive tests for elevated hormones. By learning how adjusted people benefit from their animal companions, positive psychology also contributes to interventions that can bring people back from depression or high anxiety, conditions that have traditionally interested the field of psychology. Since so many people own pets, the human-companion animal relationship has become a very big business for veterinarians and consulting psychologists. There is plenty of room for discovery in this field even though it is better known for its applications. One promising technique is the use of dogs as therapy animals. Other species have been used as well, but dogs seem to be the most reliable. Dogs are good at bonding with people, but research has demonstrated that they also readily bond with monkeys (Mason & Kenney, 1974). With this finding in mind, I wouldn't hesitate to deploy a dog to serve as a friendly therapist for a socially disabled monkey or ape in a zoo or laboratory setting. High-strung racehorses have also benefitted from housing with nags or goats, so interspecific companionship has proven to be a reliable therapeutic technique to induce calming.

THE PROLIFERATION OF COMMUNITY WELLNESS CENTERS

During the years that wellness practitioners have been active, the wellness construct has been applied in many unique ways. In the animal realm, veterinary clinics throughout North America have marketed their wellness services. A new recipe for pet food was launched in 1997 and 2000 respectively when "Wellness" branded dog and cat food came into the market. The Wellness diet contains only whole foods with no wheat, corn, soy, preservatives, artificial colors, or flavors. The company went further when it organized the WellPet Foundation in 2007 to support organizations and activities that promote the power of natural nutrition and the benefits of healthy, active lifestyles. WellPet funding works with nonprofit corporations dedicated to helping pets thrive. In this way the brand reflects the broader meaning associated with the wellness construct. The Animal Wellness Center in Davis serves pet owners in the greater Sacramento, California, area and offers both traditional Western veterinary medicine and alternative medicine such as acupuncture. They emphasize that every animal is treated as a unique individual, a characteristic of the applied animal welfare approach. A similar practice is operated by the Ohio State University College of Veterinary Medicine where they offer a menu of wellness services as preventative medicine for pets.

University infirmaries are now routinely branded as campus wellness centers. Some universities have built elaborate physical education facilities to encourage indoor and outdoor exercise for the entire campus community branded as wellness centers. In these fitness venues, nutrition and heart-healthy diets are promoted by mentors who offer classes and administer educational programs with broad appeal. Specialists organize outdoor adventures such as rock climbing, skydiving, hiking, mountaineering, and scuba diving. Such activities represent both physical and mental challenges associated with a thriving lifestyle. At the College of Veterinary Medicine at Washington State University, the school offers professional counseling and wellness services for the student and faculty community. They offer academic and career counseling and stress management advice and help their clients to achieve excellence in all aspects of their lives. As the construct that integrates physical and mental health, wellness has truly become ubiquitous in everyday life.

In his book *High-Level Wellness* (1961), Dunn eloquently described the essence of the wellness construct:

> When we become interested in wellness as a condition, we discover that the state of being well is not just a drab, static one. Quite the contrary. It has many levels. It is ever-changing in its characteristics…High-level wellness is defined as an integrated method of functioning which is oriented toward maximizing the potential of which the individual is capable. (p. 3)

The most interesting feature of wellness is what sets it apart from welfare; wellness is aspirational. There are no upper limits to how well we seek to be. No one who is asked the question "How well do you want to be?" answers "Just a little bit well." Indeed, we want to achieve a high degree of wellness. Maximizing or optimizing wellness is the goal of every rational person. Further, Dunn regarded "maximizing" as a dynamic word, as he put it, "a *becoming* word." Becoming is the theme that connects wellness to the human potential movement of humanistic psychology. Aspirations appear also in the words of humanistic psychotherapist Carl Rogers (1980), who wrote,

People are just as wonderful as sunsets if you let them be.
When I look at a sunset, I don't find myself saying soften
the orange a bit on the outside corner. I don't try to control
a sunset. I watch with awe as it unfolds. (p. 22)

In 2008, when I was the CEO of the Palm Beach Zoo, I discussed
our emerging wellness program with two potential collaborators: the Lynn
College of Nursing at Florida Atlantic University and the Palm Beach
County School System. Both exhibited considerable enthusiasm for the
partnership. Unfortunately, the global financial crisis of 2008 hit hard locally, and funding our innovative wellness program was no longer feasible.
We thought our teaching model could also enrich the nursing curriculum
by providing opportunities to develop new ideas about health and wellness
for people. At the time we were just beginning to outline our approach to
wellness for animals, people, communities, and ecosystems—essentially
global ecological health and wellness. Working with educators at the Palm
Beach Zoo, we proposed to develop a mobile wellness unit that would visit
schools with animals and instructors. Our big idea was to teach children
that animals in the zoo have to be fit to be healthy and well. We hoped to
teach children how to approach their own health with oblique examples
from the animal world. Did they know that obese elephants cannot give
birth on their own, and they needed human caregivers and veterinarians to
assist them? Did they know that monkeys and apes can develop diabetes if
they are not fed properly? Did they know that lowland gorillas in the zoo
suffer and die young from heart failure? Because children in particular are
uncomfortable when singled out for body image issues, we proposed to
teach them without getting too personal. Mistakes can be made with the
best intentions. The Walt Disney Company had to modify their obesity
exhibit at Epcot Center in Walt Disney World after critics claimed it was
insensitive to kids. The exhibit was sponsored by Blue Cross Blue Shield
and featured animated fitness superheroes and villains who ate junk food
and watched too much television. Disney didn't want to reinforce stereo-
types that children are lazy and practice poor eating habits, so they closed
the exhibit for adjustments. I still believe our proposed wellness education

program, however delicate, would work in a partnership between health practitioners and educators, zoos and aquariums, and public or private school systems. Indeed, thinking bigger, this is the kind of program that ought to be national in scope.

As wellness centers have appeared on college campuses, they represent a new opportunity to merge our interests. Coincidentally, psychology departments are populated today by many new practitioners of health psychology, and this field should be strongly connected to wellness programs for students, faculty, and the community. We are attempting to build bridges to this discipline with our wellness partnership between the Jacksonville Zoo and Gardens and UNF. The university operates a beautifully equipped wellness center on campus, and we hope to build a complementary but more focused structure at the Jacksonville Zoo and Gardens. These facilities can be synergistic and connected in creative ways. Other zoos are putting wellness into the public space as seen with the Animal Wellness Campus at the Virginia Zoo in Norfolk, and in 2007 the Cincinnati Zoo unveiled the branded IAMS Animal Wellness Plaza to make their visitors more aware of the zoo's strong institutional commitment to health and wellness. This structure connects the zoo's animal hospital with its conservation and research center.

Many practicing veterinarians have embraced wellness as a brand for their clinics. Looking up wellness online, you will find scores of veterinary wellness centers and clinics throughout the nation. Domestic animals were the first to receive attention from wellness practitioners, but many zoos are now beginning to use the word openly. On the websites of the Brevard Zoo, Detroit Zoo, North Carolina Zoo, Palm Beach Zoo, San Francisco Zoo, and Virginia Zoo, wellness is promoted and described. However, while wellness is proposed as a synonym for welfare, many zoos have yet to acknowledge that wellness practices go far beyond the norms of traditional animal welfare. A full-service zoo or aquarium wellness center must be designed to encourage teaching and mentoring so visitors can achieve wellness in their own lives. The new generation of zoo and aquarium wellness centers will be based on what we have learned about the unique abilities of all taxa exhibited in zoos and aquariums and those that live around us in the natural world.

FIGURE 2.2. STUDENT WELLNESS COMPLEX AT THE UNIVERSITY OF NORTH FLORIDA.

But we can achieve wellness only when we fully understand the animals in our care, so the wellness-inspired zoo must become an empirical zoo. Wellness, or optimal animal welfare, cannot be achieved without an evidence-based management system. In the pages to follow, we will explore how to build evidence-based institutions with dedicated scientific personnel and an outsourced team of academic collaborators or some combination of both. While wellness is becoming important to zoos and aquariums, its reach is much greater in the global economy. It is also a factor that is beginning to influence governments as they cope with the rising cost of medical services, pharmaceuticals, and hospitalization. Organizations that promote wellness understand that prevention and proactive health practices are cost-effective alternatives to treatment. As zoos become ever more naturalistic and resemble a walk in the park, visitors will be encouraged to exercise among the exotic animals and plants in a simulated ecosystem. Research in environmental psychology supports the notion that human psychological well-being is enhanced when people are exposed to natural places (Devlin, 2017; Maple & Morris, 2017). This effect is especially important to citizens living in highly urbanized areas. Surprisingly, zoos and aquariums have rarely acknowledged this noble purpose for zoos. Our commitment to naturalism and authentic landscape immersion is a powerful contributor to the positive mental health of our guests, and naturalistic zoos and aquariums appear to be just as effective as local, regional, and national parks and gardens. Understood in this way, zoos are not exploiting animals for entertainment; they are in fact locating people, animals, and botanicals in a common landscape to enhance health and wellness for all. This is not merely an important social trend; it is also a promising research opportunity as we learn more about the positive effects of well-planned zoological gardens and aquatic parks. City planners organize these settings into categories of green and blue environmental variables. The context of both is essential in designing biophilic architecture. Steven Kellert's *Nature by Design* (2018) is a beautiful example of this approach based on Kellert and Wilson's (1993) familiar concept of biophilia. It is a promising model for planning future zoos and aquariums that exceed today's standards. I will examine the form and function of biophilic zoo and aquarium design in Chapter 9.

THE BUSINESS OF WELLNESS

The wellness industry, comprised of tourism and real estate, preventive health care, antiaging products, fitness and nutrition, workplace wellness, coaching and counseling, and public health has become a market behemoth with an estimated value of U.S. $4.2 trillion in 2017 (Global Wellness Institute website). Wellness tourism alone generates U.S. $639 billion in revenue. From these market data, we can see that wellness is widely accepted by generations of consumers who are committed to a fit and healthy lifestyle. People who live this way are inclined to introduce their pets to a similar lifestyle, and there are many products that make this transition an easy one. As we have seen, there are wellness-branded pet foods online and in supermarkets that contain the most appropriate food for dogs and cats. Pet food vendors recommend variety by offering specialty supplements and treats to keep dogs and cats interested in their food. Just as it is with people, we have learned that domestic animals prefer choices and change in their diets. Because people have accepted wellness as a factor in their lives, it should be relatively easy to convince them to support wellness in zoo and aquarium settings. Zoos and aquariums are perfectly positioned to teach and mentor visitors and members about the value and importance of a wellness lifestyle. The power of wellness as a brand will be tested as zoos and aquariums attempt to raise money for wellness-inspired exhibits and programs.

WELLNESS AT HOME

In our neighborhood in North Florida, we acknowledge our pug Maisie's need for exercise and play. We walk with Maisie frequently and give her the opportunity to renew relationships with neighbors and their pets. At least once each week, she visits with other dogs at a supervised "dog's day out" recreation center where she runs and plays with other small dogs. We have only one dog, so these friendly play sessions are important to her. To keep her busy, we supply her with many toys, and she loves them all. Fetch is her favorite game. Maisie shares our house with a 13-year-old tuxedo cat, Duckie, who has learned to play with our puppy. It took a little time for Duckie to learn how to play safely with a dog, but they worked it out. We live an active life, thanks to our pug and our kitty, and this is the kind of wellness lifestyle that prevails in a growing number of households in North America. In fact, Maisie's demand to move and explore is the key to our own activity.

Medical studies have repeatedly demonstrated that interacting with our pets contributes to good health in tangible ways. We are learning that hormonal changes associated with interactions with pets may help people cope with depression and other stress-related disorders (Allen, 2003). Here are a few other findings that support the positive effect of pets: (a) heart attack patients with dogs were eight times more likely to be alive a year later than patients without dogs (Friedmann & Thomas, 1995); (b) when 24 stockbrokers taking medications for high blood pressure were studied, the addition of pets reduced their stress levels (Allen, 1999); and (c) Swedish children exposed to pets during the first year of life had fewer allergies and less asthma (Hesselmar et al., 2018). An inclusive approach to dogs is incorporated in the Jacksonville zoo director's policy of encouraging dogs to join their owners in their offices in the zoo administration building. I'm confident that this pet-friendly policy is helping our staff to enjoy their work environment in a less stressful setting thanks to our director's open-door invitation to commune with humankind's best friend.

Walking a dog regularly contributes to weight control for the dog and the owner and gives people opportunities to socially interact with other pet owners, interactions that contribute to our sense of well-being and community. Unfortunately, a lot of people do not walk as much as they should, but a wellness lifestyle should include walking and interacting with the best therapists known to man: their pets. A wonderful combination of canines and parks is the proliferation of dog parks in urban settings. Governments, community humane centers, and private vendors have all developed low-cost facilities that encourage dog walking and dog play. These facilities are particularly important to apartment dwellers with little space for their pets. Due to the importance of pets in our lives, more and more businesses including restaurants and hotels have become pet friendly. I first encountered pet-friendly dining when I visited Switzerland in 1988, but it is becoming much more common in North America. Because it is now so much easier to find pet-friendly accommodations, my wife and I travel with our pug whenever we drive to see our daughters in South Florida or Charleston, a four-hour drive south or north of our home. Driving on interstates is always stressful, but a friendly pug in the back seat converts our drive into a heart-healthy travel experience. Fortunately, Maisie is an accomplished sleeper.

FIGURE 2.3. MAISIE, A FRIENDLY PUG PUPPY (A. G. MAPLE).

Dogs are going to work with the family breadwinners all over the world. In the United Kingdom, the corporate headquarters of Nestle Company permits its 1,000 employees to bring their dogs into its headquarters building daily. When the Nestle story was published in 2016, 56 employees had elected to go through the company's "pawthorisation" process. Once an independent dog authority has reviewed a dog, the animal gets its "passpawt." Nestle's commitment to a dog-friendly workplace is understandable since they own Purina, a prominent pet food brand, but there are many workplace benefits from the program. Employees find the atmosphere of the office much warmer and more sociable. The dogs stimulate conversations, and people stop to pet the dogs in the hallway. As one employee put it, "There's something about it that feels so right." More than 50 companies in London have agreed to permit dogs to regularly visit the workplace (Ferguson, 2016). In our North Florida subdivision, we find it easier to recall the names of our neighbors' dogs, so they help us stay connected and make new friends from these daily interactions. Although we see many of our neighbors daily, at our age we need name tags to identify them—not so with our neighborhood of dogs. For some reason, remembering dogs is easy.

In 2008, I read a fascinating book, *The Art of Racing in the Rain,* by Garth Stein. There was a dog featured on the cover of the book and it caught my eye. Disney is now advertising their new movie based on this book with the dog, Enzo, promoted as the main character. In the book, Enzo offers his narration of events and we learn many things about him based on his observations and reflections. Longing to be human, Enzo looks directly into the eyes of his owner and listens to every word he utters. After reading the book, I noticed that my pug Darwin was just like Enzo; he frequently fixed my gaze and seemed to be communicating. I'm not sure all dogs are like Enzo or my first pug, Darwin, but we tend to underestimate our pets. I continue to apply what I learned from him as I communicate with my new pug puppy, Maisie. Our little pug is getting pretty good at controlling her owners.

FITNESS NOT FATNESS

As a young college professor, I was surprised to see so many animals that seemed to be overweight in labs, primate centers, and zoological parks. In many of these traditional facilities, the animals did not live in socially appropriate social groups, and they were confined to uncomfortable, restricted steel and concrete cages devoid of climbing structures. Many of their caregivers also seemed to share my concerns. I believe this is why so many of them overcompensated by overfeeding. In the days of predominantly hard architecture, there was nothing a caregiver could do to lighten the burden of captivity other than pile on the food. This pattern was not an anomaly; it happened repeatedly in many institutions. With good intentions caregivers were enabling obesity with each passing day. Enlightened feeding regimes have dramatically changed the way we provide nutritious food to zoo animals. The more we have learned about how animals live in the wild, the more their lives have improved in managed care. We don't want to produce a generation of couch potatoes in the zoo, so it is essential to activate them with low-calorie food rewards and opportunities to run, explore, and play in zoos designed for that purpose. Zoo Atlanta elephant caregivers worried about the fitness of their African elephants and chose to activate them with operant methods. Acting as their personal trainers, the staff stood above the exhibit and barked orders to the animals to move about the exhibit at a rapid pace. Because of their history of show training, these animals responded well to the instructions. If a challenging walking trail cannot be constructed, activation through training in their home habitat is the only way a zoo elephant can exercise sufficiently. I would like to see a zoo with sufficient space to design an obstacle course for elephants situated along a walking trail. At each station along the way to a final watering hole experience, the elephants would have to complete a task: push a heavy obstacle, stand on back feet to reach a lever, pick up the pace of their walk, solve a cognitive puzzle, and take a dip in the pool. This would serve as a challenge for the elephants, and it would be highly informative if not entertaining for the zoo visitors. We are beginning to see many new exhibits that function this way.

In a paper presented many years ago at a Dr. Scholl nutrition conference at Lincoln Park Zoo, Mollie Bloomsmith (formerly Bloomstrand) and I reviewed the literature on great ape feeding and foraging in nature (Maple & Bloomstrand, 1988). We found evidence that chimpanzees, gorillas, and orangutans all spent many hours throughout the day searching for and processing food. This natural proclivity is in stark contrast to the way they were fed in labs and zoos when portions of food were delivered by staff several times each day. Where wild apes consumed a variety of plants and fruit, captive apes experienced little variety and received their meals on a predictable schedule. It was not surprising that many of these apes began to habitually regurgitate and reingest their food. This form of abnormal behavior has been investigated and confirmed by many zoo biologists (e.g., Akers & Schildkraut, 1985; Gould & Bres, 1986; Baker & Easley, 1996; Lukas et al., 1999). In the Gould and Bres (1986) study, feeding browse decreased regurgitation and reingestion (R&R) behavior and increased foraging from 11% to 27% of the day. Lukas et al. (1999) found that R&R decreased when milk was removed from the diet. It appears that gorillas engage in R&R to prolong the feeding period, an adaptation to reduced opportunities to forage and feed in captivity. The phenomenon of R&R is not unique to apes as the clinical literature has cited many examples of human beings who expressed a similar behavior pattern known as the infant rumination syndrome (Thame, Burton, & Forrester, 2000; Murray, Thomas, Hines, & Hilbert, 2018). As with nonhuman species, observers have suggested psychological variables often contribute to the onset of this behavior. Environmental constraints and high stress associated with confinement are clearly contributing factors. For confined zoo animals, wellness requires opportunities to live naturally without constraints or restrictions due to substandard facilities and outmoded operating protocols.

EATING FOR WELLNESS

In many zoos, diets are supervised by veterinarians, but the better funded zoos are working with nutritional consultants, or they may employ their own in-house nutritionist with advanced training or a PhD. It is a very challenging profession because modern zoos exhibit thousands of different species. In a candid review of the field of comparative nutrition, Duane Ullrey (1996) reminded us that "progress in the field can best be made through the cooperative efforts of qualified individuals. The ultimate personal reward should be the health and welfare of the animals we propose to feed." Many changes have been made in the approach to feeding based on wellness and psychology. To encourage movement and foraging, food is distributed throughout the enclosure. The animals must locate the food, which is sometimes distributed high in trees or artificial climbing structures. Food can also be loaded into mechanical feeders that must be operated to deliver bits of food. Cognitive problem-solving is highly beneficial, especially for nonhuman primates. Knowledge gained from field studies also influences modern feeding preferences. When I first started my studies of gorillas, they were fed leafy vegetation but not much fruit. When field studies determined that lowland gorillas preferred fruit (Tutin & Fernandez, 1993), we began to feed a greater proportion of fruit, and we tried to give them a wider variety each and every day. While zoo caregivers used to cut up all foods to facilitate distribution, we now understand that animals prefer to process foods on their own, so a banana served intact gives the animals the opportunity to peel it and consume all of it. Feeding in the zoo fulfills psychological as well as nutritional needs. Again, Ullrey's wisdom is helpful. He recommended that nutritionists learn all they can about feeding strategies and nutrient compositions of chosen and rejected foods in the natural habitat. Further, Dierenfeld (1996) listed taste, texture, odor, size, shape, color, and movement as important factors in feeding. The primates are one group of animals where diet and behavior has been extensively studied in the field (Junge, Williams, & Campbell, 2009; McGraw & Daegling, 2012; Rothman, Chapman, & von Soest, 2012). In a recent study by Bonnie, Bernstein-Kurtycz, Shender, Ross, and Hopper (2019), the investigators compared the foraging behavior of zoo-housed lowland gorillas with a group of captive chimpanzees. The groups differed in their propensity to travel to find food rewards based on their species-typical social organization. In the gorillas, the male silverback dominated the food sources, whereas chimpanzees were more social in their food habits. To feed animals or enrich them properly and effectively, caregivers and veterinarians need to fully understand the dynamics of their social proclivities and the differences recorded for each species.

Other taxa such as reptiles and amphibians need more attention from scientists with advanced herpetological training. We are very fortunate to have a credible herpetologist from UNF who is serving as a visiting professor at the Jacksonville Zoo. An expert on the American alligator, Dr. Adam Rosenblatt is working with Marisa Spain, one of our sponsored zoo students, on an enrichment study of our zoo gator population. Dr. Rosenblatt is very interested in comparing the eating habits of captive and wild alligators, so we should have plenty to say about crocodilian wellness in the coming years. Alligators are the Florida state reptile, and wild populations are ubiquitous throughout the state from north to south. The potential fusion of conservation and wellness should be considered as we begin to investigate the psychological makeup of alligators and their close cousins, crocodiles, caimans, and gharials. With a diversity of captive crocodilians regionally at DAK, Gatorland, and the St. Augustine Alligator Farm in large numbers, our scientific allies have a wonderful opportunity to conduct meaningful comparative research in the next few years. Although there is plenty of scientific information to support our focus on wellness, there are still many unknowns. Many species remain to be studied in the wild and in the zoo, and many of the clinical approaches to wellness lack sufficient management data. We must also be careful of charlatans and misinformation propagated online and in the popular media, especially in Florida where many roadside attractions are located.

Credible zoos and aquariums must be vigilant as they tap less traditional and less tested sources of knowledge, but they should always be open to new ideas. The more successful institutions are often the sources of innovations in husbandry. Veterinarians at DAK have successfully worked with 27 Nile crocodiles that live together. Because of the possibility of wounding in this group, DAK vets wanted to conduct periodic wellness examinations. They trained the animals to shift on cue into a holding area and then to walk out of the water to enter a crate. Once secured in the crate, the animals could be examined for wounds and treated if necessary, and blood was drawn from their tails. They could also radiograph the animals in the crate. The crocodiles continue to be compliant and have shown no conditioned avoidance of the procedure (Fleming & Skurski, 2012).

Some herpetologists employed by zoos have expressed puzzlement about animal welfare. Many of them believe basic husbandry procedures enable them to provide everything the animals need to experience a high quality of life. However, the most obvious problem with traditional reptile exhibits is lack of space. Warwick, Arena, and Steel (2019) found that many exhibits were so restrictive that they prevented snakes from assuming straight line body postures. The old model of exhibition was to display as much diversity as possible in a museum-like set up, with similar species side by side. Reptiles that are well fed are somewhat sedentary, so they don't use the space they are provided. The artistry of these exhibits is quite good as the substrates look real, but innovation to promote activity is rarely achieved with the exhibition of reptiles. An exception was the feeding regime at Zoo Atlanta when I was CEO from 1984 to 2003. The Atlanta herp team, led by curator Howard Hunt, activated Indian gharials (also known as slender-snouted crocodiles), *Gavialus gangeticus*, by introducing live rainbow trout on Wednesdays. We also routinely fed live trout to our rehabilitant bald eagles, while live fish have been delivered for many years as enrichment to grizzly bears at the San Francisco Zoo. Elsewhere (e.g. Maple, 2016) I have discussed the ethical problems of feeding live prey to predators in the zoo. We are generally uncomfortable with the practice in North America, and it is illegal in Australia. There is enough known about awareness and pain in fishes that our willingness to deliver them to an eagle, a gator or a bear will surely wane as the research is assimilated by zoo managers. Nevertheless, in the public situations I've described, we received no visitor complaints, only compliments about the opportunity to see the consumption of live fish that were actively pursued and captured by gharials. As we learn more about the cognitive and social abilities of reptiles (Brando & Burghardt, 2019), we should pay more attention to the interactive features of the physical environment so they can engage in playful manipulation of objects. Maslow's hierarchy of needs is applicable to many mammals, particularly the non-human primates, but we don't yet know how important the psychological variables are for many birds, reptiles, fish, and invertebrates. In the pursuit of wellness for all species, cognitive and social needs should be investigated in any species that has not been the subject of psychological research. For decades Professor Gordon Burghardt has been telling us that reptiles are remarkably clever, capable creatures worthy of our respect. His work continues to inform and enlighten architects. Designers will have to become experts on the fulfillment of higher needs, embodied in the achievement of wellness, to meet the needs of all species. Larger reptiles such as anacondas, pythons, and dragons are rarely exhibited properly, but I am hopeful that the involvement of psychologists and ethologists with herpetological interests will correct this situation.

The dualistic nature of Maslow's writings is the essential starting point for wellness. Maslow's hierarchy of needs applies to people and to animals. Every zoo biologist committed to the science of animal welfare should examine Maslow's thinking to identify research opportunities and environmental stimuli that contribute to the enhancement of psychological well-being in all taxa. Clearly, the expansion of choices, social structures, and intellectual challenges are the section of the Maslow tree where innovation will be most effective. From the zoo perspective, providing groups of chimpanzees, gorillas, and baboons with cognitive workstations where they are encouraged to activate their curious minds will be much more interesting to the paying guest. Challenging opportunities to solve mental problems also contribute to resiliency, an important attribute of thriving. A life without challenges is a life that is not worth living.

At the Palm Beach Zoo, the birthplace of wildlife wellness, the construct has been incorporated into the foundation of animal care. In a marketing brochure (Big Cat Advocate) for the Palm Beach Zoo "Big Cat Society," the following statement demonstrates the value of their training program for veterinary care with big cats and other animals:

> An important element in animal wellness is the ability for our animals to learn behaviors that motivate them to participate in their own care. For example, physical exams by a willing tiger regularly takes place with no restraints or sedation. Our animals learn to present a tail or hip for injections and blood draws and to present paws, eyes or open

mouths when asked. This allows our zoologists to conduct basic veterinary care that is fun and safe for everyone at the zoo.

Thus, wellness is manifest in both basic health and mental health. For this reason, zoo veterinarians and psychologists have good reason to communicate and collaborate.

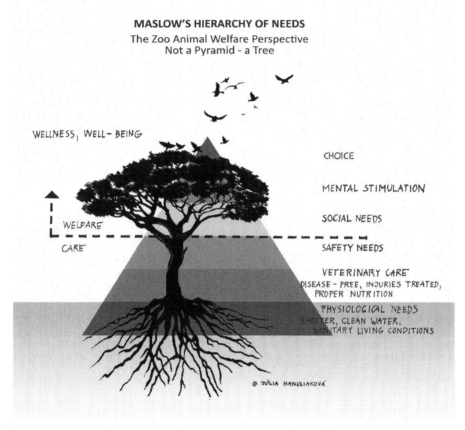

FIGURE 2.4. JULIA HANULIAKOVA'S ILLUSTRATION OF MASLOW'S HIERARCHY OF NEEDS.

CIRCADIAN WELLNESS

Given the diversity of species we exhibit and manage in zoos and aquariums, how do we determine if they are thriving? In her new book *Thrive*, Arianna Huffington (2014) defines the term for human beings. Thriving involves well-being in multiple areas: physical, emotional, social, and psychological. Each of these dimensions applies to animals. However, animals in traditional zoos live in a world vastly different than the natural world. When animals adapt to the environment human beings have created for them, they are coping with features that do not align with their nature or their origin. To encourage thriving in any form of wildlife in a zoo, we must recapture those features that stimulate natural behavior patterns. For zoo animals, thriving is indicated when the animal is behaving naturally. When past zoo designers attempted to activate animals, only one feature of natural behavior was the desired outcome. We succeeded in stimulating activity and defeated lethargy. Activating animals was a bold step, but it didn't represent the full scope of wellness. For example, lions sleep 18–20 hours per day, so they are not very active when zoo visitors arrive to observe them at the zoo. A lion can be living well even when it is not very active. So thriving must be measured according to the natural activity cycle of the species. A captive lion that is able to sleep as it would in the wild is an example of thriving; its activity pattern is normal for this species. Other species are more active at night in the wild, but traditional zoo management prevents them from going outside at night. Visitors see them in the daylight when they are less active. Once we recognize their natural habits and preferences and let them out at night, they make a different impression. In a study at Zoo Atlanta, Brockett et al. (1999) discovered that unchained African elephants in a night house were socially active throughout the night. Of course, anyone who lives among wild elephants has witnessed their nocturnal activities when they move about the landscape ripping up vegetation. Zoos such as the Singapore Zoo, which cater to their natural behavior, encourage elephants, fishing cats, giraffes, rhinos, and hippos to spend some of their evening hours in their outdoor enclosures. For example, in nature, elephants are typically active 20 hours in a 24-hour cycle. They can do this in Singapore because the operators offer nighttime dinners and entertainment and attract significant attendance at night. The animals are essentially working at night, and this makes night operations financially feasible. A 24-hour evaluation of the Singapore Zoo collection suggests that these animals are living much as they would in a state of nature. Even when innovative zoo managers have to limit nighttime exhibition by putting them inside at 11:00 p.m., they are still giving them another six hours of activity over that of a traditional zoo's operating schedule. The closer we can replicate natural activity schedules in the zoo, the closer we get to conditions that enable thriving. The night safari represents an unusual opportunity to study its effects on well-being. So far the institutions that permit night exhibition have not prioritized research, but we need to know the pros and cons of activation at night. I see evidence of an upside to this approach but no indicators that it could be harmful. However, night safaris do require a committed workforce that may need incentives to work day and night. Should it prove to be as stimulating as it appears, more zoos are going to adopt night time exhibition as a marketing strategy.

The studies we have reviewed in this chapter indicate that we still have a lot to learn about wellness. We can only advance our standards if we continue to discover what is needed for each species and each individual in the collection. A useful conclusion from Dunn's *High-Level Wellness* reveals his expectations and hope for future applications of the wellness construct. The following passage from Dunn's book is a fitting conclusion for this chapter:

> The philosophy is not a completed one. It needs further developing. It needs to be explored, pried, tested, questioned, and added to in all of its manifold dimensions. A broad search, interdisciplinary in character, is called for. (p. viii)

Chapter 3

EFFICACY OF THE WELLNESS BRAND

In 2010 I was invited to speak at an animal welfare conference hosted by the Detroit Zoo. No North American zoo is more committed to this subject than Detroit. Its CEO, Ron Kagan, has advocated for zoo-based animal welfare reforms his entire career. The Detroit Zoo is remarkable for its innovative exhibits but also for the enthusiasm of its employees. If you visit this zoo, each and every employee is capable and eager to share the story of their dramatic transformation from a traditional to a naturalistic and humane zoological park. Detroit was exceptional from the start. When it opened on August 5, 1928, the Detroit Zoo committed to the open-concept exhibit philosophy of German designer Carl Hagenbeck, whose family engineered moated zoos without steel barriers to separate the animals from the visitors. By adopting Hagenbeck's ideas, Detroit became one of America's first cageless zoological parks, a trend that has continued with the immersive architecture that has dominated zoo design since the 1970s. The most recent example of Detroit's naturalistic approach to design is the Polk Penguin Conservation Center, where 75 penguins representing four species are exhibited in a 33,000-square-foot, 326,000-gallon aquatic habitat. Gallons are a measure of volume, and this metric confirms that at 7,049 cubic feet or 75 million cubic inches, Detroit's exhibit is the most spacious penguin habitat in the world. The birds dive and interact in water that is 25 feet (7.62 meters) deep. They can locomote and investigate every cubic inch of this massive pool. Detroit is also known for the Arctic Ring of Life, an innovative exhibit accommodating polar bears, arctic foxes, and seals. At 4 acres, it is one of the most complex indoor-outdoor exhibits for polar bears in North America, featuring a 70-foot long acrylic tunnel where the bears and the seals can frolic within parallel aquatic habitats with translucent barriers. Few world zoos have invested so much capital to achieve such a high standard of animal welfare for so much of its collection.

LEADERSHIP IN ANIMAL WELFARE

The Detroit Zoo was the first of AZA's member institutions to promote animal welfare as their brand and the first to create a dedicated staff leadership position with animal welfare in its title. The first bullet point in the zoo's mission statement aims to "demonstrate leadership in conservation and animal welfare." Despite expressions of support for animal welfare reform, many AZA institutions were slow to embrace the movement. It took many years and many workshops and conferences for zoo directors, curators, and veterinarians to follow Detroit's lead. One of the first zoos to seize the opportunity was Brookfield Zoo in Chicago. Because they dedicated resources to found the unique Center for the Science of Animal Care and Welfare and chose to operate a competitive animal welfare research program, they quickly became global institutional leaders. The Brookfield team organized a series of international meetings where scientific research could be continuously disseminated and debated. These meetings brought together the world's leading experts in animal welfare: zoo and aquarium professionals, academic collaborators, and nonprofit executives devoted to higher standards and better practices of animal management. Much of this collaborative work has been published. Lincoln Park Zoo, also located in Chicago, is another leader in animal welfare research and practice. The zoo is best known for its innovative exhibits and for its long history of success in breeding and managing great apes. Lincoln Park has also pioneered new research methods and technology, and their research productivity is extraordinary due in part to their success in recruiting talented curators with doctoral degrees. During the past decade, animal welfare has become a much higher priority for accredited zoos and aquariums, approaching the first priority of conservation with some of us daring to suggest that the two priorities should be regarded as essentially coequal (Maple & Perdue, 2013; Maple & Bloomsmith, 2018). Instituting a successful animal welfare strategy in a zoo or aquarium is hard work and it takes an animal care team that is committed to implementing a working system. Often such programs are resisted at the top of an organization, so it is important to acknowledge that the support of institutional and board leaders is essential. Other North American zoos are moving in the right direction to impact conservation, science, and animal welfare including Birmingham Zoo, Cleveland MetroParks Zoo, Indianapolis Zoo, and Woodland Park Zoo. They join the bigger institutions such as San Diego, Smithsonian's National Zoo, and New York's Bronx Zoo that have made historic investments in scientific programs and personnel. Animal welfare has been a bigger challenge for aquariums due to their unique vulnerabilities, but they also have special skills to share as we work together to protect the open oceans and the wildlife that must be occasionally rescued and rehabilitated. We still have much to do to claim that our profession is operating with a strong scientific foundation but there are encouraging signs. Collaborative projects such as the gorilla heart project and the search for analogs of Dementia in apes have been set up with the involvement of some of our nation's most important scientists.

The talk I delivered in Detroit, Michigan, introduced the wellness construct to a large number of my zoo and aquarium colleagues, although I had previously published my ideas in a commentary for the journal *Zoo Biology* (Maple & Bocian, 2013). My coauthor, David Bocian, general curator at the San Francisco Zoo, was in the audience in Detroit. David had earned his master's degree in biology at San Francisco State University under the supervision of Professor Hal Markowitz, an icon of animal welfare science and one of my closest academic friends. David was intrigued with my argument that wellness was an expansion of animal welfare offering unique opportunities to improve psychological well-being in zoo animals. The San Francisco Zoo was in the midst of a slow recovery from the highly publicized 2007 death of a zoo visitor who allegedly taunted a tiger until she leapt from her exhibit and killed him. I was very familiar with the undercurrent of citizen opposition to the zoo. Hard-core opponents of zoos were also active in other coastal cities such as Los Angeles and Seattle. Seattle's cadre of adversaries were difficult to explain as the zoo had been an exemplary facility since its comprehensive reform and revitalization in the late 1970s (Hancocks, 2001). In spite of this vocal cadre of rabid adversaries, the zoo continued to move forward in a public/private renaissance with new leadership and new enthusiasm from private sector and foundation donors and sponsors.

RAISING THE BAR IN SAN FRANCISCO

I suggested that zoo leaders in San Francisco should consider going beyond welfare to embrace wellness as a solution to their public confidence problem. I didn't think it would be difficult to make this case to zoo leadership since it was essentially a commitment to better practices and higher standards of animal care. David himself was already on record as a strong advocate of animal welfare reform and ethical animal management. Professor Markowitz, David's academic mentor, contributed mightily to the institution's scientific reputation during the years he was affiliated with the zoo. However, the task for San Francisco would require more than a commitment to animal welfare reforms; it would also require an intensive marketing approach to build a wellness brand. No zoo in North America had built wellness into the fabric of its identity. The closest example was the strong animal welfare brand of the Detroit Zoo. While animal welfare was gaining traction in AZA zoos, branding was a much greater challenge. I reasoned that wellness was so well understood by people in the West that it would be relatively easy to demonstrate its relevance to animals in the zoo. We were both excited about the potential of this new idea, so David took the next step by introducing me to his CEO, Tanya Peterson. This conversation led to an invitation for me to visit with San Francisco Zoo board leaders to pitch the wellness approach. I was encouraged to submit a proposal, and it wasn't long before I was flying to San Francisco monthly to guide the change I was advocating. A native Californian, born in East LA and raised in San Diego County, I was really excited about the opportunity to return to my home state.

Wellness was a new idea for the zoo but a familiar idea to San Francisco residents. I had tinkered with the wellness construct during my six years as CEO of the Palm Beach Zoo, but my fascination with behavior change started much earlier in graduate school. My background in psychology is broader than the subfield of animal behavior, my graduate specialty at UC Davis. As a psychology major at the University of the Pacific, I sought opportunities in the field of mental health and spent one year as a student professional assistant to Robert Baird, a clinical psychologist at Stockton State Hospital. Bob schooled me on the conditioned emotional response, a phenomenon that helped me understand how fear could control behavior in people and animals. During a postdoctoral appointment at the UC Davis medical school, supported by a grant for biomedical research from the Giannini Foundation, I sharpened my focus on comparative psychopathology, a subject I recently revisited in a book I coauthored with Dan Marston (Marston & Maple, 2016). My earliest research on nonhuman primates in captive settings in zoos and laboratories provided evidence that the social and physical environments in these institutions were insufficient to promote a healthy life (Maple, 1979; Maple, 1980). For this reason, many of my colleagues began to promote environmental enrichment as a way to improve quality of life in captivity (Shepherdson, Mellen, & Hutchins, 1998). If anyone can be considered the father of enrichment, it is Hal Markowitz, so the San Francisco Zoo has a long history of contributing to this important movement.

I began my work in San Francisco in 2011 and completed the engagement in 2014. We concentrated on setting a standard for wellness within the zoo, influencing the design process to inform wellness-inspired exhibits and communicating the new operating philosophy to members, donors, media, the local government, and the general public. The marketing of this new operating focus has effectively branded San Francisco Zoo as the first zoo in the nation committed to wellness. With the passage of time, it is virtually certain that surrounding communities will acknowledge the significance of this transformation. Once animals are visibly thriving, the zoo will be perceived as a vastly different place—revitalized and fully re-freshed. Now six years into their wellness revolution, an examination of the San Francisco Zoo website provides strong evidence that the wellness program is itself beginning to thrive.

Because wellness is a new approach to zoo and aquarium exhibition and management, social media is the best way to quickly rally visitors, members, and donors to the cause. We also produced testimonials by caregivers and volunteers who were committed to innovations in animal husbandry including animal training. I continue to believe the most ef-fective demonstrations of animal welfare are the actions of dedicated staff. Wellness can be measured by what we do for animals in our care, and what we do each year should be significantly greater than the previous year. Just a 10% greater effort by staff can produce measurable improvements in the quality of an animal's life at the zoo. The story of caregivers who spend more quality time with the animals, provide them with more choices in their diets, increase their access to enrichment items, or introduce greater variance in their daily routines is a story worth sharing with zoo visitors, members, and the community at large. The San Francisco Zoo leadership eagerly promoted wellness as their unique brand. They produced a series of compelling print deliverables to drive membership recruitment and capital fund-raising (Figure 3.2).

San Francisco
Zoological Society

WELLNESS

FIGURE 3.1. WELLNESS BROCHURE. COURTESY OF THE
SAN FRANCISCO ZOOLOGICAL SOCIETY.

As the global market data revealed in Chapter 2, from the universe of entrepreneurial companies and organizations such as universities and nonprofits committed to health and wellness, there are unlimited numbers of prospects for sponsorship and philanthropy as we seek funding to advance the agenda of our visionary zoos and aquariums. Insurance companies have always been at the top of my list of potential sponsors. Throughout the West, where their brand is ubiquitous, Kaiser Permanente promotes their branded image with a simple but powerful message: thrive! Fund-raising professionals are doubtless already recruiting this company to sponsor wellness programs at zoos and aquariums in the West. *Thriving* is one of the most powerful words used in marketing today. People who select certain food items will thrive, thriving is facilitated by a vacation in California or Florida, and cruise ships are associated with an outcome of thriving. In Florida we are building zoos to encourage thriving in our animal collections, and we design zoo campuses to make sure that a visit to the zoo contributes to thriving in our visitors. As Maslow might say, thriving is a peak experience.

REFORM AS SOCIAL MARKETING

My experience as the reform leader of the rebranded Zoo Atlanta taught me that zoos and aquariums were obligated to exhibit animals in humane, stimulating, and naturalistic settings. This was the only acceptable way to educate and inspire visitors to appreciate and protect the natural world. The key to our success in revitalizing a deteriorating city zoo was our scientific foundation of management, exhibition, and education. By creating partnerships with faculty and students in colleges and universities in the Atlanta area, we opened the doors of the zoo to creativity and innovation, and we made it possible to study the changes we made. No zoo had ever been rebuilt in this way, and it hasn't been replicated in the 36 years since the Zoo Atlanta renaissance began. The story we continue to tell about this unique experiment demonstrates how powerful and compelling it has become (Norton et al., 1995; Minteer, Maienschein, & Collins, 2018). The early marketing of the reforms we implemented was carried out by the same media that had first uncovered the sensational details of mismanagement and neglect in Atlanta. I am happy to give credit to the *Atlanta Journal-Constitution* newspaper for their diligent reporting. Electronic media followed suit, and together they spread the news to every media outlet in the world. The Atlanta business community was embarrassed by the details and the failure of city government to control the bleeding. By the time that Mayor Andrew Young recruited me to become the interim director, the zoo had been named one of America's 10 worst zoos. The silver lining in all of this bad publicity is that news media chose to continue following the zoo during its recovery phase, and print and electronic reporters began to tell the story of how we managed dramatic and lasting reform. In fact, the revolutionary change that launched Zoo Atlanta as one of the world's first "ethical arks" was a feel-good animal welfare story. This outcome proved to me that advances in animal welfare could be promoted just like a new birth of an endangered, charismatic species. Eventually, I beat the marketing drum for the synergistic cause of conservation and animal welfare. With the passage of time, animal welfare morphed into wellness, a vision shaped in Atlanta and incubated in West Palm Beach. To be successful zoo directors must understand marketing, and marketing directors must understand the twin priorities of conservation and welfare/wellness. Both priorities will advance if our message is consistent, continuous and clear. We must also project a sense of optimism to persuade others to join us as members, donors, and sponsors. One of the unique attributes of wellness is its inherent optimism; there are essentially no limits to wellness. In earlier publications I have discussed the power of optimism in promoting conservation (Maple, 1995; Maple, 2016; Maple & Segura, 2017). The need to effectively spread the good news of our conservation successes and to give our partners hope has been argued by many other conservation scientists and leaders (Clayton & Myers, 2009; Swaisgood & Sheppard, 2010). A commitment to wellness can help us advance a positive perspective for conservation.

SHAPING THE WELLNESS VISION

By the time I was recruited to South Florida in my second assignment as a zoo executive in 2005, I had a pretty good idea of how to take the next bold steps beyond animal welfare. My greatest achievement at the Palm Beach Zoo was designing and building the first Leadership in Energy and Environmental Design (LEED) certified zoo animal hospital in the nation. Certified LEED Gold, the Melvin J. and Claire Levine Animal Care Complex opened on Earth Day in 2008. The complex was originally designed to include an on-campus wellness center devoted to the enhancement of mental health, a perfect complement to physical health represented in the high-quality veterinary facilities and advanced medical technology in the zoo hospital. Although I retired from the Palm Beach Zoo before the wellness center could be built, I worked with architect Gary Lee at CLR Design to develop a concept for the building and wrote about it in an article published in *Palm Beach Zoo Magazine* (Maple, 2008). This first iteration of a wellness center was programmed to emphasize the psychological approach to health and wellness. We intended to provide space for zoo staff that was devoted to enriching the lives of animals with the daily delivery of interactive technology, locally harvested browse, and useable objects and toys. Staff would also be encouraged to safely interact with the animals under their care and give them as much control over their daily activities as possible. A special feature of our wellness center concept was its utility as an educational venue where we could teach wellness to our visitors. Three people on my Palm Beach Zoo staff deserve the lion's share of credit for building our local wellness vision: Gail Eaton, Kristen Cytacki, and Stephanie Allard. My former marketing director at Palm Beach Zoo, Gail is currently a marketing consultant in Boston, Massachusetts, who still works with me on special projects. Kristen leads the education department at the Palm Beach Zoo, while Stephanie is now the director of animal welfare at the Detroit Zoo. The roots of wellness are alive in both of these institutions.

SUSTAINING WELLNESS IN ZOOS AND AQUARIUMS

Early in my career as a zoo executive, I was taught that "marketing is every-thing you do." Long lines, dirty restrooms, incomprehensible messaging, sloppy paper signage, or poor food service will defeat all the good things that we promote through advertising. Visiting DAK in Orlando with my family convinced me a long time ago that theme parks offered a superior model for managing a good time. Disney planners and managers leave no stone unturned in creating one magical moment after another. To them, a visit to their parks are performances that require skilled direction. The show must go on flawlessly each and every day. What this means for the rest of us is we have to use our financial and human resources wisely to of-fer the kind of experience that our communities expect. The Walt Disney Company appears to have unlimited resources, but my 18 years of experi-ence as a Disney advisor working with DAK leaders and planners offers another perspective. If DAK was priced differently, with a U.S. $20 entry fee rather than their current admission of more than U.S. $100, they would still exceed expectations. The Walt Disney Company has developed an operating philosophy that puts the customer first, and every employee is trained to this standard. Visitors to DAK and the other Disney properties can choose from a vast array of food service options, restrooms are meticu-lously clean, and Disney manages crowds and waiting lines better than any attraction in the world. More importantly, they have invested in superior facilities that stimulate the senses and enlarge our fantasies about travel and adventure, and Disney's research and development is second to none. They are constantly evaluating and upgrading according to their findings.

When the Walt Disney Company committed to building a new theme park with living animals, they knew they would have to prove they could meet or exceed the highest standards in the zoo profession. To accom-plish this objective, they reached out to an advisory board comprised of zoological leaders, conservationists, and experts in animal welfare. I was a member of this team for 18 years. Working with the company's elite cadre of Imagineers, we offered the design team our best advice and the benefit of our collective experience. In addition to our involvement, DAK managers recruited some of our industry's best employees to populate their park with superior caregivers, curators, scientists, and veterinarians, some of whom worked for me in Atlanta. While I hated losing these people, I knew they were entering a unique and rewarding workplace that would require their best effort. Since they also recruited some of my top graduate students who were finishing their doctoral degrees at Georgia Tech, I sent them forward to DAK with enthusiasm. All of them thrived, and several of them retired from DAK with many memories, significant stock options, and notable achievements in conservation, education, and science. Because DAK designed and built superior, naturalistic animal facilities for every species they exhibited, they immediately became international leaders in animal welfare. The DAK brand includes a commitment to animals as well as people. I'm not sure if a debate about whether animals or people were Disney's first priority could be easily settled at DAK because they have seriously invested their human and financial resources to the full benefit of both. Of course, the powerful Walt Disney Company is uniquely capable of succeeding at both. Disney learned from their mentors in the zoo business, but we have greatly benefited from contact and collaboration with the Disney team.

LINKING CONSERVATION TO WELLNESS

The zoos and aquariums in the Association of Zoos and Aquariums committed to conservation as their first priority in 1980. They unified for the purpose of organized husbandry, genetic management of populations, and sophisticated science-based methods of species reproduction. AZA's Species Survival Plan Programs influenced the way other world zoos managed their collections, leading to worldwide cooperation in reproductive animal science. Efforts to improve breeding required that zoo and aquarium animals would be exhibited in species-appropriate social groups, so our expertise had to be upgraded with the recruitment of dedicated scientific staff and outsourced collaborators from our best universities and medical centers. Eventually, our commitment to conservation led to greater support of field conservation. The institutional model for field research and protection was the former New York Zoological Society, rebranded in 1993 as the Wildlife Conservation Society (WCS). Currently, WCS manages an investment portfolio of nearly U.S. $800 million for the support of field research and field conservation in 65 countries. Other zoos and aquariums around the world also support field projects and advance protection, but none of them come close to the impact of WCS.

This noble commitment to wildlife conservation led to public relations campaigns to demonstrate our support for wild populations of animals and the wild places that sustain them. AZA member institutions enhanced the educational value of our exhibits with graphics that illustrated the plight of wild animals and our efforts to overcome these problems (Bashaw & Maple, 2001; Stoinski, Allen, Bloomsmith, Forthman, & Maple, 2002). On our websites we told the continuing story of the projects we initiated locally and globally and the partnerships that enabled our participation in the worldwide conservation movement. AZA established industry awards and raised funds to celebrate our best efforts. One example of the impact of organized zoos working for conservation is the AZA Giant Panda Species Survival Plan. Four North American zoos currently exhibit this species on loan from China with each exhibit contributing at least U.S. $500,000 annually for conservation projects in China. These funds are generated by each zoo from gate receipts and donations, with the U.S. Fish and Wildlife Service accounting for the use of these dollars. The four zoos, the San Diego Zoo, the National Zoo, the Memphis Zoo, and Zoo Atlanta, have generated more than U.S. $57 million since the start of this panda lease program in 1996. The giant panda is the symbol the World Wildlife Fund selected to represent wildlife conservation globally, so this wildlife logo is a powerful marketing tool for zoos that choose to deploy it.

At the Bronx Zoo, managed by the WCS, the Congo Gorilla Forest exhibit encourages visitors to use a computerized touchscreen to select the animals in Africa they want their admission fees to support. More than merely social marketing, this unique exhibit activates the visitor to engage in funding conservation. Following New York's lead, all zoos are attempting to link their new exhibits to conservation projects they support in nature while advocating for direct visitor participation in conservation through membership and philanthropy. The modern zoo aims to educate and inspire, but they are also strongly committed to motivating zoo guests to individually and collectively take action on behalf of wildlife and ecosystems locally and globally.

Prioritizing conservation has built goodwill for accredited zoos that have embraced the issue and contributed significant funding for this purpose. Our collective educational programs have also contributed to our good reputation. A Roper poll released in 1992 concluded that zoos and aquariums were the third most trusted messengers of wildlife conservation and environmental issues. Only *National Geographic* and Jacques Cousteau rated higher at that time (Fravel, 2003). However, our conservation message has not protected zoos and aquariums from critics who question the seriousness of our commitment. While there is plenty of evidence that the best zoos are moving in the right direction of educating, conserving and protecting, too many of the world's 10,000 zoos are substandard. More than 2,000 of these outliers are operating in the United States, regulated by the U.S. Department of Agriculture. Even the best zoos in North America, accredited by AZA, spend only a small portion of their operating budgets on conservation. While we talk a good game, we need to rise above the hyperbole and do better. Although it is likely that the gap between better and lesser zoos and aquariums will close, we will have to do much more to impress those who doubt us. While some of these critics are "haters" who want to close all zoos, the next generation of zoogoers, millennials, and their successors, are not yet fans. If we don't convert them to support us, our visitation will surely and significantly decline. It is easy to see this problem as a life or death issue. To simply survive, zoo and aquarium visionaries must design and build an entire planet of credible zoos and aquariums. These are institutions that I call "zoos of consequence." Of course, like wellness, our zoos need to thrive, not just survive.

To expand the reach of our ideas, I recently extended the life of my research unit at Georgia Tech. When I retired from Tech in 2008, the unit refused to die due to the continuation of research by my former students and collaborators, many of whom were settled in university positions in the Atlanta area. I have since reactivated our collaboration under the brand "Virtual Center for Conservation and Behavior." Wellness springs forth from the integration of the new field of conservation psychology, which is historically connected to the more mature field of environmental psychology. My virtual colleagues and I are writing papers together, planning collaborative funding, and developing infrastructure in other locations in the United States and abroad. I just added a collaborator from Australia (Heather Browning) after we published a paper together in *Frontiers in Psychology* (2019). Over the years I have learned that the visibility of a research program is a marketing tool that reflects your brand and your reputation, generating new ideas, new data, and new publications.

To sustain our scholarship and our leadership, we must continue to be entrepreneurial in our approach to problem-solving and work together to generate the financial support to keep our work going. A major focus of our planning should be a commitment to educating, inspiring, and funding graduate successors in every way we can. We must do this in the face of forces that are working against legitimate animal research. As some laboratories in universities have been closed, we can resurrect successor labs that promote higher standards and better practices in animal welfare; this is essential to the wellness approach to animal management and husbandry. Zoos will be very important in protecting our access to biodiversity, and the involvement of behavioral scientists in the work of the zoo will contribute to the advance of innovations in exhibits and facilities dedicated to the triumph of thriving over coping. Elite zoos and aquariums are becoming living laboratories for comparative psychologists and ethologists who need access to biodiversity. Academic deans are beginning to see the full potential of these assets as they contemplate ways to reduce laboratory expenses and generate external funding from new sources including private philanthropy. In August 2019 I participated in a symposium at the annual convention of the American Psychological Association in Chicago. The panel of professors from five colleges and universities engaged in zoo research shared insider information with an audience curious about how these scientific partnerships are formulated and codified.

FEWER SPECIES, LIVING LARGE

In my personal application of the wellness operating standard, I have argued that when visitors feel sorry for the animals they see at the zoo, they inevitably lose confidence in the institution exhibiting them (Maple & Segura, 2018). Any conservation message, no matter how compelling, will not be believed if the animals in the collection are perceived as bored, depressed, inactive, or unhappy. People who withdraw their support will only return to zoos when there is evidence that the animals are living well. The best zoos effectively disseminate knowledge and generate joy in their visitors. A comprehensive program of wellness, including wellness-inspired design, is the pathway to zoos of consequence, zoos that put the animals first, and zoos that stand for something other than entertainment. It must be very obvious to visitors and the community at large that zoo animals aren't suffering in captivity and their exhibitors are not satisfied with conditions that enable animals merely to cope. Thriving should be the goal of the zoo committed to wellness, and we must promote this idea with the application of bold innovations that transform traditional hard architecture into a softer, naturalistic oasis of biodiversity. The marketing goal of soft architecture is to influence the thinking of our community, visitors, and donors. They must begin to believe in our zoos again, knowing that we have achieved the highest state of the art for managed care. Once the public is satisfied with the evident quality of life at our zoos and aquariums, our conservation message will be more effective. Leaders and governing boards now recognize that we have to deliver on several fronts. Our revenue must support better exhibits, better management programs, and expanded support for conservation locally and globally. It will be no surprise that better zoos will require record attendance levels and likely as not higher admission fees. Already zoos and aquariums are diversifying their revenue models as they provide more food and gift opportunities, offer IMAX-type theater programs, and charge for parking and other amenities including contact programs for small groups who safely interact with or feed animals for a fee. Such contact programs have to be carefully planned and executed so they don't work against our overall wellness ethic. Training is good for zoo and aquarium animals as it activates them and mentally stimulates them, but trainers have to be careful not to appear to dominate the animals with aversive control or food-deprivation techniques. These discredited methods are anachronistic symbols of a bygone era when circuses and menageries were common exhibitors of wild animals. The perception that orcas were dominated by their trainers was one reason SeaWorld received such bad publicity after the release of the independent film *Blackfish* (Maple, 2016). There is a growing consensus that entertainment is no longer an acceptable justification for capturing and displaying large marine mammals including orcas and other cetaceans. We will also need to repurpose our collections, focus on fewer species in larger habitats, appropriately organize them into species-appropriate social groups, provide a varied diet and opportunities to control its delivery, and specialize in species that can successfully adapt to our respective climate zones. Size is no longer the preferred way to judge our collections. Institutions that boast about how many animals they exhibit are operating by an outmoded standard that no longer advances our reputation or standing in the zoo profession. In contrast, aquariums and zoos that exhibit successfully and reproduce and reintroduce the greatest number of threatened or endangered taxa in complex, naturalistic settings will be admired and respected by their peers. Biodiversity and wellness are not perfectly aligned since it is not the number of species that is important but the appropriate size of the groups displayed. Zoos don't need to display both African and Asian elephants, but they should try to display one species in a large herd. We will have to be creative to represent biodiversity in zoos of limited size.

PROMOTING WELLNESS IN JACKSONVILLE

The marketing team at the Jacksonville Zoo and Gardens created wonderful exhibit graphics to promote the new wellness-inspired African Forest exhibit that provides innovative facilities for bonobos, gorillas, and African monkeys. The focal point of this marketing effort is a massive artificial kapok tree also known as the "wellness tree." This structure provides arboreal opportunities for monkeys and apes, elevated tunnels to extend their travel in vertical space, and a cognitive workstation that enables keepers and scientists to interact with them via touchscreen computer technology. The naming of this enrichment device is a lesson in branding. Through the design process, *kapok tree* emerged as the working name for this impressive structure; however, the word *kapok* has no inherent meaning in terms of wellness. I preferred to connect the tree to our wellness program. The term *wellness tree* carries meaning that tells the visitor about our priorities, so I like the more effective brand.

The Jacksonville Zoo and Gardens has been on board with wellness-inspired design before they had a term for the process. Before the Philadelphia Zoo opened their Zoo360 exhibits featuring vertical pathways for primates and large cats, the Jacksonville Zoo design team built a similar elevated structure for the innovative Sumatran and Malayan tiger exhibit. This exhibit is remarkable for the amount of choice tigers can exercise. If they choose to be distant from the visitors, they can opt for a distant location through the pathways. Fortunately, the zoo has many tigers, so visitors always have a good view of some of them. Choice is a distinct feature of wellness, so both the Jacksonville and Philadelphia Zoos score high on this dimension of the construct. When visitors see the animals interacting with devices that indicate higher intelligence, they appreciate how much the zoo has invested in their psychological well-being.

When I served as CEO of Zoo Atlanta, I required that our job descriptions include psychology as a preferred degree when most zoos favored zoology. Based on my own experience, there is no more useful degree for working in a zoo or aquarium than psychology. I think this way because a knowledge of people is the most important factor in preparing better zoos for animals and visitors. It was gratifying to be able to recruit the involvement of professors of psychology and their students when I simultaneously served as CEO of Zoo Atlanta and professor of psychology at Georgia Tech. I am particularly proud of a work climate survey that was conducted by Georgia Tech graduate students working with industrial-organizational psychologist Jack Feldman. This master's level research was very helpful to Zoo Atlanta's human resources unit as it evaluated employee satisfaction.

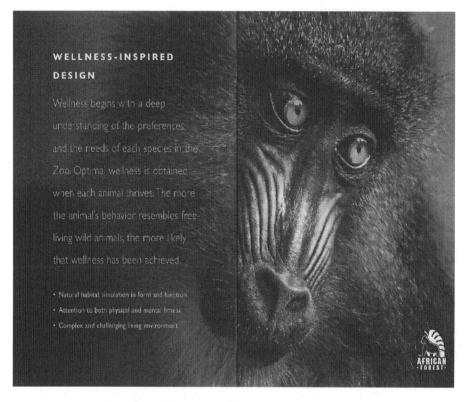

WELLNESS-INSPIRED DESIGN

Wellness begins with a deep understanding of the preferences and the needs of each species in the Zoo. Optimal wellness is obtained when each animal thrives. The more the animal's behavior resembles free-living wild animals, the more likely that wellness has been achieved.

• Natural habitat simulation in form and function
• Attention to both physical and mental fitness
• Complex and challenging living environment

AFRICAN ·FOREST·

FIGURE 3.2. WELLNESS-INSPIRED ARCHITECTURE AT THE JACKSONVILLE ZOO AND GARDENS.

The synergy between academia and the zoo was evident to Heini Hediger long ago when he served on the faculty of the University of Zurich while leading the zoo as its director from 1954 to 1973. It is interesting that early in his career as a zoo director, he took a very strong interest in public relations. His popular writings helped to advance his ideas as he shaped modern zoo management. In a videotaped interview I conducted with him in 1987 (available on YouTube), the founding father of zoo biology told me that he did not have the opportunity to study animal psychology because the subject was not taught in Swiss universities. Instead, he studied human psychology to learn the general principles that clearly applied to both human beings and animals. Although Hediger is regarded as a European ethologist, his work is an important link to the history of environmental psychology globally. His debt to the broader field of psychology is expressed in his many publications, especially his book *Studies of the Psychology and Behaviour of Animals in Zoos and Circuses* (Hediger, 1955). Hediger's behavioral ideas were a powerful influence on zoo design. He understood that zoo animals responded best to architecture that reflected the functionality of their natural habitats. Hediger abhorred the cube and felt this shape was essentially "un-biological". His answer to architects who persisted with cubic buildings was to demand curvilinear structures like the famed Africa House at Zoo Zurich.

THE PSYCHOLOGY OF MARKETING

Psychologists have contributed to the field of advertising and marketing by examining techniques of persuasion and behavior change. One of the important early contributors to the psychology of advertising was the behaviorist John B. Watson (Buckley, 1989). Principles of learning based on animal and human experimental studies generated laws of learning and memory that shaped the field. Due to Watson's influence, the psychology of advertising became more scientific in its approach (Kreshel, 1990). Two scientific findings are particularly relevant to branding in the zoo: (a) the principle of primacy (Lund, 1925) and (b) the principle of recency (Garnefield & Steinhoff, 2013). Psychological research has consistently demonstrated that people remember information that is presented first (primacy) in a sequence, and information that is presented last (recency). When we design zoos, we should try to deliver a strong message at the front gate. Usually visitors enter and depart in this area, so the message is received first and last. Too often planners are so fixated on revenue production that they only think about the strategic position of shops. Far more important is the power of our messages as people enter and depart. In a zoo dedicated to a wellness philosophy, this is where we need our most powerful example of thriving. Even better if the exhibit selected for this location is also an example of our commitment to conservation. In Jacksonville we are considering an entry plaza that presents the Florida manatee in a naturalistic pool that simulates the animal's natural aquatic habitat. Thriving manatees deliver a strong message and combined with the zoo's commitment to rescuing manatees in its recently completed rescue center, visitors will understand that Jacksonville Zoo and Gardens is fully committed to protecting wildlife inside and outside the zoo. In this case, the wellness brand is represented in what we say and what we do, and it rings true among the citizens of Florida. We will return to this idea in Chapter 6 in discussing the logistics and placement of institutional wellness centers.

SHARING AND
EXPANDING THE WELLNESS BRAND

San Francisco and Jacksonville are not the only zoos that are developing a wellness operating philosophy. In Florida, the nearby Brevard Zoo in Melbourne has created a wellness unit similar to the one we started in Jacksonville in 2014. Innovative exhibits and a partnership with faculty and students at the Florida Institute of Technology is contributing to superior management and effective messaging in the park. The Brevard Zoo staff have produced a thoughtful wellness brochure with details on how the construct has enabled better management throughout the zoo. From the 34-page, full-color document, these passages proclaim the priority of wellness at Brevard Zoo:

> Animal wellness, which has always been and will continue to be the zoo's top priority, refers to an individual's collective physical, mental and emotional states over a period of time…Our commitment to animal wellness…is a challenging continuous journey. Our initiatives will continue far and wide beyond this report as we prioritize animal

wellness as the fundamental principle in our mission of
wildlife conservation through education and participation.
(p. 1)

Another example of wellness branding is found at the Denver Zoo in
Colorado where a recent conference exploring wellness programs attracted
25 participants from AZA institutions. Since 2017 the Denver Zoo has
employed a director of animal welfare and research, reflecting an industry trend toward empirical zoos supporting the science of animal welfare.
In cooperation with the other management units at the Denver Zoo, the
program is reaching out to elevate employee morale around an expanded
wellness theme. They are creating a culture of wellness advocacy accepted
by the entire staff. The Denver Zoo is not only practicing wellness, they
are now teaching it to others by hosting and exporting wellness workshops
so AZA zoos and aquariums can prepare for the new, rigorous welfare accreditation standards. The deliverables provided for the Denver conference
(Figure 3.5) reveal what I believe is the next frontier of animal welfare:
a wellness standard adopted by every AZA-accredited zoo and aquarium
with messaging fully understood by every employee. Wellness, of course,
is everyone's concern, and we should be working to share our expertise
and advance wellness as a benefit to the communities that patronize our
institutions. In the world of sports, branding is extremely important to
the success of the team (Staples, 2019). It is so important that college and
professional athletic departments have elected to hire dedicated staff to develop and manage the brand. Zoos and aquariums that hope to influence
their audience ought to consider this option since a strong wellness brand
may determine whether zoos and aquariums thrive in the marketplace of
ideas. I foresee many opportunities to promote the brand on souvenirs and
by hosting branded events in the zoo and the surrounding community.
Wellness can be promoted just as we would promote a charismatic individual such as Atlanta's iconic gorilla, Willie B.

In just five years, the wellness construct has been embraced by a number of important zoological facilities in North America (Table 3.1), and it
is being considered by others as they work to promote their commitment

to enhanced animal welfare standards and practices. One major opportunity is the merging of veterinary and psychological management themes. The Virginia Zoo's Wellness Campus is largely a veterinary vision, but I know that they are looking for ways to add a behavioral component. Similarly, the strong behavioral dimension of wellness at the San Francisco Zoo has been strengthened by the program's new leadership role in the management of San Francisco's veterinary hospital. At the Jacksonville Zoo and Gardens, a reorganization of the board-level Animal Care and Conservation Committee will soon include animal management, conservation, veterinary medicine, and wellness components. The integration of these operating units will prevent organizational silos from forming and enable more effective communication and collaboration benefitting the synergistic function of animal health and wellness. Veterinary health and wellness may be the most promising opportunity to educate our visitors about the value of wellness. Increasingly visitors are investigating wellness products and opportunities for their domestic pets. Often, their preferred veterinary clinics have already been branded as wellness centers, so they are becoming familiar with the full potential of the ideas behind the construct. They will not be surprised to discover their local zoo has already brought health and wellness together into one familiar package. As educators, our job is to probe deeper into the potential of wellness as we teach our visitors how our commitment to new ideas is leading to significantly better zoological parks and aquariums. Worldwide, the Dublin Zoo in Ireland has been particularly successful in applying a wellness perspective to exhibit planning. Their famous elephant exhibit is a fine example of wellness-inspired design. A detailed description of their approach to design and management is represented in the forthcoming book *Wellness for Elephants* (Morris et al., 2019). I expect other world zoos to follow their lead. It is encouraging to see so many other zoos experimenting with wellness. The next few years of innovation and reform should be very exciting indeed. In the following table, Brevard, Jacksonville, and San Francisco are all-in when it comes to a broad-based wellness commitment, while the others are making progress in utilizing the construct in unique ways. It won't surprise me if this list grows substantially in the next few years. With the passage of time, the wellness construct may be adopted by other world zoos leading to significant expansion to this list of participating institutions.

FIGURE 3.3 DENVER'S EMERGING BRAND. COURTESY OF THE DENVER ZOO.

Table 3.1. North American Zoos with Emerging Wellness Programs

Palm Beach Zoo	2008
San Francisco Zoo	2011
Virginia Zoo	2013
Jacksonville Zoo and Gardens	2014
Denver Zoo	2017
Brevard Zoo	2017
Cincinnati Zoo	2018
Fresno Chaffee Zoo	2019

IN PRAISE OF STRATEGIC MARKETING

Early in my career, I thought marketing was all hyperbole and no substance. I was misinformed. By studying the field known as "social marketing" I began to realize the full potential of marketing to promote social change. One of my former students, Ted Finlay, channeled his academic interests in attitude formation and attitude change to produce a fine dissertation on the effects of natural habitats on people's perceptions of animals (Finlay, James and Maple, 1988). Dr. Finlay became so enamored of the psychological literature on attitude change that he devoted a year to study marketing after his Ph.D. was completed, and later worked for Coca-Cola and several other Atlanta companies. The emergence of superior marketing in zoos is one of the reasons zoos and aquariums have prospered and their messaging has improved. Effective marketing in a zoo requires substance and quality. If a zoo talks about conservation and animal welfare, the marketing department must provide evidence and information to document its impact. There is another way that marketing of these priorities is important. Corporate sponsors who associate with a cause are important contributors to the program's visibility and financial success. The Ford Motor Company contributed resources to the rainforest exhibit we built for gorillas in Atlanta, and their local reputation soared by association. But there are also near misses. As hard as I tried, I could never convince the Coca-Cola company to parlay their marketing of polar bear animated commercials into financial support for sponsoring the world's best polar bear exhibit at Zoo Atlanta. The real power of wellness will be demonstrated when we attract major sponsorship and philanthropy from insurance, health, and fitness companies who choose to be affiliated with our efforts to encourage wellness for all living things. I am eager to harness the power of Kaiser-Permanente's simple motto: Thrive! In cities where there is a critical mass of major corporations and small business devoted to health and wellness, I expect to see a major uptick in philanthropic and marketing contributions to zoos and aquariums that embrace wellness in the next five years.

Chapter 4

WILD ANIMALS AND WELLNESS

Modern accredited zoological and aquatic parks are designed to enable sustainable quality of life; they should not permit any suffering. However, for too long even the best zoos and aquariums have accepted coping as the performance standard for our exhibits and facilities. As we have seen, in some professional circles, coping has been recognized as a positive indication of satisfactory welfare. Many species successfully cope with captivity. Among great apes, for example, the stoic orangutan (*Pongo pygmaeus*) appears to accept without protest the most difficult living conditions, whereas the more vociferous chimpanzee (*Pan troglodytes*) never suffers captivity gladly (Maple, 1979; Maple, 1980). However, despite their emotional propensities, the Dutch zoo biologists Nieuwenhuisen and de Waal (1982) arranged conditions where chimpanzees at the Burgers' Zoo in Arnhem essentially coped with crowding when they were confined inside during a severe winter. Much like our own species, all of the great apes have the cognitive capacity to cope with change in spite of evident species-specific differences in emotion.

The utility of the wellness construct has introduced a different idea. Life in managed, human care environments should encourage thriving not coping. If wellness is equivalent to optimal animal welfare as Maple and Bloomsmith (2018) and others have argued, the wellness construct is essentially an expansion or upgrade of animal welfare standards and practices. Wellness is also clearly applicable to wild populations. One good reason for the involvement of humane organizations in wildlife conservation is the fact that wild animals are not just dying; they are suffering. When populations and species are driven to extinction, individuals also suffer from habitat destruction; fear of organized pursuit; cruel hunting practices such as snares, traps, and poisons; encroaching human expansion and intrusive technology; introduced viral diseases such as Ebola; competition for scarce water and food; and the ravages of civil wars and other forms of human conflict. Although international cartels control poaching for skins, ivory, horns, and bones, the products of local subsistence poaching frequently end up

FIGURE 4.1. PROFESSOR. MAPLE IN TSAVO NP, AT THE
SCENE OF AN ELEPHANT POACHING INCIDENT.

in local bushmeat markets where people can easily and cheaply obtain protein from an assortment of monkeys, birds, small mammals, and reptiles. No species is safe from the cruel bushmeat trade. Stanford biologist Robert M. Sapolsky (1994) argued that animals such as zebras react instantaneously to danger, but once the danger is past, they no longer worry about the confrontation. Humans, by contrast, worry about all kinds of events that they cannot control, and this can lead to ailments tied to long-term stress. However, the ability of zebras and other animals to avoid long-term stress is compromised when their environment is laden with dangerous confrontations from heavily armed poachers. Human hunters worried about meeting their quota have driven animals to suffer continuously just like we do. Apparently, elephants are beginning to adapt to the pressures of poaching in some parts of Africa by becoming more nocturnal. In Kenya, a bull elephant named Morgan hid in thick bushes during the day and continued movement during the night.

SUFFERING IN THE OPEN SEA

Historically, the greatest suffering inflicted by human hunters occurred in the open seas where the earth's great whales were hunted by spears hurled from small boats. In Viking times (800–1066) speared whales were expected to die a slow death and eventually drift toward the shore where the carcass could be butchered, but speared whales often suffered through an exhausting migration over thousands of miles before they expired. With time whales were pursued in larger, faster boats and quickly killed by powerful harpoons. Whaling drove many species to the brink of extinction. The massive blue whale (*Balaenoptera musculus*), at a recorded 170 tons, the largest mammal on earth, was reduced to a population of 10,000–25,000 animals when it was placed on the endangered species list in 1986. In 1982, when the humpback whale (*Megaptera novaeangliae*) reached a low of only 1,500 animals, the International Whaling Commission finally issued a ban on hunting this species. In the 40 years that followed, the species recovered to its current global population of 100,000. However, five genetically distinct local populations are still in trouble. These populations must contend with the effects of climate change, ocean noise, lethal entanglements with fishing gear, and traumatic collisions with oceangoing vessels (Bittel, 2016). The most endangered whale species is the North Atlantic right whale (*Eubalaena glacialis*), which numbers only 450 animals (U.S. Department of Commerce, 2018). Their numbers are so low that only 100 of the animals are breeding females, and the rate of births for this species is slowing. Entanglement is a major threat to right whales with over 85% of them showing entanglement scars.

In a candid assessment in *The Atlantic* magazine, J. B. MacKinnon discussed the plight of the North Atlantic right whale, nicknamed the "urban whale" due to the complexity of its aquatic neighborhood in the coastal waters of the Eastern United States. These migrating whales encounter a vast network of commercial shipping lanes, undersea pipelines and cables, coastal wind farms, and military operations (MacKinnon, 2018). The species range, spanning 2,000 miles of coastline from southern Canada to northern Florida, is subject to the persistent influence of human laborers who live and work along this heavily populated coast.

Noise is another contributor to whale suffering. A former Cornell University scientist interviewed by MacKinnon described day-to-day life for right whales as "acoustic hell." One of the most devastating acoustic stimuli are seismic air cannons used to probe for oil and gas deposits under the ocean floor. These cannons emit sounds as loud as 252 decibels, which is almost twice as intense as jet planes taking off from the deck of an aircraft carrier. Exposure can cause burst eardrums in animals and people. In addition to bleeding in the middle ear, intense sound can literally fracture a whale's skull and damage soft tissue. Although whales sleep differently than we do, with only one hemisphere asleep at a time, it is very likely that excessive noise is detrimental to whale sleeping patterns. We can only speculate about the ramifications of disrupted sleep on highly intelligent marine mammals, but the plight of these whales and other suffering species generates concern. A new field, wild animal welfare, is emerging to try and come to grips with these disturbing events. In captive settings Quadros et al. (2014) reported that zoo visitors, especially noisy groups at a decibel level of > 70 dB(A), have a negative impact on the welfare of individual animals. Successful zoos are often noisy, so we'll have to find ways to mitigate ambient sound to protect animals with sensitivity to noise. Buffering sound through advanced technology is a task that we cannot continue to ignore.

One approach to this problem could be the emerging new science of soundscape ecology. A working definition of soundscapes is "the collection of biological, geophysical, and anthropogenic sounds that emanate from a landscape and which vary over space and time reflecting important eco-system processes and human activities." Soundscapes provide ecosystem services to humanity in the form of life-fulfilling functions. Many sound-scapes also have cultural, historical, recreational, aesthetic, and therapeu-tic value (Pijanowski, Farina, Gage, Damyahn, & Krause, 2011). Scholars working in this domain understand that soundscape conservation is an essential priority for future research and practice. It should be possible to experiment in soundscape mitigation in zoos and naturalistic aquariums.

Other organic intrusions are also painful to whales. Right whales are the species with the highest recorded incidence of infection with *Giardia* and *Cryptosporidium* from mainland agricultural sewage and manure run-off. They are also regularly exposed to an ocean full of DDT, PCBs, oil and gas, flame retardants, pharmaceuticals, pesticides, floating islands of plastic debris, and toxic red tide algae. With a life span of up to 100 years, many of these right whales likely remember when the oceans were not as toxic or lethal as they are today. These conditions are not uniform throughout the world. In an ocean environment far less impacted by hu-man activities, a closely related species, the southern right whale in the waters off New Zealand are "fat and happy," in the words of whale ex-pert Rosalind Rolland. In contrast, the Atlantic right whale is thinner by comparison, more heavily infested with lice, and marked by skin lesions and scars. Another important difference is that the southern right whales produce offspring at twice the rate of the northern species. I feel confident in my judgment that the southern species is thriving while the northern right whale is clearly suffering. The severity of whale suffering is illustrated best by the animals that experience entanglement. These regional differ-ences suggest we can do better with whales if we make a concentrated and coordinated effort to clean the world's oceans. I will quote the writer MacKinnon directly to emphasize this contrast:

> Whale #2030 was first seen entangled on May 10, 1999, and was found dead on October 20 that year. When the end came, she had swum about a thousand miles across

several months, in pain, terribly injured, slowly dying. In other words, her death was every bit as terrible as that of a spear-drift whale found by Norse settlers in Greenland in 1385, far enough back in time that we tend to think of humans then and now almost as different species.

In a recent review in *Science* magazine, Preston (2019) examined growing evidence that ocean fish populations have been impacted by a kind of "sensory fog" produced by a combination of pollution, acidification, and noise from the shipping industry. Scientists fear that compromised senses will affect fish communities and ultimately disrupt the entire ecology of the ocean network of living organisms. These are large and complex issues that are not easily solved, but some efforts to mitigate the effects of unwanted sound show some promise. Essentially, sound from commercial vessels can be regulated by governments or by treaties. It seems clear that all forms of aquatic life are suffering from humanity's abuse of the seas. Through the intrusion of our advanced technology, we have poisoned the aquatic environment and altered its chemistry in significant ways. Whales are the largest ocean creatures damaged by human activities, but the greater damage may be the collective effects on millions of small animals that populate the world's oceans. Fortunately, fish demonstrate some resilience in response to these adverse conditions, but the cumulative effects will in time work against their survival.

HEROIC INTERVENTIONS

In the waters around Maui, in the Hawaiian Islands, more than 12,000 humpback whales spend the winter calving, nursing, and breeding. The health of these whales is monitored by Ed Lyman, who works for the Hawaiian Islands Humpback Whale National Marine Sanctuary. Many of the humpbacks arrive in Hawaii carrying marine debris such as fishing lines, netting, buoys, ropes, mooring lines, and anchor chains. Whales suffer from these entanglements as they wound them and cause painful injuries that can even kill them if the entanglements are not removed. Since 2003 Lyman and his associates have freed 27 whales from their burdensome entanglements. His expertise is in demand in other parts of the globe as well. He has rescued whales in Alaska, Canada, Mexico, New England, and the South Pacific. Data from the International Whaling Commission estimates that 300,000 whales, dolphins, and porpoises die from the effects of entanglement annually (Casey, 2018). Rescuing entangled whales is a dangerous but necessary business. During Hawaii's most recent humpback visitation, Lyman received 80 reports of distressed marine animals, resulting in 21 rescue attempts and five freed whales, so some rescues are unsuccessful. Every rescue is a unique challenge; some take hours, and some take days, but Lyman and his team experience great satisfaction whenever a 40-ton whale is untangled to swim freely in the water once again. The process of disentangling whales is a wonderful example of wild animal welfare at work due to altruistic human heroes who assist wild whales through the transition of suffering to thriving. Average citizens are easily activated to help whales in an emergency. Recently, a pod of pilot whales beached themselves on St. Simon's Island in Georgia. Sunbathers and swimmers rushed to the scene to assist the whales and return them to the ocean. Remarkably, the intervention worked and the animals were observed swimming toward the open ocean, another remarkable demonstration of collective altruism directed to another species.

The exhibition of whales, even the smaller and more adaptable beluga, is also controversial. Justifying their capture, translocation, and exhibition in questionable holding tanks is getting more difficult, but some governments in Asia are permissive and unethical. Animals that migrate long distances in the open ocean are not good candidates for confinement in aquariums. The massive whale shark, the world's largest fish, is also a poor candidate for exhibition, although the species has been exhibited in one North American and several aquatic facilities in China, Japan, and Taiwan. Based on the limited information available, the Asian whale sharks live in relatively small facilities. The Georgia Aquarium has been more successful with the species. Although two of six whale sharks exhibited in a 6-million-gallon tank at the Georgia Aquarium have died, the remaining animals are receiving high-quality care and seem to be coping. Given their needs and the physical limitations of world aquariums, however, whale sharks cannot thrive outside their natural habitats. It can be argued that whale sharks on exhibit help visitors to appreciate and perhaps even protect at-risk populations that are living in the open ocean, but to win this debate, whale sharks cannot just survive; they must live well in human care.

The suffering of whales in the open ocean has sparked outrage globally, but it hasn't stopped the killing. The leading critics of whaling include the Humane Society of the United States (HSUS) and Greenpeace, but reforms will not come without pressure from governments and associations with high ethical standing. Iceland recently announced that they would kill as many as 2,000 whales over the next five years (Block, 2019). The World Association of Zoos and Aquariums (WAZA) is an organization that ought to stand up for whales suffering in the seas and for those suffering in substandard aquariums. If whaling could be ended by responsible animal advocacy groups such as WAZA, it would likely have a ripple effect to protect other aquatic species. Individual aquariums with stellar reputations, such as the National Aquarium in Baltimore, Maryland; the Monterey Bay Aquarium in Monterey, California; Chicago's Shedd Aquarium, and the New England Aquarium in Boston, Massachusetts, should advocate for whale protection and urge their peers to join them. I haven't always agreed with HSUS, but I admire their strong leadership on the whaling issue. I feel the same way about Greenpeace. Their methods are not my style, but I am tempted to send them a donation each year to encourage their continuing harassment of commercial whaling ships. It is one of the few courageous acts that just might turn the tide against whaling. The Trump administration could also provide leadership on this issue. President Trump should use his bully pulpit and his friendship with leaders in Japan, Iceland, and Norway to prod them to cease whaling. He has shown a willingness to stand up to international bullies. Let's see if he will take the side of the whales. Although Iceland announced in 2015 that they would kill 2,000 whales that year, Icelandic whaling companies have agreed that no whales will be taken in 2019. This is the first time in 16 years that no whales will be hunted in Icelandic waters, but Japan has decided to pull out of the International Whaling Commission and intends to resume commercial whaling. Their decision breaks a 33-year international moratorium. They plan to continue hunting Bryde's, sei, and minke whales. If whales were rescued from a life of suffering brought on by human penetration of their previously hospitable oceanic habitats, it would be one of the most important political victories in the history of our living planet. I urge the President to work with Congress to persuade the leaders of Iceland, Japan, and Norway to stop commercial whaling immediately.

WELLNESS INTERVENTIONS

The successful comeback of mountain gorillas in Central Africa was achieved by courageous conservation organizations such as the Dian Fossey Gorilla Fund International, whose field staff kept working for their survival even during wartime. The population of mountain gorillas has dramatically risen to more than 1,000, the highest number in nearly a century (Kerlin, 2018). One of the factors in their recovery has been personalized veterinary care provided by a team from UC Davis known as the Gorilla Doctors. Since the late 2000s, individual animals have been monitored by their own long-term health records, and their health is personally managed by vets who know them as if they were family. When gorillas are injured or ill, veterinarians do not hesitate to intervene with antibiotics, treatments for wounds, and stitches if necessary. Just as zoo biologists now recognize the importance of individual animal welfare, conservation biologists are just as concerned with the physical health of individuals as they are with populations. The success of the Davis Gorilla Doctors has influenced a new cadre of aquatic veterinarians in the SeaDoc Society. They formed to take action with individualized care for orcas in the Pacific Northwest's Salish Sea. When the SeaDocs arrived on the scene, this pod of whales had not produced offspring in three years. Disruptions in the natural food chain are responsible for their poor health. Without intervention many orcas will die from starvation. Orcas are caught in a survival struggle due to the fierce competition for salmon in the Pacific northwest. More effective management of salmon populations could resolve this issue and save many whales from a slow and painful death by starvation.

The Davis veterinarians who are helping gorillas and orcas see similarities in the two taxa. Both gorillas and orcas live in close-knit, socially complex family units, and both are highly intelligent. The people who live among mountain gorillas in Africa and the human residents of the Pacific Northwest revere the animals in their midst and acknowledge their intrinsic value. The fact that individual animals can be easily recognized contributes to the conservation support that local people give to these projects. While veterinary care for gorillas has a lengthy history, the SeaDocs have been working with orcas only since 2016. It is too soon to say that they will enjoy the success of the Gorilla Doctors, but the approach should work with whales and other sea creatures that are suffering in the oceans. Like mountain gorillas, orcas can also be treated and returned to good health. Another similarity is the value of these animals to ecotourism. Because ecotourism generates so much revenue, every country in the region benefits from their survival. Orcas will also benefit both governments and local people if tourists continue to visit them. Whales suffer from entanglement in man-made flotsam and jetsam, but they are also endangered from ingesting such materials. Victor (2019) reported the death of a beached whale in the Philippines where it was found with 88 pounds of plastic trash in its body. The ingestion of plastics leads to reduced weight, energy, and swimming speed, which makes them more vulnerable to predation. This load cannot be easily expelled, and it cannot be digested. The waters of the Philippines rank just behind China and Indonesia in the amount of floating plastic waste. It is estimated that 5 to 13 million metric tons of plastic waste is deposited in oceans annually, much of it entering rivers and streams and then passing into the ocean. Although ecotourism fuels conservation, the sheer number of tourists has invited criticism. It appears that a large piece of Indonesia's Komodo National Park may be closed to tourism to protect the resident population of Komodo dragons (*Varanus komodoensis*). In 2018 alone 160,000 tourists visited the park, and some observers believe the animals are becoming too "tame" while rampant poaching has dramatically reduced the numbers of their main prey, the Timor deer. Similar objections to ecotourism pressures may shut down some whale-watching expeditions in the states of California and Washington. The growing popularity of mountain gorilla watching has also been questioned by critics. It would be tragic if ecotours had to cease when they are doing so much to attract support for conservation.

CASUALTIES OF HABITAT DESTRUCTION

In terrestrial environments, wild animals are not just inconvenienced when we cut down a forest or drain a swamp. Instead, the process of destroying animal habitats results in maiming and killing entire populations of species. In Australia it has been estimated that 50 million mammals, birds, and reptiles die each year due to land clearing for human habitation and commerce (MacKinnon, 2018). Much of the damage to wildlife occurs when earth-moving equipment smothers or injures animals. In addition, animals that survive the clearing process are left in a hostile environment devoid of food, shelter, and hiding places from predators. Displacement is stressful since animals that survive do not have adequate protection or resources. In a review of the Australian situation, Finn (2017) observed that no state or territory has offered regulations that consider animal welfare when authorizing land clearing for development. This deficiency can be corrected if land-clearing applications are required to consider habitat impact. Further, when earth is moved, the expected damage should be calculated. More transparency is needed to prevent or reduce harm to wildlife. While suffering is clearly an issue in habitat loss, the greater damage is from extinction. In Australia 50 species including 27 mammals have been driven to extinction in the past 200 years. This loss is exacerbated by the fact that 87% of the animals in Australia are endemic; they are found nowhere else on earth.

Another threat to wildlife is roadway traffic. The endangered Florida panther occupies the Everglades landscape in Florida bisected by the dangerous highway known locally as "Alligator Alley." Since 2004, 14 Florida panthers have been killed by collisions with vehicles on this highway. In

2017 a 10-foot fence was added to protect panthers. Fencing seems to have helped protect the animals from road kills. In central Arizona, a well-traveled elk migration corridor was modified to include multiple underpasses and bridges for wildlife that were vulnerable to collisions on the highway. Biologists assisted with the design by providing sensors that warned motorists when elks were present (Dodd, Gagnon, & Schweinsburg, 2010). In the nine years following these upgrades to the highway, only seven collisions with vehicles have been recorded, a major difference when compared to the nine collisions per year prior to the road improvements. Clearly the technology exists for protecting animals that habitually enter highways, but local governments often overlook or ignore the problem. Citizens who care about animal survival will need to lobby their governments to introduce reforms to protect the migration routes of wildlife. In the long run, protection is cost-effective since collisions with wildlife damage vehicles and nearby structures and often severely injure or kill the occupants of trucks and cars.

A recent example of the intrusion of massive shifts in the quality and quantity of wildlife home ranges occurred when the federal Bureau of Land Management auctioned 57,800 acres of prime sage-grouse habitat in Wyoming (McGlashen, 2019). The auction yielded U.S. $88 million split equally between the state of Wyoming and the federal government. While the sage grouse was once abundant in the West, their numbers have declined by 50% in recent years. There are fewer than 500,000 sage grouse remaining in their historic range, with 40% found in Wyoming. Sage grouse are vulnerable to the effects of road building, noise, and other activities associated with drilling. It is likely that the sale of formerly protected habitat will further disrupt sage-grouse reproduction. The familiar cycle of trauma, morbidity, and mortality will occur once the plains ecosystem is damaged by construction. It is not too late to save the remaining healthy habitat for sage grouse and other species, but the temptation to monetize the land is difficult to resist.

Human beings have damaged ecosystems by destroying keystone species, those whose activities create habitat and nourish entire webs of life. This trend has been reversed for predators and large herbivores, but other species, burrowing rodents such as ground squirrels, for example, are the new targets for extirpation. Persecuted as pests, ground squirrels are rarely included in conservation management plans issued by governments. Because attempts to repopulate them have largely failed, scientists at the San Diego Zoo recently translocated 707 ground squirrels captured at sites around San Diego and moved them to new locations. The team used a variety of habitat preparation strategies and eventually established new communities in six of the nine sites they tested. The team, led by San Diego Zoo biologist Ron Swaisgood purposely attempted to create a hybrid of new and old habitat rather than replicate what had previously existed. The squirrels are expected to transform the ecosystem with their own efforts and increase its value for native plant and animal conservation (Swaisgood, 2019). The scientists are hopeful they can also restore populations of other persecuted burrowing species such as prairie dogs, European rabbits, and plateau pikas. It is no surprise to me that a group of honorable zoo biologists would have the backs of animals that others regard as pests.

THE RELEVANCE OF SANCTUARY

A recent article in *Science* examined the need for people to share land with nature. Ellis (2019) noted that most people live longer, are healthier, and live more comfortable lives than their ancestors, but the opposite is true for other living things as space for wild creatures has greatly diminished. Ellis drew an interesting conclusion:

> The call to manage land toward a better future is not a call to end development, but rather a call to develop better. Progress will come when people aspire to live in a world where nature is given enough space to thrive." (p. 1228)

Well-run sanctuaries for nonhuman primates and elephants serve an important purpose by offering a safe alternative to the lives they led in backyard cages, medical laboratories, roadside menageries, and circuses.

Organizations such as the Center for Great Apes in Florida and Chimp Haven, a 200-acre facility in Shreveport, LA, built for chimpanzees retired by the federal government have created superior social habitats and continue to provide high-quality care for hundreds of animals. Lincoln Park Zoo recently formed a research partnership with Chimp Haven. For decades chimpanzees have been rescued from a solitary life and introduced to new companions in sanctuaries. Even the semi-solitary orangutan can benefit from social opportunities. In fact, 21 of them are living a social life at the Center for Great Apes. Zoo professionals have also been involved in helping this unique center. Architect Jon Coe offered his ideas for the first overhead transfer tubes built there for great apes. This facility was designed to give them complex, elevated space and sufficient separation to choose social or solitary time. Sanctuary apes in the United States represent some of the most extreme cases of abuse and neglect, but they respond to tender loving care when integrated carefully into managed social groups. Sanctuary caregivers have learned so much about how to rehabilitate abandoned apes, we are now exporting this expertise to sanctuaries in Africa and Asia. A recent study by Wobber and Hare (2011) examined the psychological health of orphaned bonobos and chimpanzees in a sanctuary in Congo where they are coping but not thriving.

Elephant sanctuaries are less common in North America, but one of them, Hohenwald in Tennessee, provides 2,700 acres for African and Asian elephants retired from zoos and circuses. There are currently 11 elephants enjoying individual care and the opportunity to live in a managed herd at Hohenwald. Certified by AZA, older elephants and those with no companions can live better after translocation to Hohenwald. Sanctuary should be a retirement strategy for aged zoo animals that cannot be retired in place. Although we still have problems breeding elephants, half of the offspring are males. Due to the difficulty of managing multiple males to adulthood, sanctuaries provide an acceptable option. For that reason alone, zoos and aquariums should support high-quality sanctuaries. However, sanctuaries have not always been acceptable to zoos, largely because they have marketed their services at the expense of zoos. When sanctuary supporters and animal rights allies have lobbied governments to remove elephants from zoos perceived to be substandard, they have interfered with the operating standards of accredited zoos. City governments are not permitted to override a zoo director's authority to make animal decisions. Zoos that have suffered this fate have lost their accreditation. Clearly, with so much at stake, zoos and sanctuaries need to negotiate their differences and work together for the benefit of the animals in their care.

Operations of ape and elephant sanctuaries should be extended to assist with the surplus of aging, injured, and retired sea mammals. There is a particular need for facilities that can accommodate cetaceans. Cetacean sanctuaries are challenging because they require so much space, and aquatic filtering technology is quite expensive. Retiring whales is even more difficult due to their great size. An interesting experiment is underway in Iceland where two beluga whales are being retired in the world's first open-ocean sanctuary. The animals will be confined in a 32,000-square-meter sea pen abutting Klettsvik Bay in the Westman Islands. This was the location of the film *Free Willy*. The two belugas will be moved from Changfeng Ocean World in Shanghai in the spring of 2019. Although the animals cannot be returned to the wild safely, they will no longer be used in public performances. Belugas can live 50 years in the wild. One question that can be asked about this experiment is whether the whales will benefit from a cessation of training. Training contributes to psychological well-being when it is carried out correctly. To thrive in the sea pen, some positive training would be a helpful bridge to their retirement. As this book goes to press, Mystic Aquarium in Connecticut is preparing to receive three captive-born belugas from Marineland of Canada. The facility will keep them with five other belugas in a large aquatic tank built for exhibition and performances. This transfer of belugas from one aquarium to another will lead to upgrades in their management and exhibition, but it will be difficult to craft an exhibit large enough and complex enough for the animals to thrive.

I believe a new aquarium should consider setting up a contiguous sanctuary where cetaceans and pinnipeds can be retired but managed with human contact and compassionate training methods. This way, the aquarium could educate the public about cetaceans living in our oceans without exploiting them in undignified entertainment venues. We desperately need sanctuaries for these abandoned sea creatures, and our ability to finance their retirement generally depends on some public involvement. While the aquarium could provide the financial support to build it, the sanctuary could be operated as a nonprofit charity, and visitors would pay a fee to see them living but not performing. There are new public aquariums in the planning stages in many American coastal cities—at least three in Florida—and all of them should seriously consider a dedicated sanctuary for marine mammals as part of their plan. Even aging, injured wildlife can thrive in facilities designed to cater to their mental, physical, and social needs. Like chimpanzees in biomedicine, such marine mammals have spent their lives in service to humanity; the least we can do is to provide them with a high-quality facility where they can age gracefully. Our commitment to lifelong care is now codified in the high standards and best practices of all accredited zoos and aquariums, and we must do our best to honor this ethical commitment. This is why the tragic culling of an otherwise healthy young male giraffe in the Copenhagen Zoo in Denmark offended so many citizens around the world. The leaders of this otherwise respected zoological garden chose to cut the animal's life short because they believed he could not lead a normal life in their zoo. He was not identified as a breeder, and to prevent inbreeding they shot him and fed his carcass to the lions in full public view. I wrote an op-ed for the *San Francisco Chronicle* (Maple, 2014) condemning this particular act of management euthanasia as unnecessary and cruel. In my opinion, zoos cannot ask their supporters to celebrate the birth of an animal and then abandon it months later as if its life no longer has value.

In a thoughtful survey of zookeeper attitudes about culling, Powell and Ardaiolo (2019) cited the perspective of animal ethicist Bernard Rollin: (a) a proposed ethic must resonate with existing personal beliefs, (b) a new ethic should not aim to be quickly established, (c) a new ethic should hold middle ground between extremes, and (d) a new ethic must agree with common sense and be communicated in simple language. I believe the Copenhagen decision to kill Marius violated several of Rollin's principles. An interesting finding in the Powell and Ardaiolo survey was the differentiation between taxa that were acceptable candidates for culling compared to those that were not. For example, there was widespread agreement among keepers that the culling of primates, marine mammals, pachyderms, and carnivores was not acceptable. Clearly, culling otherwise healthy animals is a difficult assignment that employees are not eager to carry out. However, our difficulties with population management in the zoo are not going away, and ethical solutions must eventually be found. One solution is to create more living space devoted to retired individuals or to encourage cooperative partnerships with credible sanctuaries. A lack of qualified sanctuaries for specified taxa may lead to a consortium of zoos that work together to build sanctuaries of their own. Zoos have some experience in doing this, but it has not always been successful, and it has always been very costly for the participants. Building sanctuaries is not as challenging as keeping them going. Given the emotions surrounding culling, it took considerable courage for the investigators to carry out this important project. Its value as a baseline will be useful in future years as we attempt to monitor any consensus that may eventually emerge.

SYNERGY OF WILDLIFE CONSERVATION AND ANIMAL WELFARE

In a paper by Paquet and Darimont (2010), the authors confirmed that human activities tend to deprive wild animals of their "life requisites" and cause trauma and suffering by destroying or impoverishing their habitats. In this publication, the authors' objective was to integrate ethical aspects of wildlife conservation and animal welfare to encourage a new "wildlife welfare" ethic among conservationists. In their introduction Paquet and Darimont elected to quote Albert Schweitzer (1924) who advocated a universal set of ethics that applied to all living things:

> "We need a boundless ethics which will include the animals...the time is coming when people will be amazed that the human race existed so long before it recognized that

thoughtless injury to life is incompatible with real ethics. Ethics in its unqualified form extends responsibility to everything' that has life."

Some of the species at great risk from human habitat disruption include keystone carnivores such as the gray wolf. Other species affected by the construction of roads, railways, agriculture, and logging include grizzly bears, cougars, wolverines, lynx, black bears and coyotes. We know that preservation of habitat quality requires linkages, connectedness, and dispersion into geographic areas large enough to merge individuals into populations. Riparian corridors, unique plant communities growing near a river, stream, lake, lagoon, or other natural body of water, are essential to the livelihood of carnivorous species and must be protected. Given what we know about the habits of predators and other wildlife, we ought to create construction guidelines that protect biodiversity. Instead, man-made barriers such as highways and railways are contributing to the fragmentation of landscapes. The permanence of these structures has prevented future opportunities to restore impaired habitat (Paquet & Carbyn, 2003).

In most of North America where wolves persist, human disturbance has already displaced them from favorable habitats. It appears that wolves prefer to avoid human contact, but the pressure from human activities is increasing. For example, wolves are threatened by purposive aerial hunting, deadfall trapping, large fishhooks, poisoning, and the presence of snares and traps. These human actions kill many wild wolves, but many others are subjected to injury, trauma, and suffering. Whenever a single species is targeted, collateral damage is always a by-product of the mission. This is particularly true when species are eradicated through the application of breakthroughs in technology.

In their comprehensive discussion of the fusion of animal welfare and conservation biology, Paquet and Darimont recommended the following adaptation of the Five Freedoms of animal welfare originating in a U.K. government report in 1965: (a) the freedom from thirst, hunger, and malnutrition caused by humans; (b) the freedom from fear and distress caused by humans; (c) the freedom from pain, injury, and disease caused by humans; and (d) the freedom to express normal species-specific behavior. To ensure these freedoms are enforced, the authors also emphasized the need for conservation and welfare advocates to promulgate a vision of nature that supports an ethical, aesthetic, and spiritual set of motives for conservation rather than countable, measurable, and monetary considerations. As Birch (1993) argued, since most of us do not intend to cause suffering, we should be willing to assume the responsibility to protect all living things from human interventions that endanger animals. Paquet and Darimont's conclusion is worthy of emphasis:

> "We believe the primary cause of environmental destruction is deeply rooted in anthropocentrism whereby natural laws are easily disregarded because there are no imminent adverse consequences for people. From an ecological perspective, human dominance of nature manifests as an extreme case 'of competitive exclusion,' where wild animals have no voice and human priorities always prevail." (p. 186).

COMPASSIONATE CONSERVATION

Compassionate conservation is a movement that prioritizes the protection of animals as individuals rather than populations. Compassion and empathy are emphasized to help resolve the issue of land sharing and the alleviation of suffering due to human domination of the wildlife landscape. A guiding principle of this new movement is the following statement: "First, do no harm." Leaders of the compassionate conservation approach believe that setting aside protected areas is not sufficient to protect individual animals. There is a need to advance coexistence so that humanity can compassionately share space with other living things. To achieve this outcome, land developers must take a critical look at projects to make sure that animals and ecosystems are acknowledged as stakeholders when highways, housing, shopping centers, and other human habitations are under consideration. Harmonious development takes into account how a community makes room for biodiversity and creates naturalistic features that benefit wildlife and human occupants of such spaces. Balanced and biodiverse communities result in a better, more sustainable world.

Compassionate conservation has attracted a following among both conservationists and advocates of animal welfare. The wellness construct actually facilitates integration from these two perspectives. With its origins in human health, wellness is a condition that applies equally to all animals, people, communities, and ecosystems. The goal of wellness is to encourage thriving in all living things as individuals, groups, populations, and communities. Thus, we can apply the term *wellness* in our evaluation of animate organisms, structures, and places. We seek to live well, but we also want to create environments that enable and encourage wellness. As we seek to elevate animals to a level of compassion that will reduce suffering, we will have to be careful not to create additional conflict with human beings. For example, if a construction project will relieve human suffering through the provision of a new medical complex or education center or access to a scarce resource such as water, the need to consider animal welfare has to be balanced with human aspirations. Ultimately, we have to be wise enough to identify win-win solutions that will protect both human needs and the needs of wildlife. Planning for both will be more expensive and likely lead to delays in project timelines, but the enlarged benefits to all stakeholders will be worth the effort. Too often we are forced to choose between "guns or butter," but we can do better than that. To avoid these conflicts, architects and engineers may need additional tutoring in biology and ecology to recognize the importance of compassion as they contemplate the downside of disruptive construction. In the end, we must design and develop a world where we all can thrive with a minimum of conflict, disaffection, and loss. The challenge of developing for human aspirations while protecting wildlife and habitat afflicts both developed and developing countries. Conservation organizations like the Dian Fossey Gorilla Fund International found it necessary to build health clinics and schools to help the people occupying the villages adjacent to prime gorilla habitat in Rwanda and Congo. The pressure of rapid population growth and civil war throughout the African continent has put tremendous pressure on the remaining forests and riverine ecosystems that sustain so many species. Conservation nongovernmental organizations and friendly Western governments are working with local people to protect the future of wildlife and future generations of citizens. A broad-based wellness strategy is a good place to start advancing the best ideas for wise land management that can be shared among all the inhabitants of an ecosystem. Humanity's greatest challenge is to find a way to share the bounty of this planet with all creatures great and small.

Compassionate conservation brings the practices and sciences of animal welfare and conservation biology closer together. The leaders of the Born Free Foundation were the originators of this movement. They considered it to be a new paradigm for protecting animals and their habitats, and they gave voice to an idea that is a theme of this book. Conservation is synergistic with wellness, and it is quite possible to work in both domains so that one commitment enhances the other. For people and animals to thrive in interconnected communities and ecosystems that are healthy, we must be comprehensive in our planning. No living organism can be left out. In many ways, this fusion is similar to the One Health movement that combined traditional medicine and veterinary medicine in combatting viruses that were capable of jumping from one species to another. Prior to this integration of separate disciplines, information was siloed and unavailable. Breakthroughs became possible when the two sides began to converge for the greater good. Compassionate conservation is another way forward that promises to benefit the whole planet.

To bring leaders of governments, conservation, animal welfare, and enterprises together, the big ideas will have to dominate. Our history has been marked by conflict, not cooperation. The Born Free Foundation, like PETA and HSUS, has been a severe critic of zoos. Their leaders have more often fought to drive them to extinction rather than oversee their revitalization. Perhaps this was true because of the limitations of the scope of animal welfare. The wellness construct makes it possible to think bigger about the welfare of animals, and it can be easily extended to conditions in the natural world. We should expect a new approach to achieving compassion and empathy for animals in accredited zoos, aquariums, and parks. Our ability to cooperate depends on our ability to communicate. Workshops and conferences where speakers from all sides are welcome represent the best opportunity to generate cooperation for the benefit of the animals we love and respect. The best work of zoos led to the recovery of species such as the California condor, the American bison, the golden lion tamarin, and Przewalski's horse. At the same time, zoos that could not properly exhibit elephants are now spending more money and building innovative habitats that resemble in form and function an elephant's natural habitat. Modern zoos taking these bold steps are encouraging elephants to live in herds that are encouraged to thrive in managed human care. We can do this with almost any species if we understand its needs and make a commitment to meet those needs. This is how wellness works to benefit the world's wildlife. Wildlife wellness and compassionate conservation share a common purpose. The Detroit Zoological Society, through its dedicated Center for Zoo and Aquarium Animal Welfare and Ethics, developed a universal framework for animal welfare and shared these ideas with participants in two important symposia in Detroit in 2012 and 2014. In the

FIGURE 4.2. DETROIT ZOOLOGICAL SOCIETY'S UNIVERSAL
ANIMAL WELFARE FRAMEWORK.

audience there were zoo professionals, academics, and representatives of nonprofit humane organizations. Some observers complained that the audience favored the latter category, but as Detroit's commitment to dialogue has continued, a growing number of zoo leaders have responded. I only regret that in the meetings I attended, open debate between some of the most strident speakers was not arranged in a balanced way. One issue that continues to bother me is the idea that zoos can be saved if they will just stop breeding animals. People who take this position consider all zoo animals as prisoners held against their will. But the best, accredited modern zoos have become so successful at simulating nature that the animals don't live in prisons; they live in their own homes—spacious, naturalistic, complex, and socially appropriate in their composition. This was the position of Heini Hediger decades ago (Hediger, 1950, 1969), and his conclusion still applies today. With more active debate and discussion, Kagan's enlarged podium will gain added value in reforming all zoos that pay attention. I am very grateful that Ron Kagan chose to recruit my former student, Stephanie Allard, who has become such an important member of his leadership team in Detroit. Dr. Allard is in a unique position to evaluate and connect Detroit's approach to great welfare and Jacksonville's synergistic interpretation of the wellness construct. Hopefully, with Dr. Allard in place, Detroit will take its place as one of the nation's more engaged scientific zoos. They are blessed with great colleges and universities nearby who should become active partners in the future.

In their excellent review, Kagan and his colleagues discuss the many different ideas about the meaning of animal welfare. Since they define the future zoo as one where animals don't just survive but thrive, from their perspective welfare and wellness are synonymous. This is a key difference in what we used to call "good" welfare and the revised aspiration to achieve "great" welfare. Essentially, we are all working toward a global commitment to design and build zoo exhibits and facilities that encourage thriving. Another powerful word that indicates our shared commitment is *well-being*. Chuck Gillespie, the CEO of the National Wellness Institute, recently commented on the difference between wellness and well-being. According to Mr. Gillespie, we should "be less concerned with what it is called, and be more focused on what wellness is accomplishing. Wellness is the program, the initiative, the event, the strategy. Wellbeing is the result." An interesting new development is the formation of Wellbeing International, an organization founded by Dr. Andrew Rowan, formerly an executive and active scientist with HSUS and the Humane Society International. This dynamic, new organization (wellbeinginternational.org) is supporting and disseminating a positive agenda to encourage a more balanced world where animals and people share our good, green planet. I am encouraged by the strong and intelligent leadership of Dr. Rowan and his team, and I am hoping that Wellbeing International will prosper on the world stage. Enlarging the universe of true believers in welfare, wellness, and well-being is our common mission. Mutual support for the science of animal welfare may yield international funding opportunities for cooperation and collaboration. I would expect nothing less from Wellbeing International under Rowan's capable leadership.

Chapter 5

WELLNESS-INSPIRED ZOO DESIGN

O ne of the essential building blocks in my long career was the time I spent coteaching a course on the psychology of environmental design at Georgia Tech. This unique course was cross-listed in the College of Sciences and the College of Architecture. After the sudden death of Professor Richard K. Davenport, I was hired to replace him in 1978. Davenport and Professor Richard Wilson, a colleague in architecture, had set up the course a decade earlier. It was one of the first courses in the nation in the field of environmental psychology and was one of its most enduring. I started teaching the course in my first year at Tech along with Professor Wilson and Professor Jean Wineman. I treasure the many hours I spent over the years interacting with talented architects and students in our struggle to examine the key features of good design. To students with little or no experience with wildlife, opportunities to design new animal habitats were much like an introduction to alien life-forms on Mars. They had to read about natural history and animal behavior and then interview caregivers, curators, and educators at the local zoo in Atlanta. Their plans were drawn up and presented to their peers and juried by their professors. It was a very enjoyable learning experience for all of us, with a huge diversity of animals surveyed over the 20 years I taught the course. I didn't know it at the time, but the course I was teaching was an exercise in exhibit programming. Careful planning, based on research, is the way to implement innovative exhibits and facilities. The program consists of the design ideas that are subsequently transformed into drawings and blueprints and executed as a finished product by construction teams. I told the students that if their ideas were good enough, they might influence the actual exhibits we were planning in the formative stages of Zoo Atlanta's revitalization. Indeed, there were many ideas that originated in the class and later appeared in the form of successful exhibits. On one occasion, I presented my fantasy on how to exhibit elephants at night. I envisioned a trail from the zoo downtown in Grant Park all the way to north Atlanta in Buckhead, a distance of seven miles. I told them I wanted to let the animals enter the trail and slowly walk to a refreshing waterhole. At the end of this safari to Buckhead (coincidentally the location of many student watering holes), the animals would turn around and walk back to the zoo, a conceptual all-night excursion for the elephants. This idea became known as Buckhead Elephant Park, drawn by one of my students and later published in a chapter in the book *An Elephant in the Room* (Maple, Bloomsmith, & Martin, 2009). Many zoos have subsequently designed and built walking trails for elephants in their new approaches to exhibit design for both Asian and African species. It is gratifying that crazy ideas can morph into practical solutions.

Whenever I had the chance, I invited experts in behavior and design to lecture to our students. One of the earliest visitors was the famed zoo architect Jon Charles Coe. He visited us in 1982, early in his career. At the time I was trying to organize my ideas for exhibiting great apes in ways that would encourage natural behavior and reduce or eliminate abnormal behavior. I first met Jon in Chicago in 1983 at a conference. I later visited him in Seattle where he offered me a tour of the revolutionary new Woodland Park Zoo. His firm, Jones & Jones, was known as the iconic landscape architecture firm that literally invented landscape immersion design. Woodland Park Zoo was led by another architect, David Hancocks, who subsequently wrote *A Different Nature*, the most important book about zoos since Hediger's *Wild Animals in Captivity* (1950). In Atlanta I asked Jon to sketch on a lined yellow pad the ideas we discussed and debated to produce naturalistic, species-appropriate chimpanzee, gorilla, and orangutan exhibits. When he finished his sketching, it was the first time that I was able to see a vivid picture of what I had been thinking about for so many years. With his permission, I subsequently published some of the sketches to illustrate behavioral concepts (Finlay & Maple, 1986) in hopes that somebody somewhere would actually build such an exhibit. Little did I know that scarcely two years later, I would become the zoo director empowered to build a revolutionary new gorilla exhibit based on these early plans. At this point Jon and I became serious collaborators on a project that was no longer theoretical. Jon was also a superb salesman as he spoke to our board and potential donors to eloquently explain how these new ideas would change the world of zoo architecture.

DESIGNING FOR DINOSAURS

Another academic exercise that generated wild ideas was our in-house conversation about "Tinkering with the *T. Rex.*" The travelling robotic dinosaur exhibitions in zoos, gardens, and museums made me think about what I would do if I had a chance to exhibit a real, live dinosaur. In the 1980s this was a zoo director's nightmare, but it intrigued me. With each passing year, genomic science has brought the world closer to realizing the ambition of cloning a long-extinct creature such as a woolly mammoth, Tasmanian tiger, or saber-toothed cat. In these cases, a living relative of the extinct cousin would be used to create the clone. A dinosaur may also be possible if you believe Dr. Jack Horner, the famed paleontologist who served as an advisor to the film *Jurassic Park*. Horner and his colleagues have experimented with the genetic makeup of birds, and they have manipulated them to produce animals with reptilian teeth and other primitive features (Brennan, 2008). Because reptiles and birds share so many genetic traits, scientists believe we will soon know enough to produce a living dinosaur from a genetically altered chicken or a reptilian velociraptor from an emu. There is no scientific reason why a *T. Rex* cannot be one day unleashed to live on an isolated island much as they did in the movie. Who can say that future zoo directors will not one day be blessed or cursed with the management of a diverse collection of resurrected and revitalized dinosaurs? Today's challenge of designing species-appropriate exhibits for elephants, polar bears, gorillas, and the like will be child's play compared to the task of successfully managing exotic saurids and raptors of many sizes and shapes. The fact is that by substituting dinosaurs for large, charismatic megafauna that actually exist, this mental exercise helps a design team or a group of students to think outside the box. By no means have we exhausted all of the creative possibilities in exhibiting wild animals. There is much more to do.

WELLNESS FOR GREAT APES

After the success of Woodland Park's naturalistic gorilla facility, many zoos stepped up to build better exhibits for great apes. Our vision of excellence was possible because Zoo Atlanta had fallen into such a state of disrepair that the entire city put their full support behind our recovery. It took just one year to complete our conversion to nonprofit governance with the autonomy to market the dream and fully fund it with both private and government money. We had only one lowland gorilla at the time, but he was quite extraordinary and well known throughout the south as he bore the name of the longtime mayor of Atlanta, William B. Hartsfield. Willie B, as he was known, had been captured as an infant in Central Africa and moved to the zoo in 1961. He was isolated from his own kind for 27 years and did not seem to be a prospect for resocialization. Even I could not be optimistic because I knew too much about the debilitating effects of social isolation. Early on we used the original ideas that Coe and I had discussed in 1983. Our aim was to build a gorilla exhibit unlike any other world facility by exhibiting not one, not a pair, not even a family group of gorillas but a population of them in contiguous habitats. This might have been regarded as a pipe dream were it not for the fact that I had been discussing collaboration with colleagues at the Yerkes National Primate Research Center of Emory University. Once we designed a superior exhibit, I took it to Yerkes director Dr. Fred King with the support of Dr. Ken Gould, who was serving on the board of the Atlanta Zoological Society. We identified three adult male gorillas and six females as candidates to occupy three separate habitats suitable for breeding. We reserved one small section for Willie B., who would represent those solitary gorillas that are found at the edges of established breeding groups in Africa. Our priority was to stimulate breeding in this population of gorillas. The Yerkes administration warmed up to the idea of moving their animals to a better facility where they could be fully appreciated by vast numbers of zoo visitors.

FIGURE 5.1. EVIDENCE OF BREEDING SUCCESS WAS ALMOST IMMEDIATE IN 1989

My colleagues at Yerkes also appreciated my offer to pay per diem support for the animals until they were moved to the zoo. Our esteemed donor Jay Crouse contributed U.S. $50,000 to ensure the animals would be committed to our project when the exhibit opened in 1988. Our partnership facilitated a continuation of research on natural social groups that included my student, Mike Hoff's, benchmark studies of social development (Hoff, Forthman, & Maple, 1994; Hoff, Nadler, Hoff, & Maple, 1994; Hoff, Hoff, & Maple, 1998) and the eventual resocialization of Willie B. himself (Winslow, Ogden, & Maple, 1992). We had no idea if our social strategy would work, but we were obligated to try. It took some time to get around to Willie B.'s resocialization because the other animals hit the ground breeding. Nine months after our spectacular opening in 1988, the first two babies were born and their mothers (Figure 5.1 courtesy Joe Sebo) proved to be perfect gorilla parents. Our marriage of research and exhibition turned out to be the perfect zoological storm.

ACCOLADES IN ATLANTA

Starting with the acquisition of Willie B., Zoo Atlanta continued managing lowland gorillas for more than 50 years when it was honored in 2011 with AZA's prestigious Bean Award for its institutional contributions to gorilla conservation, husbandry, reproduction, and research. As an indication of the strength of the partnership between Yerkes and Zoo Atlanta, from 1975 to the present, no world zoo has published more research on the behavior of great apes. Currently the Atlanta region is populated with a cadre of brilliant scientists who continue to use the zoo as a major behavioral research center. These scholars, some of whom were my former graduate students at Emory and Georgia Tech, have broadened the base from their positions at Agnes Scott College, Dalton State College, Emory University, Georgia State University, Kennesaw State University, and the Yerkes National Primate Research Center.

Best known for studies of chimpanzees, gorillas, and orangutans, the zoo strengthened its reputation in reptiles when we hired Dwight Lawson and he hired Joe Mendelson. Following his extraordinary achievements in Atlanta, Dr. Lawson became the CEO of the Oklahoma City Zoo. A first-rate scientist, Dr. Mendelson is now director of research at Zoo Atlanta. He has continued the research collaboration with scientists at Georgia Tech while publishing a string of papers in prestigious journals such as *Science*. It is gratifying to me that research continues to be important in Atlanta, but it will likely continue as long as there is access to the dedicated, permanent endowment funds put there in 1995. I do worry that the young scientists who are driving research will not be replaced when they retire. Already,

Mike Hoff has retired from Dalton State College, and Mollie Bloomsmith may be the next one to take this step. In Mollie's case, Yerkes would be foolish not to plan for succession.

Our research in Atlanta preceded my development of the wellness construct, but it anticipated the utility of this term. We sought to design and build the most open and naturalistic facilities we could imagine and to evaluate how these innovations contributed to gorilla welfare. The strongest indicator of our success was successful reproduction and normal parenting. Years of restricted living conditions did not prevent the animals from responding naturally to their new, complex habitats. For all practical purposes, our groups behaved like wild gorillas but without the dangerous intrusion of human habitat encroachment or poaching. Earlier in my career, I lamented the fact that so few gorillas were born in zoos and so many that were born were immediately removed for hand rearing by human caregivers. As elected members of the AZA Species Survival Plan committee for gorillas, my colleague Ben Beck and I were strong and continuous proponents of the better practice of leaving newborns with their biological mothers (e.g. Maple and Hoff, 1982; Beck and Power, 1988). Eventually this practice prevailed. In Atlanta I was able to preside over unprecedented reproductive triumphs where all of our socially housed gorilla mothers raised their offspring successfully. The integration of landscape architecture and animal behavior research worked for gorillas, and it was the perfect combination to pave the way for wellness. It takes time and money to turn a substandard, traditional zoo into a simulated Garden of Eden, but the ideas behind wellness-inspired design generate hope as each new exhibit takes shape. Fortunately, managing to wellness standards and practices provides opportunities to introduce solutions and interventions that improve animals' lives immediately. The design team has to be committed to rapid and continuous reform through innovations in management and husbandry. In fact, the architects who worked with us, Gary Lee and Jon Coe, have always maintained that good architecture requires equally good management. Many excellent exhibits have been defeated in the long term by management lapses.

In my opinion, the benchmark Philadelphia Zoo360 design program is one of the most important advances toward the achievement of wellness standards. With the assistance of Philadelphia-based architecture firm CLR Design and their former partner Jon Coe, the zoo planned facilities for a variety of animals that permitted them access to vertical travel tubes outside the confines of their normal exhibit spaces. These elevated mesh tunnels gave animals an opportunity to explore the zoo campus from a new perspective. The visitors found this to be fascinating as they now had to look up to find animals in surprising locations. This array of translucent trails provides an experience of novelty and adventure for a variety of species. The original trails were named Gorilla Treeway, Treetop Trail, Great Ape Trail, Big Cat Crossing, Meercat Maze, and Water Is Life. Ten species of small monkeys, gorillas, orangutans, gibbons, tigers, lions, and meercats are among the animals enriched by this innovation. When I visited Philadelphia soon after they opened Zoo360, I was encouraged by their creativity, but it didn't surprise me. In 1987, when I was making a film in Indonesia, I visited the Jakarta Zoo. They exhibited a large group of orangutans at the zoo, but I was not prepared for the unique way they provided enrichment. Several times a day, a horse-driven cart arrived at the back of the exhibit and keepers ushered several orangutans into the cart with no shackles or restraints. They willingly and enthusiastically rode the cart throughout the zoo, among visitors, and made no attempt to escape. Clearly these rides were enriching and the most novel approach to animal welfare that I had observed in a zoo to that point. The Philadelphia trail system reminded me of the Jakarta experiment. Elevated pathways for orangutans were the perfect enrichment for this arboreal species. The state of the art for this system was pioneered in 1995 at the Smithsonian National Zoo by my colleague Ben Beck, who developed the Think Tank exhibit for great apes that included tall platforms and ropes the animals could use to brachiate from one exhibit to another. What was especially daring about this pathway was the fact that orangutans could locomote over the visitors walking through the zoo below them. And, yes, there was the occasional accident when orangutans defecated on guests, but the zoo carried on in the best interests of animal welfare. Dr. Beck was determined to encourage orangutans to exercise their natural propensities as tree-dwelling creatures, so he took the risk that the exhibit would work. I had championed arboreality for zoo orangutans since the 1980 publication of my book on the species, but Ben's innovations at the National Zoo moved the standard well beyond my own modest expectations. Other examples of vertical innovation for orangutans have since been installed in Tokyo, Japan, and Guadalajara, Mexico (Coe, personal communication). Verticality is now the gold standard for primates in zoos, and this significant reform to exhibits ensures that monkeys and apes are able to behave naturally and zoo visitors are able to observe and appreciate the complete behavioral repertoire of these facile creatures.

The Jacksonville Zoo and Gardens in Florida has also experimented with travel trails. The zoo's tiger exhibit encourages verticality within its elevated pathways for Sumatran and Malaysian tigers. AZA honored Jacksonville with an exhibit award for this innovative facility, which was built along wellness programming ideas before the word was commonly in use. The most unique feature of this exhibit is the way tigers are managed. Keepers are trained to encourage the animals to make their own choices about where they want to go in an array of exhibit destinations. Freedom of choice is our primary goal in managing these animals. We are also experimenting with giving tigers access to their exhibit at night since tigers are nocturnal in the wild. Trails function differently for specialized animals. For elephants, trails are essential because they must be able to walk to maintain circulation in their massive feet and legs. They are huge, powerful animals and need to exercise as they forage. Big cats like the trails so they can explore and for the opportunity to distance themselves for privacy. A more recent example of wellness-inspired design in Jacksonville is the new African Forest exhibit that houses gorillas, bonobos, and mandrills sharing the elevated trails and an iconic artificial kapok tree known locally as the wellness tree. This gigantic structure houses advanced computer technology that will provide the animals an opportunity to solve cognitive problems, receive food rewards, and interact with their keepers. Portable cognitive workstations have also been constructed in cooperation with scientists at the Indianapolis Zoo so more animals can take advantage of this form of periodic enrichment. Portable units are more cost-effective than the construction of many installations throughout the zoo, and we can introduce the technology to a greater number of animals this way. A study of the effectiveness of this innovative exhibit is underway, so we'll know soon just how much we have changed the daily life of these animals. Whenever we build a new exhibit, we try to carry out an objective post-occupancy evaluation so we understand how it works. Other zoos are experimenting with choice. The new "Primate Canopy Trails" exhibit at St. Louis Zoo provides eight interconnected habitats providing access to novel outdoor space and opportunity to explore each and every day.

FIGURE 5.2. LEMURS NAVIGATE ELEVATED TRAVEL SYSTEM
AT THE PHILADELPHIA ZOO (JANET MINER).

FOUR DECADES
OF RESEARCH ON RED APES

My initial research in Atlanta starting in 1975 examined the social behavior and social development of Sumatran orangutans at the zoo. Richard K. Davenport had studied orangutans in the field, and he wanted to learn more about them in artificially constructed social systems. He introduced a group of animals in a large group enclosure at the zoo to see how this largely solitary species would adapt to close quarters. After Professor Davenport's untimely passing, I began to study the zoo orangutans. On my first day observing the group, several extraordinary events were recorded. I was there with my new graduate student, Evan Zucker, who is now a professor of psychology at New Orleans's Loyola University. On the way to the zoo, I had told him that I didn't expect much action because of the stoic, asocial nature of this species. Atlanta's orangs proved me wrong. We saw a very active adult male who was playing vigorously with his five-year-old offspring. There had been no published reports of paternalistic play in orangutans, so we wrote a paper about it (Zucker, Mitchell, & Maple, 1978). Several other papers on play and social development followed (Maple & Zucker, 1978; Maple, Wilson, Zucker, & Wilson, 1978). When I presented my findings at the Baltimore meeting of AZA in 1976, I was gratified by the response of zoo professionals who were surprised by the unusual sociality displayed by these normally solitary apes. We also observed the phenomenon of "proceptivity" in an adult female orangutan, confirmed by following the animal for a 90-day hormonal cycle. The data clearly showed a peak of sexual behavior midcycle when the animal aggressively pursued the male and engaged in aggressive copulations with him. We made an interesting Super 8-millimeter film of the interactions and an undergraduate student, Mary Beth Dennon, gathered the data for her 1976 honors thesis at Emory. We later published this material in the first confirmation of the phenomenon of proceptivity for this species (Maple, Zucker, & Dennon, 1979). I believe that other investigators had not reported this behavior in orangutans because they were not typically housed in groups. When males and females meet in the wild or in the zoo, the males immediately chase the females and copulate with them. In a group, an atypical housing arrangement for them, the females respond to their sexual opportunities and their internal hormonal state to initiate aggressive copulations of their own. Our film is a remarkable record of this unique behavior.

After five years of research on zoo orangutans, I wrote *Orang-utan Behavior* (1980), a reference book published by Van Nostrand Reinhold. This was one of the first books on this species written by a psychologist. I used this knowledge to help me plan a future orangutan exhibit concept that would cater to the orangutan's special needs. In those days most zoo orangutans had very limited opportunities to climb. Orangutans are specialized to live in trees, and they do not locomote well on the ground. When you see a large male on the ground, it delivers the impression that he is depressed. In a benchmark paper published in *Zoo Biology* in 1985, Jon Coe argued that when animals are presented in a position below zoo visitors, they do not command our respect. This is the reason Coe and Lee advocated exhibits where zoo animals were presented on slightly higher ground than visitors. The elevated position, a profound design innovation, seems to produce a universal feeling of awe in the humans below, a factor in our willingness to protect them.

The behavioral program for orangutans called for artificial trees with simulated lianas to encourage their species-typical hand-over-hand brachiation. We wanted to create contiguous enclosures where males could be separated from females at the perimeter. The idea was to permit females to crawl through openings smaller than the males so they could exercise female choice. Unfortunately, our funding provided just enough money to build a superior gorilla exhibit. The orangutan exhibit was good but not great. It was, however, dramatically vertical, and orangutans could climb to a height of 54 feet (Figure 5.4). Coe and Lee executed our modest budget beautifully and offered their characteristic creativity to the benefit of the animals. Clearly wellness will not be achieved if orangutans cannot move in naturalistic, arboreal spaces. Fortunately, zoos no longer ignore the natural history and evolutionary specializations of orangutans. There are now many excellent examples of naturalistic orangutan exhibits throughout the world with food distributed in high places to encourage locomotion while providing opportunities to search and forage in a simulated arboreal eco-system. One of the most recent examples is the U.S. $21.5-million Simon Skjodt International Orangutan Center at the Indianapolis Zoo. The designers chose to build a "functional forest" with impressive verticality. The orangutans at the Indianapolis Zoo have so much vertical space (up to 80 feet), the apes are able to choose where they want to go as they explore horizontally and vertically the top of the zoo campus from elevated trails.

FIGURE 5.3. IN THE WILD AND THE ZOO, ORANGUTANS PREFER TO LIVE VERTICALLY.

In the wild, orangutans are losing their arboreal habitat as deforestation advances. They cannot live let alone thrive in deforested conditions. The primary reason for this trend is the proliferation of palm oil plantations in Indonesia, but zoos are fighting back to protect populations of orangs in the wild. Recently the Chester Zoo in England was named the world's first "sustainable palm oil city." To help the zoo, more than 50 organizations in the city of Chester have altered their supply chains and committed to sourcing palm oil from entirely sustainable sources. Hopefully, other cities around the world will follow Chester's example and stop the advance of deforestation that is bringing indigenous wildlife to the brink of extinction. The Chester Zoo's actions illustrate how modern zoos are fusing conservation and animal welfare to formulate meaningful public programs. Chester is an example of principled leadership—a zoo of consequence.

DESIGNING FOR DOLPHINS

We carefully study animals in part to learn how to deliver facilities and services that enhance their lives in captivity. What we learn from both wild and captive animals helps us to understand their basic biology and behavior. The design of facilities that are focused on entertainment fail to deliver sufficient space for bottlenose dolphins to thrive. On the other hand, dolphins are highly intelligent social creatures, so it is possible to enhance psychological well-being with human contact. A study by Clegg, Rodel, Boivin, and Delfour (2018) revealed that dolphins anticipated human-animal interactions more than the provision of toys, suggesting that dolphins perceive human interactions and toys as rewards. The authors equated dolphin responses to the construct of happiness and concluded that better bonding with human caregivers indicates better welfare. Although dolphins seem to adapt well to captive settings, aquarium operators have become increasingly concerned that visitors believe that the animals are being coerced to perform. For this reason, many zoos and aquariums are giving dolphins more opportunities to withdraw from contact. They can opt in or opt out. Essentially, they are giving their consent to work. It is also becoming more common for aquariums to provide opportunities to swim with dolphins as an educational experience. There is no compelling reason to capture wild dolphins, orcas, or whales to entertain us, although the historical justification for keeping dolphins was to learn more about them. Bottlenose dolphins have been studied more than most zoo animals.

Opened in 1961, the Brookfield Zoo dolphin exhibit is remarkable because it is connected to a long-term field study of the species. Brookfield scientists have a deep understanding of dolphin biology and behavior and continue to publish their findings from both field and zoo studies. As a demonstration of their credibility among peer institutions, they have taken responsibility for the world's largest international study of cetacean welfare. In a study that includes 44 accredited zoos and aquariums in seven countries, the Brookfield scientists aim to determine best practices and best facilities as well as the value of training. Since this is a long-term project, results are not expected until the year 2020. Commenting on the Brookfield website, Vice President Lance Miller stated,

> "When you think about animal care and welfare, there's the art and the science to it. I think 30 years ago it was more of an art form. You had a lot of people with a lot of great knowledge because they had worked with the animals for so long. What we do now is we don't try to take away from that art, but we try to use science to kind of mesh the two."

ORCAS AND WHALES AND BEARS

With proper care, we can keep orcas and whales alive in large aquatic facilities, but their quality of life is not optimal. SeaWorld built the world's largest aquatic habitats for killer whales and kept them in many locations for many years. The film *Blackfish* severely criticized the company for ignoring the needs of these highly intelligent, social creatures. The fact is, until recently, guests were amazed at the ability of SeaWorld trainers to control the behavior of these giant animals. It was thought to be the apex of training expertise, and it appeared to be interaction that orcas enjoyed. With time the public soured on the idea of dominating killer whales, just as they began to avoid circus acts with elephants and big cats. We have learned so much about the special cognitive and emotional makeup of these animals that it is no longer deemed acceptable to force them to entertain us. However, interaction between humans and charismatic megafauna is not inherently bad. As dolphins and orcas are retired from the performing arena, it may be necessary for staff to continue training sessions to activate and enrich the daily lives of animals that cannot be returned to the wild. Retired performers will also be valuable subjects for psychological studies that contribute to their well-being. SeaWorld's new Orca Encounter show is decidedly naturalistic with a measured pace and demonstrated concern for the future of orca populations and their vulnerable habitats around the world. With this creative public program, SeaWorld is demonstrating its corporate commitment to education and conservation. Beluga whales have proved to be more adaptable than killer whales and one recent report (Hill and Nollens, 2019) indicates that it may be possible to enrich their experience in captivity to enable thriving. Whether this finding is robust enough to generalize to other settings remains to be confirmed.

It was previously believed that polar bears suffered in captivity because they could not hunt, but important research from University of Oxford scientists came to a different conclusion. In a research paper published in *Nature*, Mason and Clubb (2003) found that polar bears, lions, and other animals with very large home ranges in the wild developed abnormal behaviors due to their inability to roam widely in zoos and aquariums. The authors observed that polar bears were especially prone to repetitive pacing as a result of being confined in space that is typically one million times smaller than their natural range (as estimated by Mason and Clubb). The authors acknowledged that zoos have attempted to remedy the loss of hunting opportunities by simulating prey capture, but it may be even more important to provide more and better space to activate the animals in a natural way. Innovations at the Detroit Zoo and a few other institutions with superior polar bear exhibits have built extensive aquatic pathways to encourage natural movements and play. If these aquatic features are too small, polar bears will resort to pacing while swimming. Effective simulations of polar bear habitat including both complex terrestrial and aquatic opportunities will bring out the natural behavior patterns of these active bears. Enrichment is very effective in bears. They clearly enjoy the presentation of ice encased fruit or fish, and they work busily at extracting the morsels of food within the ice. Caregivers who are not overly concerned with technical intrusions into naturalistic exhibits have used the ubiquitous Boomer Ball with some success as the bears will actively pursue the ball in the water and out. Polar bears are particularly aroused by the presence of viewing windows at the lower levels of their pools, and they will dive down to play or pursue visitors, especially small children. This experience can be quite exhilarating for both the bears and the kids but not so much for their concerned parents. People come away from a close encounter with a free-swimming polar bear with a feeling of awe and respect. Although zoos can never duplicate the vast arctic space available to polar bears in the wild, the best exhibits are growing larger and more stimulating for the bears. Many of the newer exhibits include other species such as seals and waterfowl to increase the complexity of the habitat. If captive polar bears are actively exploring their deep pools and visiting people who observe them from the other side of the glass, we will not feel sorry for them; in fact, we will experience them as we would if we visited their wild habitats. Polar bears are another species that should not be exhibited in every zoo. Only zoos and aquariums that have sufficient resources to provide large, immersive environments should acquire them. Exhibited properly, active, curious polar bears will inspire zoo visitors to do all they can to protect this majestic species in the wild.

For many years, polar bears were exhibited in warm climates with insufficient sources of water and little shade. In the south, it was not uncommon to see green polar bears covered with algae. I was involved in the rescue of six polar bears on the road in a travelling Mexican circus. The circus made a stop in Puerto Rico, within U.S. legal jurisdiction, when I was contacted by officials of People for the Ethical Treatment of Animals (PETA). The organization mistakenly believed one of the polar bears had come from Zoo Atlanta. I disputed this conclusion because I knew there were only two polar bears born at the zoo, and I knew where they were. One of the bears was sent to Germany by the previous zoo director. The animal died there. The second bear, Andy, had been living at our zoo in a substandard enclosure when I was appointed director in June 1984. Because Andy was named after our mayor, Andrew Young, my decision to send the bear to San Francisco on breeding loan had been a delicate one. Mayor Young did not object to my judgment that Andy would live better in a cool climate with other bears, and we successfully moved him with the mayor's blessing. Years later, San Francisco veterinarians discovered that Andy was actually a female. She had been misidentified by zoo staff in place at the time of her birth. Because we had blood from all of the polar bears that lived in our collection, we were able to compare the DNA to the bear in Puerto Rico. Since we could prove it was not our bear, I suggested to federal authorities from the U.S. Department of Agriculture that they prosecute the Mexican circus for identity fraud. This approach was adopted by our government, and they moved quickly to repossess the bear. In conjunction with volunteers from AZA's Bear Taxon Advisory Group, federal officers arrived at the circus compound in the dark of night, used bolt cutters to bypass security, and loaded the disputed bear into a travel crate. The bear was transported to the airport, loaded on a cargo plane, and flown to Baltimore where it was received by the Baltimore Zoo. PETA was so pleased with this transaction (which facilitated the confiscation of all of the polar bears), they sent me a nice plaque for my office. The PETA official who served as my contact reluctantly confirmed that the bears were better off in AZA-accredited zoos than they were in the traveling circus where the Feds rescued them. To achieve wellness, decisive action is sometimes required. As a zoo leader, I learned from this unusual bear repo that I could find common ground with an organization that was usually at odds with my profession.

Another exemplary exhibit for polar bears is the new U.S. $16-million facility in St. Louis, Missouri. This exhibit encompasses 40,000 square feet of simulated sea, coast, and tundra, the three types of habitat that typify a wild polar bear's life. It is large enough for five bears should the zoo be able to acquire them. In spite of its size, this new exhibit may not provide enough space for polar bears to roam. As we do with elephants, the zoo may have to activate the bears with training programs tailored to the bears' needs. Our goal of promoting fitness in zoo animals illustrates how labor-intensive zoo management has become. In considering what can be done for polar bears, it is useful to look outside the box. My colleague Nevin Lash (Ursa International) designed a polar bear exhibit for a township in Canada for nuisance bears that were raiding the town and disturbing the people. Nevin's solution was to arrange a semi-wild setting where the bears were safely confined but able to roam widely. Within their "exhibit" they can exclusively use an entire lake at the perimeter of the fencing. This innovative space has to be the largest and most natural polar bear exhibit in the world. What we learn from this experiment is the importance of optimizing space for active animals like bears.

WELLNESS FOR REPTILES

In our book *Zoo Animal Welfare* (2013), Bonnie Perdue and I suggested that the most neglected taxa in zoos and aquariums are the giant snakes: anacondas, pythons, and boa constrictors, species that can grow to a length of 29 feet (O'Shea, 2007) and a weight of more than 500 pounds. Traditional zoos and aquariums exhibit these massive creatures in small enclosures where they are usually inactive and distant from the visitor. This issue was recently reviewed in the *Journal of Veterinary Behavior* by Warwick, Arena, and Steedman (2019). The authors argued that snakes may be the only vertebrate where management policy commonly deprives the animals of the ability to freely extend the body to its natural length. They further recommended that future policies for snake husbandry should require a paradigm shift away from erroneous traditional practices to recognize the greater spatial needs of these reptiles. The authors took the additional step of providing guidelines for essential absolute minimum containment conditions for a variety of snakes.

FIGURE 5.4. LIKE MANY GIANT REPTILES, THE GREEN ANACONDA
IS USUALLY EXHIBITED IN CRAMPED SPACES.

The most interesting feature of these giant snakes is their size, but a visitor cannot appreciate their size unless the animal is stretched to its full length. In many zoos, staff occasionally stretch them to evaluate their health. It takes a large number of people to accomplish this task as the animals do not like it. The crafty zoo director will always instruct staff to take a selfie on such occasions so the huge body can be appreciated by visitors. The largest snake in the world is the South American green anaconda (*Eunectes murinus*), a largely nocturnal aquatic species that is sluggish on land but quite fast in water. They are also capable of pursuing prey in trees. An animal with such abilities should be activated in naturalistic zoo exhibits that permit the animal to show its size and its species-typical movement. Designers planning a zoo exhibit for anacondas should experiment with large translucent tubes similar to rodent habitat trails. Encouraged to travel through these tubes, anacondas would be incredibly popular, although a little scary if not terrifying to some. A wellness-inspired exhibit for giant snakes would be unique while turning a sedentary animal into an active one. Since wild anacondas eagerly pursue and consume fish and other animals, a zoo diet of living fish could be presented in these travel tubes, providing the additional enhancement of predation. A bit of creative technology could also be employed by training constricting anacondas to envelope and squeeze a device that provides an accurate reading of their strength. Because so many reptiles are relatively sedentary, it may be necessary to provide video technology in reptile exhibits to teach visitors about their habits in the wild. Nocturnal species like the anaconda are very active at night. Films are not a substitute for the living animal, but film records can complement what we see in the zoo by showing us more from audiovisual recordings. I once observed a huge python moving on the ground in Kenya at night. The animal passed in front of our car and surprised us with its speed. In my 25 safari visits to East Africa, this is the only active giant snake I have ever seen. Of course, many people fear snakes, so we have to be careful how we exhibit them to engender respect and appreciation but not hate. Venomous snakes have been subjected to roundups in Georgia, Texas, and other locations throughout North America. The tactics of these snake hunters include pouring gasoline into the burrows used by snakes and tortoises to kill them with fire and smoke. Collateral damage is inevitable as endangered and nonvenomous species such as indigo snakes, king snakes, and gopher tortoises are also killed. Recognizing the danger that venomous reptiles may pose to nearby communities, we should adopt more humane methods to protect the important role of reptiles in our complex ecosystems. We don't have to love them, but we must avoid driving reptiles to extinction. Zoos and aquariums have an important role to play so visitors learn to appreciate and value reptiles, and to make sure that people learn to respect them at an early age.

THE HUMAN CONNECTION

Developed to its full potential as a naturalistic, landscape immersive oasis, zoos and aquariums at their best encourage people and animals alike to thrive. Evidence strongly suggests such places contribute significantly to the mental health of visitors even as the exhibited animal population is expressing its full repertoire of natural, species-typical behavior (Maple & Morris, 2018). Indeed, the enhancement of human psychological well-being has to be acknowledged as one of the primary purposes of modern zoos and aquariums. Oddly, in many of North America's most populous cities, animal rights groups routinely denounce zoos and advocate their abolition. It is clear to me that we must do a better job of promoting the full-service features of zoos including their revitalizing function. The wellness construct allows operators to dedicate zoos and aquariums to serving their communities in new ways. Many zoological institutions offer peaceful walking trails among the sounds and sights of a simulated botanical Eden. At the 500-acre Minnesota Zoo in Apple Valley, visitors can cross-country ski the campus during winter months. Many zoos are also dedicating programs to the health and wellness of visitors and staff. The Lincoln Park Zoo in Chicago offers outdoor yoga and meditation classes at their Nature Boardwalk outdoor pavilion. It won't be long before zoos with giant pandas and other Chinese taxa will be offering tai chi classes for visitors to encourage their personal health and wellness. Following the lead of DAK, many zoos are also designing buildings that inform visitors about the cultural context that prevails in the landscape that sustains biodiversity around the world. African and Asian animal exhibits are contiguous to markets where food and souvenirs are themed for the visitors' enjoyment and education. For example, a creative way to teach visitors about Indonesia is to offer them slices of durian fruit, a sweet but stinky item that orangutans and local people consume with enthusiasm. To eat it you have to hold your nose. For orangutans, wellness is in the taste of the beholder.

Zoo animals in a state of happiness remind us of ourselves. When groups are intact as in the wild and stimulation is all around them, they explore and play and enjoy the enriched habitats zoos have created for them. It is difficult to dislike zoos that operate this way. With elephants, as described in this chapter, just watch how they use their bodies. Are they digging with their toes? Are they extending their trunks to interact and communicate with others? Can they stand on their back feet to obtain low-hanging fruit? If they do all these things and more, the designers have succeeded in creating a naturalistic habitat in form and function. Zoos designed and built to such naturalistic, functional specifications are authentic simulations of the natural world. This, in essence, is the epitome of wellness-inspired design. The only approach that may be superior is Jon Coe's "UnZoo" concept. Jon advocates bringing the audience to the animals in managed settings that are essentially the wild state. For aquatic iterations, he has designed boats that take visitors out to the open ocean to see dolphins and whales in their natural habitat or skirt coral reefs to visit with sharks, dugongs, and manatees. The UnZoo eliminates the need for captivity; no bars, no cages, no enclosures. Instead, it encourages wild animals to cooperate with visitors who come to observe and enjoy them. We do this now with organized safaris to see mountain gorillas in the Virunga Volcanoes region of Rwanda and Uganda. Chimpanzees can also be observed on hiking safaris in Central Africa.

Photographic safaris in East Africa confine the visitors to vans and Land Rovers while the animals are living free. This was also the concept behind the original Lion Country Safari Parks in North America. One drawback to this approach is the increasing pressure that popular visitation programs put on wild animal populations. In Puget Sound in the Pacific Northwest, critics have argued that orcas are bothered by too many tourists. It won't be long before the people who have abandoned zoos because they are opposed to animal captivity will be deprived of viewing wild animals from a close but safe distance. There is plenty of evidence that watching animals in zoos and in the wild can promote conservation attitudes that will help to protect wildlife and wild ecosystems. There is really nothing like seeing living animals behaving naturally. As much as I value film, it is not an effective substitute for viewing living animals up close.

The architects that bring us close to wildlife with authentic simulations of the natural world continuously refine their technology and expand their horizons. Innovations such as Zoo360 influence advanced versions of the art so the experience gets better each time it is introduced to another location. I have been fortunate to work closely with architects my entire career who have exchanged ideas with me and kept me engaged at the cutting edges of design. Gary Lee and his colleagues at CLR Design, his partner Jon Coe, and Nevin Lash of Ursa International have all creatively examined the wellness construct and applied it in their best work. It is fair to say that wellness has evolved and improved as a design approach due to the synergistic collaborations we've experienced for the past 40 years. CLR's development of "activity-based design" was a relevant precursor to wellness. Their idea of keeping animals at the back of the house in reserve allowed the exhibitor to release members of the group when they were ready to explore. This was a win/win for visitors and the animals. I do hope that a new cadre of zoo directors and designers test the boundaries of wellness by introducing bold, new approaches that bring out the best in the next generation of zoological gardens. One way to do this is to invite free-thinkers from the entire staff to submit their wildest ideas and partici-pate in the vetting of the final design. In my experience, graduate students are especially good at offering untested but often extraordinary ideas for consideration but they must be empowered to speak up.

Chapter 6

INSTITUTIONAL WELLNESS CENTERS

The most endearing feature of the wellness construct is its universal application to human beings and their communities and to wildlife and ecosystems. A wellness center located on the zoo campus will serve the purpose of interpreting wellness for visitors while clearly demonstrating how zoos and aquariums have committed to higher standards and better practices to benefit all living things. Accredited zoos and aquariums are evidence-based institutions committed to exhibit enhancements that educate and inspire. Animals behaving naturally and living well are the most effective ambassadors for wild populations and the ecosystems that support them in the natural world. Future zoos embracing the wellness construct will reveal its meaning in the construction of complex, naturalistic exhibits based on immersive design principles. Every exhibit in the best zoos and aquariums will present animals in natural groupings with ample opportunities to live normal lives. True to our empirical foundation, we will carefully monitor these animals to ensure they enjoy the highest quality of life we can provide. As good as exhibits can be, we will gather systematic data and always seek to improve them. In our superior habitats, animals will never suffer. With time, coping will transition to thriving. Many new exhibits in the best zoos and aquariums have already delivered wellness, but it will take a generation of design and development to provide environments that meet the needs of each and every species that we manage. The story of how zoos and aquariums evolved into repurposed and revitalized gardens is worth telling again and again. Zoos were not always noble, and they once reflected anachronistic attitudes about humanity's superiority over the rest of the animal kingdom. From 2,500 BCE, there is evidence that empires in Egypt and Mesopotamia collected animals from the known world to be displayed for entertainment and to demonstrate their power over adversaries (Kisling, 2000). With the passage of time, the wealthiest nations built the biggest zoos. In epochs of peace and prosperity, animals were collected by explorers and traders for display in public places. Great zoos such as those in Berlin, Germany; London, England; New York, New York; and San Diego, California advanced the state of the art to a sophisticated standard based on science and artful management practices. Zoos and aquariums in the 21st century are no longer mere menageries; they are built with the form and function of natural habitats, providing visitors with adventures that resemble in every way a trip to exotic, lost continents. The creativity required to design and build a great zoo matches the artistry of a great symphony or a piece of fine art. Wellness is the road map guiding the future of all zoos and aquariums.

THE MISSION
OF ZOO WELLNESS CENTERS

As we have seen, the wellness construct is a new idea in the zoo world, and wellness centers are newer still. The broad mission of a wellness center is to provide guests with a locus for advocacy and interpretation. It is here that educators explain through words and deeds the strategic approach to a superior quality of life. The model for this transformation is the natural world. Managers are only satisfied when the animals are behaving like wild animals. The only exception to this demand is that predators and prey are not usually exhibited together. However, there are some situations where animals are fed live prey; insects can be fed to lizards and birds, and live fish can be fed to crocodilians and raptors. This practice is still condoned for enrichment even though there is growing evidence that fish may feel pain like mammals do (Balcombe, 2016; Brathwaite, 2010; Sneddon, 2011). Elsewhere I discussed this issue as a trade-off where zoo caregivers may have to give preference to the recipient of the enrichment (Maple &

Perdue, 2013; for example, the provision of live fish to grizzly bears or bald eagles). A controversial subject such as this one is an appropriate debate topic in a wellness center discussion group as enrichment strategies should be described in detail for visitors. The science that supports the conclusion that fish feel pain has already influenced some anglers who have devised more humane methods for quickly killing fish to prevent suffering. A fishing vessel named *Blue North* harvests Pacific cod from the Bering Sea. Within seconds of capture, the crew moves a fish to a stun table where they deploy 10 volts of electricity to render the animal unconscious. The owners of this ship follow the humane slaughtering techniques developed by Temple Grandin, who has taken the unique perspective of the animal selected for slaughter. As others join this movement, pain and suffering may be greatly reduced in the global fishing industry. The use of live prey in the zoo and aquarium profession, a practice that is not widespread, will certainly be debated as scientists continue to examine the nervous systems and emotional makeup of fish. A good source for generating a discussion of this kind is the book *What a Fish Knows* by Jonathan Balcombe (2016). Historically, zoos have exhibited contiguous rows of predators and prey to give the illusion they occupy the same landscape, and CLR Design pioneered the concept of exhibit rotation where prey and predators moved in and out of the same enclosure sequentially.

One way that wellness centers can help us understand the distinction between coping and thriving is to present films of active wild species in high-definition images. As the technology evolves, exposure to virtual reality will provide a strong immersive effect. Large populations that an ecotourist can see in Africa, for example, are difficult to portray in a zoo, so film augments what we can see. We should deploy film in a wellness center to expose the visitor to the power and speed of wild animals and their specialized array of vocalizations. The complexity of life in socially appropriate natal groups is easily discerned by trained observers. Images of active social life can be projected within a smart entry and exit portal for a zoo or aquarium. This portal delivers a powerful emotional message about activity, complexity, and wellness, and it sets the tone for understanding how wellness-inspired design affects the lives of animals at the zoo. An important decision about any wellness center is its placement on the zoo campus. The most appropriate location is the public entrance/exit to and from the zoo. If the wellness message is strong, its retention is facilitated by the psychological law of primacy and law of recency discussed in Chapter 3. We remember information when it is the first thing we see, and we won't forget it if it is the last thing we see. So powerful imagery is essential at the zoo entrance/exit. To generate emotion and make an impression early in a zoo visit, the wellness center has to be placed in the most technologically sophisticated location in the entire zoo campus. From this spot at the beginning of the zoo adventure, the entire experience must be teachable with technology and with articulate spokespeople.

THE WELLNESS THINK TANK

Since no zoo or aquarium has actually built a comprehensive wellness center, we have a wide variety of options available to us. If the wellness portal is designated as the ground floor of a wellness building, the entire structure becomes a locus for the discovery and practice of wellness. Every empirical zoo and aquarium should provide space for thinking, debating, collaborating, and discovering together. A think tank approach will provide office space, small conference rooms, a digital library, a media and reading room, and a high-tech theater suitable for lectures and audiovisual presentations by visiting scientists and educators. Academic partners, faculty, and students should be involved in designing these facilities to meet the quality standards of our colleges and universities. Thoughtful design will also permit members, donors, and friends to use these facilities for board and committee meetings and benchmark celebrations. In this way the wellness think tank helps to generate the revenue and the support to expand its mission. The think tank section of our wellness center must be prepared to focus on both human and animal wellness. To this end it serves the greater needs of the community as well as the zoo. Because wellness is evidence based and always evolving to higher standards and better practices, a dedicated think tank is a good way to facilitate continuing reforms and innovation. I have always believed the best zoos and aquariums are distinguished by their intellectual capital and the systems and resources that support it. Local social, political, and service clubs will eagerly flock to rent such stimulating space in the zoo. Although it is more of a wellness laboratory, San Francisco Zoo designated creative space for Jason Watters' wellness department at the back of the zoo. It was named for Senator Dianne Feinstein and her husband Richard Blum. It has much in common with a wellness think tank.

Planning for a future of leadership requires that we design a center where colleagues can gather for professional meetings, workshops, and conferences. The size of the wellness center will determine just how extensive these sessions can be. Local and regional meetings require modest allocations of space, but national and international meetings can only be hosted by institutions with at least a 250-seat theater, many meeting rooms, and space dedicated to catering. Unlike zoos, major aquariums are designed to host large conventions. Meetings of this size are a major contributor to the annual revenue stream of aquariums and the host city. Thinking bigger about the scope of wellness centers, they could offer a way to focus on collective issues that all zoological institutions must face together. For example, a major conference on aquatic animal welfare is long overdue. If aquariums are going to continue to exhibit aquatic megafauna, drastic changes will be necessary to accommodate the needs of animals that have suffered in many substandard world facilities. Unlike the terrestrial elephant, now living in wellness-inspired habitats in many zoos, money is not the reason cetaceans are not living well in aquariums. Rather, it is a lack of new ideas that plagues the profession. The manufacture of bigger circular tanks is certainly not the answer. Aquarium professionals and expert design firms will have to literally think outside the box to create facilities that encourage thriving. Contemporary aquariums are a long way from featuring exhibit innovations that will be game changers on the animal welfare front.

FEELINGS THAT MATTER

In Chapter 5, we discussed the importance of wellness-inspired design principles. Wild animals live in harmony in the natural world. They are not always safe, but they adapt to danger and do what it takes to escape and survive. When animals are hunted by others, the danger passes until another day when the prey species are again challenged by other predators. If we design to mimic nature, we should create situations that temporarily elevate heart rate and pose a perceived risk sufficient to generate a moderate amount of fear. It is controlled fear, of course, and it must be defeated by something the animal does to escape or overcome the stimulus. By overcoming the challenge, we build in resilience. A life worth living isn't free of danger; living well requires some degree of risk or perceived risk to be a good life. Designers who understand this principle provide enough space so managers can use it to create challenging situations. Predatory cats may be presented with a zip-line experience where they must pursue an object as it moves through its habitat on the zip line. Once the object is captured, the cat can be rewarded with a meal. You don't have to teach cheetahs to pursue prey presented with movement, and it is much more rewarding for the cat to work for its reward than to have it delivered with no life in it. Don Lindburg had great success with lures to activate cheetahs at the San Diego Zoo (Maple, 2019). This kind of active enrichment is also thrilling for zoo guests. Because we advocate wellness for all living things, it is not unimportant to generate arousal in the people who visit the zoo.

We can experiment with human emotions in our wellness centers and find ways to build it into the zoo experience. For example, psychologists have investigated how the sense of awe can promote altruistic, helpful, and positive social behavior. Awe is recognized as that sense of wonder we feel in the presence of something vast that transcends our understanding of the world around us. People experience awe when they are in touch with nature, religion, art, and music. In a study by Piff, Dietze, Feinberg, Stancato and Keltner (2015), the investigators exposed human subjects to awe-inducing stimuli and then tested their willingness to engage in pro-social behaviors such as helping. The feeling of awe was associated with prosocial behaviors in every experiment they conducted. The investigators concluded that awe induces a feeling of being diminished in the presence of something greater than oneself, shifting an individual's focus away from their own needs toward that of the greater good. In the presence of threatening natural phenomena such as tornadoes and volcanoes or immersed in a grove of towering eucalyptus trees, the feeling of awe consistently generated cooperative, helpful behavior. The investigators wondered about how powerful awe could be in generating a better world.

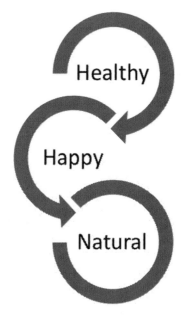

FIGURE 6.1. KEY FEATURES OF HEALTHY HABITATS IN THE MODERN ZOO.

Might the experience of awe cause people to become more invested in their communities by giving more to charity, volunteering to help others, or doing more to reduce their impact on the environment? The strength of these findings strongly suggests that the answer is yes. Clearly any institution that exposes its visitors to powerful emotions has a chance to induce changes in attitude and behavior. For this reason alone, I believe a dedicated wellness center should generate emotion through the effective deployment of powerful images and audiovisual stimuli using 3-D and virtual and augmented reality technologies. These techniques deployed as visitors enter through a portal to the zoo campus can set the tone for the entire day. Realistic sounds and sites from the zoo itself can be generated as the visitor examines artifacts and abstract images of the full experience. Visitors can also investigate immersion techniques using a computer interface that enables the visitor to design or change any exhibit available in the program. This computer engagement might be particularly effective as visitors exit the zoo or by providing them with computer games they can order online. Long-lasting behavioral effects and playful involvement are possible with the assistance of computer technology. At the San Diego International Airport, I recently witnessed a visual display of silhouetted swimmers moving through the airport above the crowd. It was fascinating and very realistic.

Technology has been embraced by both zoos and aquariums. At the Aquarium of the Pacific in Long Beach, California, a new U.S. $53-million, 29,000-square-foot expansion opened to the public on May 24, 2019. The new wing is packed with advanced technology rather than large fish tanks and is comprised of media-friendly oceanic art, a cinema with a 132-foot curved screen (the Honda Pacific Visions Theater), and a large exhibition gallery. Effective simulations of living structures such as corals immerse guests in a multisensory landscape. Special effects include fog, wind, aromas, vibrating seats, and ultrasound waves. This array of technology is there for one reason: to inform and to inspire change. This West Coast aquarium is betting that combined with the beauty of ocean-going creatures, powerful media images will provide visitors with the information they need to interpret the world and make a difference in the choices they make as consumers. The North Carolina Zoo has also experimented with advanced technology by providing guests access to virtual reality experiences in a simulated African landscape. Zoo Atlanta was the first North American zoo to introduce virtual reality when a partnership with Georgia Tech enabled students to enter the gorilla exhibit through a portal available with a virtual reality helmet. The sounds and behaviors of gorillas were authentic, based on the behavior of living gorillas in the Ford African Rain

Forest exhibit (Allison, Wills, Bowman, Wineman, & Hodges, 1997). We also provided authentic vocal sounds of lowland gorillas to the producers of the film *Congo*. Special effects are becoming more common in zoo design.

AFFECT AND CONSERVATION

Emotion can work against conservation when zoo visitors perceive that animals in the zoo are not doing well. When visitors feel sorry for zoo animals, they are prone to withdraw their support, visit less often, and communicate their disappointment to family and friends. A substandard animal facility, such as the many roadside attractions that are still in business, confuse visitors by showing the dark side of animal exhibition. We should not tolerate such abuse of the public trust. In my career as a zoo executive, I assumed leadership in Atlanta when the entire staff was angry about the neglect of city fathers who had long ago abandoned the zoo. Needless to say, support groups longing for reform cannot raise money when zoos are mismanaged or neglected for a long period of time. The lesson I learned from this experience was a simple one: people don't give you money because you need it; they give it to you because you deserve it. A dilapidated zoo must experience organizational change before it can alter the landscape of philanthropy, sponsorship, and community commitment. Leaders committed to revolutionary change must step up to defeat the chaos and rally reform. As my mentor Carolyn Boyd Hatcher courageously put it in 1984, "the zoo must change or it must be closed."

Zoos that have crossed the threshold of reform and revitalization can change behavior by creating a reason for people to support the establishment. If they are touched emotionally by the sight of a gorilla raising its infant, two magnificent gibbons singing their characteristic duet, a herd of elephants enjoying a dip in a full-immersion pool, or the squawking vocalizations of a pair of Australian kookaburras, zoo visitor emotion may morph into liking, giving, and returning. In a study by Powell and Bullock (2014), visitors to the Bronx Zoo in New York were surveyed after they viewed tigers, African wild dogs, and spotted hyenas during baseline conditions or when the animals were provided enrichment to stimulate natural behavior patterns. The investigators asked visitors to rate their predispositions toward nature, their positive emotional experiences when viewing the animals, and how the experience affected their "conservation mindedness." In this study, conservation mindedness was indicated when participants rated wildlife issues as meaningful, expressed their intention to support conservation organizations, and confirmed their willingness to alter their own behavior.

In the Bronx Zoo study, female participants reported stronger emotional experiences than males, and older participants reported stronger emotions than younger adults. Visitor predisposition toward nature was strongly correlated with emotions, while strong predispositions toward nature and emotional experiences produced significantly stronger reports of conservation mindedness. Many other studies have demonstrated that women have more positive attitudes toward animals than men (Herzog, Betchart, & Pittman 1991; Schlegel & Rupf 2010). Women exhibit a stronger identification with animals (Hills, 1993) and respond to animals with more emotion and sympathy (Serpell, 2004). Within the zoo environment, women perceive animals more positively and respond to animals with greater empathy (Myers, Saunders, & Birjulin 2004), especially those they conclude are bored or sad (Reade & Waran 1996). Other studies cited evidence that emotions and learning are highly interrelated (Damasio, 1994) and linked their findings to developments in positive psychology. For example, positive emotions foster environmental consciousness, environmentally responsible behavior, and a variety of other personal outcomes, including good health and enhanced problem-solving, creativity, and resilience (Frederickson & Cohn, 2008; Carter, 2011). The Bronx Zoo study found that tigers elicited more positive emotions than the other two carnivores, wild dogs and hyenas. In addition, behavior affected emotions as visitors were influenced by the amount of activity displayed by the animals they observed. Participants also reported stronger emotions when they were closest to the animals and when they made eye contact with them. This is an important finding because other data have indicated that animals can suffer stress from exposure to visitors. Zoos that choose to distance visitors from key species or deprive them of contact experiences may be losing their best opportunity to generate positive emotions and changes in attitude. If conservation mindedness is a goal of zoos, they will have to think long and hard about how to produce and sustain this outcome.

Wellness centers are the logical venue in the zoo where findings such as these can be shared with visitors. As intellectual think tanks, they can also investigate the role of emotions in learning to see how the zoo itself is changing the behavior of our guests. One field that should be explored in wellness centers is conservation psychology, defined as the scientific study of the reciprocal relationships between human beings and the rest of nature. A relatively new specialty, conservation psychology originated at the Brookfield Zoo in Chicago (Saunders & Myers, 2003). The field has always been concerned with proactive measures to ensure the protection and survivability of wildlife and ecosystems. Because zoos have such high visitation, more than the combined visitation of all major-league sports teams, they are well positioned to influence millions of people (estimated at 140 million by Ballantyne, 2007). It is quite feasible to designate zoos and aquariums as the primary institutional communicators of reliable factual information about wildlife conservation. Their obligations as the disseminators of conservation science are consistent with the role of zoos as the acknowledged experts on exotic animal biology and behavior. Wellness centers with provisions for imbedded think tanks serve this purpose well.

EATING WELL, LIVING WELL

In Chapter 2 we discussed the psychological variables associated with nutrition in the zoo. In a zoo that recognizes that wellness applies to man and beast, healthy eating habits can be described in a way that appeals to all ages. Given the prevalence of obesity in the modern world, how and what we eat is a delicate subject for a zoo and is most appropriate when delivered in a dedicated wellness center and reinforced at themed restaurants and food courts throughout the zoo. The opportunities to present food in a cultural context have been exhaustively introduced in Disney properties, most recently in DAK, but many zoos and aquariums are experimenting with culturally diverse and healthier cuisine to appeal to zoo visitors who take wellness seriously. As we provide greater opportunities for choice for our animals, we cannot ignore the need for visitors to experience choice also. The most significant advancement in human nutrition is arguably the availability of a vast menu of plant-based protein options. Popular accounts of this nutritional strategy are widely available, for example, in *Forks Over Knives* and *The China Study*. The ideas in these and other sources can and should be taught in zoo wellness centers. Even Burger King has successfully introduced a plant-based protein Whopper burger, and it has been well received so far (Fickenscher, 2019). It will be interesting to see if zoo visitors will accept significant changes in the composition of zoo food.

Animal stories are fun for children, but they can also inspire adult behavior change. In Atlanta, when I reached a point where I needed to lose weight, I was inspired and informed by the approach of our veterinarian, Rita McManamon, who trimmed nearly 100 pounds from our famed gorilla, Willie B. She accomplished this by changing his diet and the way he was fed. He also benefitted from the new exhibit when it opened in 1988. He spent all day outside and moved around much more than he had in his steel and concrete cage. Once he was introduced to female gorillas, his motivation to move around was accelerated. I realized that if I adopted a similar plant-based diet with lots of fruits and vegetables, I would lose weight too. As we did with Willie B., I adopted portion control throughout the day, but for me it was daily swimming that really burned the calories. With zoo animals, caregivers can actually serve as personal trainers and help the animals to exercise. Animals that are living well are truly inspirational models for people who spend time with them at the zoo. Willie B. inspired me to lose 70 pounds. I will always be grateful that I knew him and learned from his example. Of course, our growing knowledge of wild animal nutrition can make a real difference in our journeys to superior health and wellness. In our work in the zoo, we enjoy one distinct advantage over most folks; we can walk daily among wild animals and gorgeous botanicals to get our daily exercise. My advice to zoo directors who are trending to the portly side; avoid golf carts. It is also helpful to surrender medical oversight to an expert like Dr. McManamon. Since she couldn't practice human medicine without a license, I turned to West Palm Beach internist, Dr. David Dodson, who deserves the lion's share of credit for my success. A strong proponent of plant-based protein diets, he has served as my personal physician for more than a decade.

FIGURE 6.2. JACKSONVILLE BONOBO SAUNTERS DOWN THE ELEVATED SAFARI TRAIL.

One dimension of veterinary medicine that fits perfectly in a wellness center complex is the art and science of nutrition. In our original plan for the Palm Beach Zoo wellness center, we provided space for a nutrition team with the task of educating visitors about our commitment to providing healthy diets. By introducing the science of nutrition as it applies to zoo animals, visitors learn how to apply this knowledge with their own pets and their family at home. As we have seen, obesity is a difficult subject to discuss openly with family. By using animal models, the information can be delivered in a way that is more oblique. Of course, the zoo that is practicing good nutrition won't have many living examples of obese animals to showcase their ideas, but it is easy enough to use photographs and illustrations to tell the stories of how obesity affects various taxa in the zoo and how we defeated it. By providing access to veterinarians, nutritionists, and keepers who feed the animals, visitors can ask questions and learn more about their favorite animals. Good nutrition can be shared with inspirational accounts in the wellness centers. Some of the most interesting stories are how zoos use browse as enrichment. Visitors are always amazed when they find out how much planning is required in organizing a successful browse enrichment unit. At the San Francisco Zoo, the horticulture department works five days per week collecting browse for their koala collection and three days a week collecting material for hoofed stock, primates, birds, and other species. It takes two dedicated vehicles to collect *Acacia longifolia* and *Coprosma*, which are delivered to most of the animals, and *Eucalyptus* tips that are delivered to the koalas. About 20% of zoo browse is collected from the zoo campus with the remainder found in other city parks, city-owned land, and private and federal properties that cooperate with the zoo. Reliable partners are required to ensure no dangerous pesticides are used on this material. All cuts of browse are made to encourage new growth and protect the plants for future harvest. Most browse is delivered within two hours of harvest, so it is always fresh. The San Francisco harvest of browse amounts to 61 tons of material annually, and it takes 54 staff hours per week to carry out the program (Steve Beach, personal communication). Supplementing the animals' diet with browse is the zoo's most important enrichment program, and it also involves some creative applications that are introduced less frequently. Fruit and fish icicles, for example, are made by freezing food in water so the animals have to break the ice to obtain the food. This technique is particularly popular with bears and big cats. If the ice contains colorful fruit and veggies, primates will eagerly take it apart.

Herpetologists elicit activity from many smaller reptiles and amphibians by introducing live insects. Kids are fascinated by insects. Since they take so little space, an insect zoo could be placed in a wellness center for a close-up look at crickets, walking sticks, praying mantises, and Madagascar hissing cockroaches. Zoo directors with a sense of humor have been known to grab a few of the robust but gentle Madagascar species as a lecture prop at service club meetings. Media celebrity and former zoo director "Jungle" Jack Hanna liked to position them on his tie to serve as a living tie clip. The roaches stayed perfectly still during his talk, but they always made an impression. Apparently, these spectacular roaches crave attention because they seem eager to occupy the stage with public speakers, docents, and charismatic media figures. If you want to know if your son or daughter has a future in the zoo business, ask them to put their hand into a bowl of wriggling roaches. If they fearlessly handle hissing roaches, you know you have a future zookeeper in the family.

PROGRAMMING FOR HAPPINESS

In the wellness center think tank, zoo staff and their academic collaborators will be able to discuss and debate tough issues, and these debates should be shared with our visitors in every way we can. During my long career, I have been asked repeatedly to give my opinion on whether animals are happy in the zoo. It has become easier to answer this question now that so many behavioral scientists have agreed that the term *happiness* is now an acceptable term for some species, notably dogs, cats, and great apes. This shift to accepting happiness as a welfare outcome fits the new paradigm of positive psychology. We are no longer content to merely avoid discontent; instead, we do what we can to promote "positive affect" or happiness. What was once forbidden as anthropomorphism is now freely discussed in scientific journals and textbooks. Indeed, happiness can be observed, measured, and facilitated in the zoo.

One good example of "happiness-inspired design" is found in the master plan from the Paris Zoo (Fiby & Berthier, 2007). The authors' subtitle for their plan is entitled, "How to make anteaters happy." By providing enrichment through a naturalistic substrate, anteaters were able to express a broad range of natural behaviors. Reaching their full behavioral potential evokes the finding that anteaters were indeed happy in such an enriched living space. Our visitors should be able to recognize that naturalistic design elements enable natural, species-specific behavior including evidence of happiness.

Psychologists have equated happiness with subjective well-being (Myers & Diener, 2018). There has been a renaissance of research on the subject in recent years. In their review of the subject, Myers & Diener plotted the growth of published research from 1960 to 2018. It is an impressive curve, ranging from fewer than a dozen articles in 1960 to more than 1,300 per year in 2018. The traditional methods for assessing happiness in human subjects uses life-satisfaction scales and simple survey questions, for example, "Are you very happy, pretty happy, or not too happy?" Other studies have examined real-time records, reconstructions of daily experiences, brain activity, and the use of positive and negative words across time and place. Four traits of happy people have emerged from these studies: optimism, extraversion, personal control, and self-esteem. As Myers and Diener asserted, we are social animals, adapted to group living with a need to belong. Human beings thrive when they receive and provide social support. It is likely that these findings can be extended to animals. Thriving, for example, requires harmonious, species-specific social groups. Elephants naturally live in large herds, so we have begun to build exhibits that are sufficiently complex to accommodate large social groups. In constructing a theory of happiness, Myers and Diener (2018) observed that in poor countries, the satisfaction of Maslow's basic needs are more important, whereas wealth leads to a focus on higher-order need satisfaction. In the zoo where basic needs are readily being met, we now believe it is essential to provide opportunities to satisfy cognitive, emotional, and social needs for each species and every animal exhibited. As we have learned, this is the progression from welfare to wellness. With growing acceptance of the term *happiness* in both the human and animal literature, research productivity on this subject will increase exponentially in future years. While scientists have accepted a measure of anthropomorphism, zoo professionals are still offering resistance. It will take some adjusting for zoo people to accept the idea that animals too can be happy. In order to effectively communicate with our visitors, donors, and sponsors, we may have to address this issue head on. I frankly think it will be comforting for most of our supporters to know that we are okay with the idea of animals that are happy. Since visitors are always asking if the animals are happy at the zoo, it is important for zoo professionals to have a satisfactory answer to the question.

SATISFACTION AND CHOICE

One of the highest priorities for animal welfare is expanding opportunities for choice. Advocates for choice have included Maple (1979), Markowitz (1982) and Mellor, Hunt, and Gusset (2015). At the Jacksonville Zoo and Gardens, tigers are provided with elevated pathways and plenty of space so they can choose to distance themselves from noisy visitors. Gorillas and bonobos can use computer technology at their convenience and earn rewards in the process. There are many zoos with high-tech apparatuses that are ape friendly and easy to maintain. There is so much opportunity to choose in zoos worldwide that we may soon be able to examine whether choice by zoo animals follows the principles derived from studies of human choice. Grant and Schwartz (2011) acknowledged that giving individuals choices has important well-being and performance benefits. It was once assumed that more choice was better. As Seligman (1975) determined, individuals with choice had control, and a lack of control led to helplessness and clinical depression. Other findings demonstrated that autonomy was a robust predictor of well-being and therefore regarded as a basic need (Ryan & Deci, 2000). The relationship between choice and well-being was thought to be monotonic; as choice increases, well-being increases also. However, recent research indicates that at high levels, choice can have negative effects. For example, Iyengar and Lepper (2000) found that too many choices can cause decision paralysis, dissatisfaction, and disengagement. These findings support the inverted-U model for the number of options and both the likelihood of choice and the satisfaction with one's choices. Without delving into the many explanations offered for this phenomenon in human subjects, we have an opportunity to examine whether zoo animals respond in a similar way. Advocates of choice for its positive effects on animal welfare would never know its limits without the data obtained from human subjects. It is imperative that animal welfare scientists formulate testable hypotheses to see if too much choice produces distress in zoo animals. I learned recently about one young investigator, a graduate psychology student at Georgia State University, who has been working on this problem with great apes. Maisy Bowden has developed a methodology to test choice using joy sticks in a cognitive workstation adapted for chimpanzees. She understands that choice for great apes, like human subjects, may be less satisfying and more distressing when there are many options. In a zoo where there are many species available to study, a true comparative analysis can be run to see whether the inverted-U can be generalized to a wide variety of species or whether the findings are confined to species with a similar genetic profile. I feel comfortable predicting that closely related bonobos, chimpanzees, gorillas, and orangutans will respond in a nearly identical way when presented with many as opposed to only a few choices.

From here we may be able to find a general primate model that can be tested against other cognitively complex species such as bears, big cats, cetaceans, elephants, and pinnipeds. As a comparative psychologist, I believe that comparative cognition research will prosper as more and more of my colleagues discover the value of zoo collections. Comparative studies of closely related apes, big cats, and bears should yield interesting results. A good example of what can be accomplished in the zoo was recently published in *Zoo Biology* (Wagman et al., 2017). The investigators from the Cleveland Metroparks Zoo found that daily variable-schedule feeding enrichment with the intermittent presentation of unique enrichment items increased behavioral indicators of positive welfare and decreased behavioral indicators of negative welfare in four species of bears (the Andean, sloth, brown, and black bear species). Their experiments confirmed the meta-analytic findings of Swaisgood and Shepherdson (2005) that enrichment increased natural, active behavior in 74% of studies.

PSYCHOLOGICAL
SCIENCE AND WELLNESS

Although conservation and education centers and even specialized museums have been constructed on zoo grounds, a comprehensive wellness center has yet to be built. The reason for this omission is that animal welfare and then wellness had to be widely accepted in the zoo world before the idea could be implemented. The closest embodiment of a wellness center that I have been involved in is Zoo Atlanta's Conservation Action Resource Center (ARC). This unique facility was envisioned as an integrated building for employees and collaborators from four distinct operating units: conservation, education, research, and technology. The ARC building, as it was labeled, prevented these units from drifting apart. We reasoned when it opened in 1994 that educators needed to teach the latest findings from conservation and science and that the effectiveness of our educational outreach depended on sophisticated information technology. Integrating these operating units into one department managed by a doctoral-level biologist was a management innovation at the time. In addition, we designed the building as a curvilinear structure, following the ideas of Hediger, with a living roof for sustainability. Reflecting the essence of a wellness center, the ARC building attracted scholars from Emory University, Georgia Tech, Georgia State, and the University of Georgia. Smaller colleges in the region have subsequently joined this academic network, making Zoo Atlanta one of the most scientifically accessible zoos in the world. To facilitate public programs, we designed a major auditorium with advanced audiovisual technology for classes and presentations K-college level. In the 25 years since the ARC was opened, we have learned plenty about how to teach and inspire others in a dedicated center of learning at the heart of the zoo. It is time that we imagine, design, and build more centers like this one, organized around the depth and breadth of the wellness construct and dedicated to understanding why wellness is so important to animals, people, communities, and ecosystems. Our wellness journey would start in such a place and take our guests through each unique example of taxa our ingenious designers have encouraged to prosper.

FIGURE 6.3. LOWLAND GORILLA RUMPEL WORKING WITH
COMPUTER IN JACKSONVILLE (M. MORRIS).

ENVIRONMENTAL WELLNESS

The field of environmental psychology began as a way to study how the
built environment affects human behavior. My contribution to this field
was to extend the science to cover environments that influence animal

141

behavior. Early in my career, I borrowed from architecture the research technique of post-occupancy evaluation and enjoyed some success evaluating exhibits for a variety of species in the zoo (e.g., Clarke, Juno, & Maple, 1982; Maple & Finlay, 1986; Maple & Finlay, 1987; Finlay, James, & Maple, 1988; Ogden, Finlay, & Maple, 1990; Ogden, Lindburg, & Maple, 1993; Hoff et al., 1994; Hoff & Maple, 1995; Hoff, Powell, Lukas, & Maple, 1997; Chang, Forthman, & Maple, 1999; Stoinski, Hoff, & Maple, 2001; Lukas, Hoff, & Maple, 2003; Wilson, Kelling, Poline, Bloomsmith, & Maple, 2003; Bashaw, Kelling, Bloomsmith, & Maple, 2007; Browning & Maple, 2019). Although our primary purpose in conducting post-occupancy evaluations was to understand if we had succeeded in improving the exhibits for animals, we also tested many facilities for their impact on zoo visitors and staff.

Our wellness center think tank concept is well suited to the task of teaching our visitors about the relationship between environment and behavior. While zoos and aquariums have promoted their noble objectives through their collective commitment to conservation, education, and animal welfare, they also serve an important purpose in the enhancement of human well-being through exposure to the natural world. This may turn out to be the most important justification for operating zoos and aquariums built to the exacting naturalistic standards prevalent today. In Chapter 9 we will explore the WELL building certification process and examine how buildings and naturalistic settings contribute to the mental health of visitors, staff, and the animal collection. Based on a significant body of evidence, the therapeutic potential of naturalistic zoos and aquariums seems to be unlimited. Exhibits that offer teaching opportunities are especially welcome in settings where they can be properly interpreted by staff. A new elephant concept by Nevin Lash, illustrated in Chapter 8, suggests wellness features that will engage the Jacksonville Zoo elephants in exercise and provide them with a nice view of the adjacent Trout River. When it is complete, it will likely become a popular gathering place for visitors who will immensely benefit from the tranquility associated with this natural simulation of Africa.

One of the most important lessons we can teach our visitors is that we cannot save every species we value. Painful as it is, we will have to choose those that have the best chance for protection and survival. Our SSP programs now reflect these priorities. Similarly, we cannot offer optimal welfare to every animal in our collections. By carefully choosing species, we can do a better job of exhibiting and managing those we encourage to thrive. For many species, thriving requires sufficient space and zoos are limited in the space they can provide.

In the fifth decade of my long career, I am happily engaged in planning for future exhibits within the Jacksonville Zoo's current master plan. I do this to help my colleagues envision how wellness will impact our zoo's reputation. Right now, we are one of the leaders of wellness globally, and we hope to stay in that position. I never thought my ideas would lead to exhibits when I was a full-time college professor, and now that I am no longer calling the shots as a working CEO, I rely on others to decide whether my ideas have merit. The fun of it is in the design, discussion, and debate about building better exhibits. I stay engaged for the sheer joy of exercising my creativity, anticipating that the wellness revolution is just beginning and we have much to achieve in future years. *Beyond Animal Welfare* is intended to stimulate discussion, debate, and decisions that lead to meaningful reform.

Chapter 7

TEACHING THE WORLD
ABOUT WELLNESS

In 2018, after many years serving the zoo profession in Gland, Switzerland, The World Association of Zoos and Aquariums relocated to Barcelona, Spain. WAZA Leaders and staff had barely adjusted to the change when the local zoo found itself mired in controversy. From what I've read about the situation, government authorities and local citizens have concluded that the Barcelona Zoo does not meet public expectations for animal welfare. Because the zoo has not upgraded to meet international standards, the government has already ordered that the popular Barcelona dolphinarium must be closed. The entire zoo is under threat of evisceration. The Barcelona City Council on February 14, 2019, gave initial approval to an amendment that will severely downsize the Barcelona Zoo collection, reducing the institution to 11 exhibited species and calling for the transfer or relocation of the nearly 2,000 animals that remain to sanctuaries or rescue centers. The amendment also requires the Barcelona Zoo to resign from all national and international membership associations, including WAZA. The board of directors of WAZA strongly condemned the extreme position taken by the local government and offered to work with authorities in solving problems at the zoo. This sudden shift in public sentiment was likely building momentum that was unnoticed by the operators. Failure to address long-standing problems in exhibition and management can stimulate a crisis such as the one that has challenged the very existence of the Barcelona Zoo. If cooler heads prevail, it is not too late to formulate plans to upgrade and revitalize a zoo in this situation. A wellness framework is made to order for change of this magnitude. Zoo leadership will have to think bigger about their welfare standards and practices, and they will have to rally the community behind a plan to make significant improvements quickly. An important international city like Barcelona should have a superior zoological park. As this book goes to press, online media report that the city plans to invest 64.5 million euros (U.S. $72.9 million) to prioritize animal welfare, conservation, and education. Authorities claim the zoo will become Europe's first "animalist" zoo. It will be interesting to see how this transformation turns out.

It is often the case that zoo crises begin with an animal that visitors perceive as long suffering. Media have been discussing the evident "depression" of an elephant named Suzi at the Barcelona Zoo for nearly a decade. During this period, animal rights groups demanded the animal be moved to a sanctuary. The failure of the Barcelona Zoo administrators to find an acceptable solution surely contributed to the dramatic turn of events in 2019. There is no species in the zoo that generates more public concern than elephants. My advice to any zoo in this position is to be certain your elephant exhibit is up to international standards. If it is not, then the organization should face the issue head on. If the problem cannot be rectified, leaders should seriously consider moving the animals to a better facility. The alternative is to accept the challenge to design and quickly develop a state-of-the-art elephant facility regardless of the cost. The process of revitalizing a failing zoo requires proactive planning. This is where talented architects are necessary. Illustrations that vividly reveal the future of a zoo can change public opinion and rally support for the cause. I've always tried to have a plan on my desk to show how I would change my worst exhibit. I like to put my design team into the public arena as often as possible to keep optimism alive. After decades of experience programming for exhibits and facilities in zoos, here are five key principles of environmental design that I have found conducive to the achievement of wellness for exhibited megafauna such as great apes, elephants, giraffes, hippopotamuses, and many others.

1. Provision of space sufficient to encourage a range of natural loco-motion and exploration while ensuring critical distances and some measure of privacy.

2. According to the natural proclivities of a species, sufficient atten-tion to verticality and complexity so that animals can live as they would in nature.

3. Purposive recruitment of sufficient numbers to obtain a species-appropriate critical mass of individuals to form a group or herd similar to the species' group size in nature.

4. Opportunities to roam widely through the creative use of elevated travel tubes or contiguous safari trails so animals are encouraged to exercise and explore their surroundings.

5. Sufficient variation in routine so that animals are provided choices in lighting, food, shade, schedule, manipulable material, inside or outside access, and a soft, comfortable substrate.

CONSTRUCTIVE REFORM IN BRAZIL

While I have had no direct involvement in the Barcelona dispute, I am often called upon to assist other zoo professionals by offering constructive criticism. Given the severity of the situation in Barcelona, I would certainly advise them to reach out to experts in Europe to elevate the discussion and push back against their adversaries. Since I began writing and lecturing about the psychology of zoo animals in 1975, I have served the profession as a consultant to dozens of zoos in North America. In 2018 I accepted a generous invitation to visit Brazil to lead three workshops and deliver a keynote lecture on animal welfare standards and ethical leadership to the annual conference of Brazilian zoos and aquariums hosted by the Jardim Zoológico de Brasília. This invitation was timed to generate conversation and support for reforming Brazilian zoological institutions. My colleagues have been worried about the future of Brazilian zoos due to growing public pressure from animal rights groups. According to insiders familiar with the political situation, the newly elected federal government appears to be taking the side of critics who want to close zoos and aquariums that do not meet international norms. In my presentations I shared my experiences as a reform leader in North America and offered ideas and remedies to transform low-achieving zoos into naturalistic facilities committed to scientific standards and ethical practices. These are new ideas in Brazil that need to be nurtured, debated, and widely disseminated.

FIGURE 7.1. PROFESSOR MAPLE WITH BRAZILIAN
COLLEAGUE MARIA FERNANDA IN 2018.

There are some excellent zoos in Brazil, but many more are in need of upgrades. The participants in my workshops were well prepared and eager to find answers to their questions. I returned to Florida impressed with the young people who are working in Brazil's zoos and aquariums, but a zoo revolution in Brazil is still a distant objective. I am grateful for their interest in my book, and I signed copies that were for sale at the conference (Figure 7.1). To increase the book's value to Brazilian zoo biologists, students, professors, and private citizens, I agreed to have the book translated into the Portuguese language and to return to Brazil soon to continue the conversation on reforming zoos and aquariums throughout the country. On my next visit, I would like to tour the country to visit many of their zoos and aquariums and talk to zoo staff and students. Since *Beyond Animal Welfare* will also be published in a Portuguese-language edition, I expect to be involved in helping my friends in Brazil as long as it takes to get results. Because I am known for leading the revitalization of Zoo Atlanta, I know how to respond to a crisis and rally support for troubled zoos. In a country rich in biodiversity and ecosystem services, it would be a shame if all of the nation's zoos were not active contributors to advancing conservation and animal welfare.

Zoos are unique urban resources; there is nothing else quite like them. Organizations whose purpose is to close zoos and aquariums are not satisfied with institutional upgrades and improvements, but the loss of a zoo deprives communities of an important physical and social asset. The full potential of a zoo can be realized by contracting with design firms that specialize in the conversion of substandard facilities to meet present and future operating standards. When there is a critical mass of citizens who can see clearly the future of their local zoo, they must rise up to rescue it. I can attest to the fact that Atlanta residents were prepared to close their zoo if it could not be rehabilitated. Fortunately, they were patient enough to participate in its complete transformation, but it took 18 years to get it done. Because of my experience in Atlanta and the experience of other cities in North America, I would never give up on a zoo as long as there is momentum and opportunity to change. During my lifetime, American zoos of all shapes and sizes in Albuquerque, New Mexico; Birmingham, Alabama;

Columbus, Ohio; Detroit, Michigan; Fresno, California; Dallas, Texas; Houston, Texas; Indianapolis, Indiana; Jacksonville, Florida; Knoxville, Tennessee; Melbourne, Florida; Miami, Florida; Minneapolis, Minnesota; New Orleans, Louisiana; Omaha, Nebraska; Phoenix, Arizona; Pittsburgh, Pennsylvania; Portland, Oregon; Seattle, Washington; and Tampa, Florida, have all been completely re-imagined and rebuilt. In fact, a great zoo is never really finished; it must be continuously evaluated and upgraded to meet public expectations and advancing standards and practices. Such institutions are dynamic, nimble, and comfortable with change. Designers and operators also understand that zoos must be positioned to earn more in-park revenue to be able to fund the renewal and extension that modern zoos require. Every one of the zoos I've mentioned host significant tourism from out of state. Local membership programs also contribute to the bottom line.

EUROPEAN INNOVATORS

Throughout their history European zoos have generated visionary innovation. From Hagenbeck to Hediger, ideas from Europe have influenced zoo design throughout the world. In the Netherlands, where there are many fine zoos, Dierenpark Emmen was an early innovator but ran into financial difficulties and resumed operations under a new name, Wildlands Adventure Zoo Emmen. Emmen was known for its naturalistic hippo exhibit where the animals were encouraged to thrive. My colleagues who have visited Emmen recently continue to sing its praises. Another good Dutch zoo, Apenheul Primate Park, specializes in monkeys and apes. Its gorilla exhibit was unique in Europe with an outdoor forest for the animals and indoor housing with an expansive tunnel system connecting all rooms to facilitate socialization. Apenheul used an elevated system of roped pathways to enable smaller monkeys to move about the entire zoo above the visitor pathways. This innovation preceded the covered tunnel systems that the Philadelphia Zoo pioneered many decades later. I first visited Apenheul in 1978 to see firsthand what happens when a design team thinks outside the box. Apenheul's neighbor, the Royal Burgers' Zoo in Arnhem experimented with the exhibition of a large group of chimpanzees before anyone succeeded in doing this in the United States. By partnering with the University of Utrecht, primates at the Burgers' Zoo were not only exhibited in a functional social group but also systematically observed by faculty and students with a serious interest in primate biology and behavior. Two icons of primatology were associated with Arnhem: Professor J. A. R. A. M. van Hooff and Frans de Waal. De Waal's recent book *Mama's Last Hug* takes its name from an event that occurred at the Burgers' Zoo when Professor van Hooff bid goodbye to a dying 59-year-old female chimpanzee named Mama. The online account attracted 10 million views. The complex space provided for chimpanzees at Arnhem qualifies as an example of wellness-inspired design. However, optimal welfare was insured only when the animals had the use of both outdoor and indoor space. The 110-acre Burgers' Zoo was an early leader in animal welfare, and with its partnership with leading primatologists, it has been the epitome of an empirical zoo. The innovative Burgers' Zoo approach to managing chimpanzees was described in an important and influential paper published by van Hooff in 1973. Professor van Hooff's findings and ideas have helped zoo designers in north America to build better ape exhibits. Because of this rich history of European expertise and innovation, the leaders of the Barcelona Zoo should never give up. I'm not sure why Barcelona isn't a higher priority with other European zoo leaders, but there are plenty of experts throughout the continent who could help get the zoo on track. A major city zoo should never be allowed to fail.

ZOOS VICTORIA—
GLOBAL LEADERS IN ANIMAL WELFARE

An invitation to lecture at a conference hosted by Zoos Victoria in 2017 provided my first opportunity to visit Australia. The Future of Animal Welfare conference was a gathering of 125 zoo and academic professionals who met in Melbourne for three days of intensive discussion and debate.

It was a stimulating examination of the animal welfare vision of Zoos Victoria led by CEO Jenny Gray. Dr. Gray, whose academic training is in philosophy, is the current chair of the board of WAZA and a world leader in zoo ethics. The coordinator of the conference, Sally Sherwen, did a masterful job of multitasking as she presented big ideas and managed a sequence of presentations by locals and visiting guests. The underlying theme of the meeting was the demand for higher standards and better practices of animal welfare in Australia and throughout the world. The model advanced by Zoos Victoria at this meeting is depicted in the illustration below (Figure 7.2). The CARE model links conservation to animal welfare to engender respect for wildlife and ensure effective operating standards and practices. The animal welfare commitment of Zoos Victoria is a value system shared by all employees who work at the three zoos under the Zoos Victoria organizational structure. Collectively, Zoos Victoria is committed to protecting all twenty-seven endangered vertebrate species in the region, promising that none of them will be lost on their watch.

Slightly different in form, each of these institutions provide a unique approach to exhibition. The Melbourne Zoo is somewhat traditional with a large and diverse collection of 320 species, while the Healesville Sanctuary is a refuge for native Australian wildlife located in rural Victoria. A special feature of the Healesville facility is its Australian Wildlife Health Centre where guests are introduced to comprehensive animal care by veterinarians committed to preventive medicine. Conservation education is accomplished with many personalize demonstrations including a free-flying bird show. Healesville was the first world zoo to breed the rare duck-billed platypus (*Ornithorhynchus anatinus*). The third facility in the Zoos Victoria partnership is the Werribee Open Range Zoo covering 225 hectares of habitat for African animals. Werribee is a safari experience with animals living without barriers obstructing the visitors view. Naturalistic exhibits at Werribee encourage thriving in the large mammals that are managed on the open range together: giraffes, zebras, rhinos, and soon elephants will be exhibited in a new state-of-the-art facility.

FIGURE 7.2. ANIMAL WELFARE AT ZOOS VICTORIA.

Local design icons David Hancocks and Jon Coe have become residents of Australia, and they too have provided ideas for the elephant project. A unique feature of animal welfare in Australia is the participation of leading academics in their university community. The nation's international experts on animal welfare have expertise in agriculture, biomedicine, and zoological exhibition and they pay attention to each of these areas in papers and conferences where issues are discussed and debated. The comprehensive nature of these collaborations ensures that only tested ideas vetted through the academy will be advanced and implemented in Australian zoos and aquariums. A new scientific institute is under construction in Sydney where the Sydney Zoo has also become known as an international leader in the science of animal welfare. Australian zoo biologists are in a unique position to mentor other world zoos on conservation and animal welfare issues. Anyone who has taken the time to study their formal programs will acknowledge that they are the world's leaders in zoo animal welfare.

WELLNESS AND HUMANE EDUCATION

The Detroit Zoo has demonstrated extraordinary leadership in humane education. Dedicated to animal welfare science and practice, their exhibits and their public programs all reflect a total institutional commitment. In their iconic Center for Zoo and Aquarium Animal Welfare and Ethics, Detroit's partnership with local, regional, and international humane organizations is a highly visible feature throughout the zoo. An example of their concern for general issues in animal welfare is their willingness to share their campus with others. They often invite rescue organizations to bring adoptable dogs and cats to temporarily occupy their parking lot so they can offer these animals to zoo visitors. This way, the rescue organization is able to appeal to a high volume of animal-loving prospects among the one million people who visit the Detroit Zoo annually. Guests who visit a naturalistic zoo with high standards of welfare/wellness will soon understand that a zoo like Detroit is kind to animals. If there is one message that children should retain from a zoo visit, it is that ethical treatment of animals is imperative in the zoo, in nature, and at home. It is not so easy to keep a consistent message on ethical treatment when so many zoos have traditionally encouraged contact with zoo animals. Bringing visitors close to zoo animals is tempting, and many zoos have generated additional revenue by providing contact for a fee. Some forms of contact are no longer practiced by accredited zoos: for example, elephant rides, chimpanzee tea parties, and photos with baby lions and tigers. One of the most controversial contact programs was close contact and a photo op with an adult female orangutan marketed as "Breakfast with Ah Meng" at the Singapore Zoo. There are some other programs that are still considered acceptable that could be questioned. Stingray petting pools can only be operated if the animal's stinger is surgically removed. Similarly, the act of pinioning a bird to prevent flight is no longer considered a best practice. There is no question that a pinioned bird has limited locomotor options. Even the less invasive practice of feather-trimming prevents birds from flying normally, and birds that cannot fly are reduced to coping rather than thriving. The ethical ark will choose to debate these questions and try to avoid ethical conflicts.

Reacting to concerns about their ambassador animal programs, Lincoln Park Zoo leaders recently agreed to ensure that animals could exercise choice and control when participating in public programs. This resulted in a cessation of programs that required animals to be removed from their habitats. Formal evaluations of the zoo's penguin program determined that touching the animals was not essential to elicit emotion or empathy from the guest. Since the goal of these programs was to stimulate caring, the Lincoln Park Zoo is betting that the actions of their caring staff will be sufficient to influence empathic attitudes in guests. At this zoo, less handling by staff and fewer removals from habitats are considered a better welfare outcome. What is important about this decision is the fact that it is evidence-based. It is unclear whether this idea will engender change in other zoos since there are so many cases where human-animal interactions are an integral part of daily enrichment. For example, free-flight programs for raptors and other birds provide opportunities to exercise and interact for food rewards and attention. To abandon these programs would require evidence that flight is a negative rather than a positive experience. It seems to me that inactivity is an indicator of poor welfare. Skilled bird trainers are now able to fly birds longer distances in the zoo, delivering greater opportunity for natural behavior and providing visitors with the surprise of seeing large birds flying freely among them. Hornbills have been successful deployed in such programs. I await the day when Marabou storks are routinely flying above a simulated savannah exhibit just as they do in Africa. Empirical zoos will determine whether innovations like free flight produce stress that is good or bad, but the number of zoos that now operate free flight bird shows has grown by leaps and bounds. As an educational tool, the success of such programs is beyond dispute. In an interesting study of Detroit Zoo visitors, identified by local media as a wellness study, collaborating scientists at Michigan State University and their partners at the zoo concluded that viewing the animals on exhibit actually reduced stress in the visitors. Detroit zoo director Ron Kagan concluded that "these findings confirm what we at the DZS have always known—the Detroit Zoo is a sanctuary not only for animals but for people as well, a place to relax and recalibrate."

HOW CLOSE IS TOO CLOSE?

I strongly believe that psychologists should be involved in the evaluation of training methods in zoos and aquariums. The psychological field of applied behavior analysis does not require domination of the subject nor is it punitive. Operant control of animals does not require that the trainer enter their exhibit space. The debate about protected versus free contact for elephants is over, and protected contact is the preferred training platform. Because elephants and orcas are dangerous animals, responsible zoos and aquatic parks prefer to train these animals from a distance. Caregivers and trainers cannot be injured or killed by elephants and orcas if people are not permitted to occupy a space when the animal is in it. As the CEO of a zoo with elephants, I took a stand to support protected contact in 1994, a decision supported by research we conducted on the efficacy of kinder, gentler forms of elephant management (Brockett et al., 1999; Maple, Bloomsmith, & Martin, 2009; Wilson, Bashaw, Fountain, Kieschnick, & Maple, 2006). The protected contact approach has the extra advantage that distance removes the perception that trainers coerce or dominate the animal. By riding on the animal, striking it with a bull hook, or forcing the animal to perform inane circus tricks, the subject is diminished and victimized. Aversive control methods should always be avoided. Verbal or hand signals are sufficient to direct the animal to carry out trained behaviors. With food or social rewards, the animals can be trained using positive control methods. The fact is that many zoo animals like to be gently patted or stroked by their keepers, who do so carefully, but few zoos permit visitors to touch potentially dangerous animals even under supervision. Feeding animals is a different story. Many responsible zoos operate giraffe-feeding concessions and a few permit visitors to feed fruit to rhinos and lettuce to manatees. To be considered ethical, animals cannot be overfed, and they must be fed items that are nutritious and safe. There is no question that visitors are thrilled by this experience, which must be carefully planned to avoid any undue stress on the animals. Sometimes the animals decline their opportunity to participate, but they must never be deprived of food or penalized to evoke compliance. It should be remembered that the way we treat zoo animals in view of the public will help build empathy and appreciation for the wild and domestic animals that our visitors encounter in their own lives. At Zoo Atlanta, I authorized VIP visits to our male rhino, Boma, who was fed apples and carrots by dignitaries under close supervision by his caregivers. He was a very tractable animal who eagerly approached the station where he placed his head to be fed. At the time I considered these moments to be enriching for the rhino and the guest as Boma thrived on the attention of his caregivers and was never coerced to cooperate. Two very important people who I accompanied to feed Boma were President Jimmy Carter and author Pat Conroy. They didn't pay to feed Boma; they just wanted to meet one of Atlanta's leading zoo celebrities.

A number of studies have determined that zoo visitors can be a source of stress for zoo animals (Davis, Schaffner, & Smith, 2005; Quadros et al., 2014; Sellinger & Ha, 2005; Sherwen, Hemsworth, Butler, Franson, & Magrath, 2015), but the effects are not universal. In 1980, during my first academic leave to work in a zoo, I proposed a study of siamang vocalizations that seemed to be more intense when crowds of visitors were at their peak. The zoo director, fearing my hypothesis might be confirmed, asked me if I would omit this study from my list of priorities. Not wanting to offend administrators responsible for generating attendance, I agreed. Nearly 40 years after I passed on this opportunity, my question was answered in a study of siamangs and gibbons at the Cleveland Metroparks Zoo (Smith & Kuhar, 2010). The investigators found no difference in aggressive or affiliative behaviors in low- versus high-attendance conditions. However, they did find that the animals used their enclosures differently due to larger crowds, suggesting that visual barriers and the ability to distance themselves reduced the potential negative effects of crowd size. This finding agreed with conclusions from a similar study of gorillas by Kuhar (2008). It would appear that wellness can be protected from the intrusions of visitors with careful design practices. A surprising admission in the *China Daily* acknowledged that visitors in Chinese zoos cause stress for the animals. The article noted that zoo animals were subjected to large crowds, noise, and abusive behavior during the eight days of China's national holidays. This criticism is highly unusual for a Chinese publication and may indicate growing awareness of animal welfare issues in China.

A challenge for those who seek to teach wellness to others is the mixed message that we sometimes send with our public programs. Now that SeaWorld has dramatically changed their orca shows, they are still obligated to retire these unique animals for a lifetime in human care. Performing pinnipeds and cetaceans in retirement greatly benefit from the attention of their caregivers/trainers. This is not exploitation any more than we are exploited when we hire a personal trainer to help us work out. The SeaWorld orcas cannot be safely returned to the open ocean, so they are now a special population with special needs. Elsewhere I've recommended that SeaWorld organize a formal wellness program for these animals (Maple, 2016) so that visitors can still observe their interactions with caregivers. These orcas could become ambassadors for wellness if their routines are thoughtfully developed for their benefit. The Orlando SeaWorld park also manages a small group of pilot whales rescued after a request by the federal government. These animals are also at SeaWorld for their lifetimes with no prospects for reintroduction, so they are candidates for a specialized wellness program to keep them healthy and well. It will be interesting to see how SeaWorld solves the problem of keeping them mentally active. A cognitive workstation adapted for large aquatic sea mammals might be just what the doctor ordered. Going forward, whales at SeaWorld could serve the primary purpose of educating the public about their advanced social and cognitive skills and the importance of protecting their threatened populations in the open ocean. It appears that SeaWorld's new Orca Encounter show offers the correct mix of conservation and animal welfare messaging. At this point, the semi-retired orcas at SeaWorld are living well.

TEACHING ETHICS
WITH THE INVASIVE PYTHON ISSUE

Burmese pythons are now the dominant species in the Florida Everglades ecosystem. No one knows exactly how this happened, but they seem to have originated in the pet trade and a single breeding center in South Florida destroyed by Hurricane Andrew, a Category 5 hurricane. From this moment on August 23, 1992, pythons entered the Everglades wilderness and began to reproduce. It is inexplicable that this collection of dangerous animals was not secured against the highly probable high winds of hurricanes and tornados. The current population of these invaders is estimated to be in the tens of thousands or perhaps many more. Small mammals such as racoons and opossums in the ecosystem have declined by 99%; rabbits and foxes have completely disappeared from the Everglades. Without any predators, Burmese pythons can devour birds, fish, mammals, and other reptiles with impunity. Although hunting of pythons has been authorized year-round without the necessity of permits, only 1,000 of the animals have been captured or killed. At this rate the population will continue to grow unimpeded by government intervention. There are important lessons from this ecological disaster. Both private owners and some unscrupulous zoos or roadside attractions have either purposely released giant snakes into wilderness areas or lost them in the swamp due to escapes. Coincidentally, while the pythons were multiplying, imports of Burmese pythons were also growing. Under no circumstances should these imports have continued, but proposed legislation that would have limited trade was strongly opposed by animal dealers and, surprisingly, some vocal members of the zoo and aquarium community. The Burmese python has upset ecosystem wellness in the Everglades with serious consequences that may never be rectified. It is unclear whether the python invasion can be slowed sufficiently that the indigenous creatures can make a comeback. As this book goes to press, a major study of the invasive pythons in the Everglades has been proposed by the Division on Earth and Life Studies of the U.S. National Academies. The attention of the National Academies may elevate the problem for consideration by federal authorities with sufficient funding to eventually degrade if not eradicate Burmese pythons from the Florida Everglades. The all-too-convenient relationship of many zoos to the pet trade is a subject that will be seriously debated by animal ethicists, zoo biologists, and government regulators. If something isn't done to solve the problem of invasive pythons, the Everglades experience will go down in history as the most extensive destruction of a mature ecosystem by an alien species. The Everglades invasion by Burmese pythons is a teachable moment and must be fully discussed and understood by all serious students of wildlife. There are other invasive species such as Bufo toads, green iguanas, tegu, and curly-tailed lizards, but none of these compare to Burmese pythons in terms of their impact on the ecosystem and their danger to humankind. Human error certainly played a role in this zoological nightmare, but it is proving to be a difficult problem to solve.

Chapter 8

RECONCILING WELLNESS
AND WELFARE

We are at an early stage in our understanding of the wellness construct. Our knowledge of the many species exhibited in zoos and aquariums is not sufficient to be certain that the higher standards and better practices associated with wellness will guarantee thriving for each and every one of these animals. Moreover, since so many factors are involved in controlling biology and behavior, it will take a long time to program, design, build, and evaluate exhibits that ensure wellness has prevailed for every taxon in human care. Proclaiming, as I have done, that wellness is a superior construct that extends animal welfare to a higher platform will surely invite criticism from without and within. Indeed, as it is with all aspects of animal welfare, we will have to deal with potential revolutions of rising expectations. Already, as we introduce wellness tactics in the zoo, frontline employees expect that wellness practitioners will respond equally and urgently to the needs of apes, bears, birds, cats, cetaceans, fish, hoofed stock, lizards, snakes, and everything in between. Until wellness units obtain budgets and human resources that are equal to the task, some species will be left behind. Zoo and aquarium leaders and managers will have to endure a period of adjustment until the entire organization and its supporters commit to funding a comprehensive wellness program capable of responding to demand. If we are not defeated by our own expectations and limitations, we will have to win the debate with adversaries who will have yet another reason to oppose the existence of zoos and aquariums. They will argue that unless animals are thriving, they should not be living in zoos and aquariums at all, and they may soon begin to complain that few zoos are anywhere close to achieving the stringent standard of thriving. They will use our own high standards against us. During my lecture engagement in Brasilia in 2018, I was approached by an animal rights attorney who confronted me on my use of the term *wellness*. She argued that this idea could distract from the legal gains made on behalf of animal welfare in Brazil and elsewhere and didn't think wellness would help the cause. Of course, I never said that animals had a right to thrive, only that thriving was better than coping. Laws as they stand prevent suffering, but they do not guarantee thriving. I disagree with those who fear that welfare will lose out to wellness. They are not competing ideas; they are in fact complementary. All the accumulating evidence that supports the necessity of animal welfare reform also applies to wellness.

I believe wellness can be a feasible living standard for all zoo animals, but it will not be easy or inexpensive to achieve this outcome. Because it takes decades to completely rebuild a zoo, it is essential that daily management reflect advances in wellness. The frontline operators of every zoo bear the responsibility for managing the reforms that lead to a thriving population of zoo animals. As wellness becomes better understood, it will be impossible to ignore. For this reason, wellness services should be a high priority until the architecture of exhibits and facilities catch up to the new standard of wellness-inspired design. Wellness services include behavior intervention, training, schedules of reinforcement, human-animal relationships, useable space, social opportunities, comfortable substrates, autonomy, and mental stimulation. There is a lot that caregivers and curators can do for animals while they are waiting for the million-dollar exhibit to be built. In Atlanta we retrofit many exhibits during the early days to generate as much change as we could as we awaited revenue bonds for construction. I closed and renovated the entire feline house to improve the lives of the cats who suffered in the old facility. The most important change was the introduction of soft, sand floors to get them off broken cement. We also repainted the walls pastel colors associated with calming and provided the animals with connected cages to give them more space. These small changes made a big difference to the cats and to those who came to see them.

Eventually we replaced the feline house with large, naturalistic exhibits for Sumatran tigers and African lions. Following the mantra, "fewer species, living large," we became feline specialists. Of course, the most important investment a zoo can make is to be sure the animal care staff is sufficient in number and training to get the job done. A wellness culture means that the entire team is all-in, but the team must have the resources and the time to make wellness a high priority each and every day.

ZOO TALES

When the public loses confidence in a local zoo, it isn't long before citizens demand action. It takes strong leadership from dynamic zoo directors, elected government officials, and outspoken citizens to stand up for reforms that lead to revitalization. It also helps when print media, television, and social media begin to beat the drums for change. When these forces come together in unison, as they did in New Orleans, Louisiana, in the late 1970s; Atlanta, Georgia, in the mid-1980s; and Oakland, California, in the 1990s, zoos formulate innovative, new operating standards and ultimately prosper. Atlanta and Oakland experienced the humiliation of being listed on HSUS's annual "worst zoo" list published in *Parade Magazine*. As bad as it was, this dishonor represented a turning point, and both zoos recovered to become beacons for the zoo animal welfare movement. Just as Ron Forman did before him, Oakland zoo director Joel Parrott asserted his core values and turned the Oakland Zoo into a model of animal welfare reform. It is a privilege and an honor to lead a zoo that is at the forefront of change. Each time it is done, the achievement makes it easier for other institutions to take bold steps to transform their operating standards and practices. It is very important for such zoos to widely share what they have learned with the global zoo community. Talks should be given, papers should be published, publicity should be generated. These are the greatest stories that zoos will ever tell. Impoverished zoos in developing countries are particularly in need of cost-effective solutions. Jon Coe is one of the big-name architects who regularly offers pro bono solutions to small zoos and nature centers. Those in a position to change zoos need to understand that small changes will lead to greater demands. Wellness standards are the most difficult standards to achieve and sustain.

Every employee in a substandard zoo dreams of its rehabilitation and revitalization by an infusion of public and private funding and powerful new ideas. If you are lucky, your career path will take you to institutions that turn the corner on your watch. I worked for Ron Forman at the Audubon Zoo in the early years of its transformation, arriving in the city in 1980 while on leave from my faculty position at Georgia Tech. It had been four years since my first introduction to the zoo while attending a psychology conference in New Orleans. When I visited the zoo in 1976, the dilapidated physical plant was on its last legs. However, many of the photographs I took in New Orleans in those early days have served me well in the classroom as they depict so vividly the antipathy and the consequences of traditional hard architecture in a bygone era.

Mr. Forman is still the CEO of the Audubon Zoo and his 45 years of service have borne fruit. Because he studied business and marketing in college, he understood that a zoo with suffering animals could never succeed in the marketplace. The master plan he put together was unusual in that he took the initiative to form a consulting group of young zoo directors and local architects. He also invited the esteemed Marlin Perkins to help him promote the change. At that time, Marlin Perkins was undoubtedly the best-known animal advocate in the world. When Ron assigned me the responsibility of guiding Marlin through the zoo, it was a very slow journey because visitors interrupted us every step along the way to ask Marlin for autographs and photographs. Marlin's congenial visibility called attention to the urgency of Ron's vision. Leading the Audubon Zoo on a path to respectability required immense focus on the community's capacity to deliver funding and support while the zoo was still mired in disrepair. Ron also had to overcome personal setbacks such as the loss of a curator who was killed by an elephant. Virtually all of the exhibits had to be rebuilt, although in retrospect many were small by today's standards.

FIGURE 8.1. AUDUBON ZOO GORILLA BEGS FOR FOOD
FROM VISITORS, C. 1976. (T. MAPLE)

How the zoo and its animal collection was perceived by the community was important to Ron, and their collective enthusiasm confirmed he was on the right track. By building naturalistic exhibits with landscape immersion properties, he was laying the foundation for animal welfare and conservation commitments. He also paid close attention to aesthetics and visitor services, ensuring that revenue production was paramount. One of the most important features of the Audubon Zoo story is the model it provided for all zoos struggling for respect in the early 1980s. If I had not worked for Ron, however briefly, I could not have been selected to lead the revitalization of Atlanta's troubled zoo. The Audubon model certainly influenced my thinking when I was named interim director in Atlanta in 1984. I insisted on the title "interim" because I only intended to stay long enough to stop the bleeding. I retired 18 years later knowing that our success was now the new model for city zoos on the road to recovery and respectability. Revitalizing Zoo Atlanta was the high point of my career and a reminder that no zoo is a lost cause.

Atlanta's misfortune was not unprecedented, but animal welfare was at the forefront of its failures. The zoo was dilapidated and badly in need of renewal. The Parks and Recreation budget had been depleted to find funds to move the Milwaukee Braves to Atlanta in 1961. Two decades after the Braves were successfully relocated to Atlanta, it took a management crisis of epic proportions to elevate the priority of a new zoo. Fortunately, government and business leaders agreed on the formula to restore public confidence in Atlanta's zoo by creating a new entrepreneurial, nonprofit governance model for the zoo with a board comprised of businesspeople who would resist bureaucracy. These changes were welcomed by our community and long overdue. The fascinating history of Atlanta's zoological park from its humble beginning in 1889 to its rebirth and renewal as the revitalized and reimagined Zoo Atlanta is described in a lengthy article in the journal of the Atlanta History Center (Desiderio, 2000).

PUBLIC–PRIVATE PARTNERSHIPS

My opportunity to lead Zoo Atlanta was a sudden change for me and for our city. Community leaders in synchrony with a new mayor came to agreement in a crisis resonating throughout the nation and beyond. The city zoo was the laughingstock of outsiders, but no one in Atlanta was laughing. An embarrassment to the city that was once too busy to hate, city fathers agreed to invite the business community to embrace radical reform. One leader short of a full team, they selected a young psychologist from Georgia Tech to find the best model for its proper evolution from a failed city zoo to a privatized Zoo Atlanta. At the time of my appointment, I knew very little about the business world, but the newly created zoo board was packed with brilliant business leaders, balanced by gender and by race. They were the perfect group of business mentors to guide the new CEO. By agreement, they encouraged me to lead in planning and designing a principled zoo of consequence while they steadied the new ark with business and marketing acumen. It was the perfect partnership, and our rise to respectability was rapid and unprecedented. Zoo Atlanta in 1985 became the first zoo in AZA to successfully migrate from city governance to private, nonprofit management. The city retained ownership of the zoo, but it no longer interfered with our advancement. A clever application of the funding formula that doomed the old city zoo in 1961 was the salvation of Zoo Atlanta as the Atlanta-Fulton County Stadium Authority provided the first U.S. $16 million of revenue bonds to jump-start the new zoo. Combined with another U.S. $9 million of private money raised locally by the revitalized Atlanta Zoological Society, the first four years of the new corporation saw the opening of a new entry complex with enhanced revenue centers; a lovely flamingo exhibit with 60 Chilean flamingos obtained from the wild; the spectacular, industry-leading Ford African Rain Forest exhibit for Willie B. and nine other lowland gorillas loaned by the Yerkes Primate Center of Emory University; and naturalistic exhibits for orangutans, drills, elephants, giraffes, lions, tigers, and other Asian and African species liberated from cages to habitats. Because our first chairman, Robert M. Holder, was a developer of considerable talent and means, our rate of change was accelerated. Mr. Holder gave us four years of strong leadership, ensuring that the zoo would succeed early and often.

Free from the constraints of city government, I was able to hire the first full-time veterinarian, first general curator, first qualified mammal curator, and first bird curator in the zoo's long history. I also hired a talented marketing director and a curator of education who had been mentored by Jack Hanna at the Columbus Zoo, and the zoo's first director of research. As we grew our scientific credentials were upgraded through partnerships with Georgia Tech, Emory, and the University of Georgia. Charles and Lessie Smithgall, a prominent Atlanta family, stepped forward to donate a significant endowment to support graduate students who played an important role in documenting reform. We were accredited by AZA in 1987, three years after we lost our membership. In 1994 we hosted the national conference of AZA, and for a decade the zoo won many national awards for highly innovative exhibits and facilities. In becoming one of the nation's elite zoos, our conservation education center won a local Urban Design Award, and due to our 50-year history of exhibiting, studying, and successfully managing lowland gorillas, Zoo Atlanta was awarded the prestigious

Bean Award from AZA. We followed the right path and brick-by-brick built a zoo that our community learned to love.

In 1984 we didn't have the wellness construct to drive our vision, but we simulated nature as best we could, which provided the environmental features associated with landscape immersion, including attention to botanicals. Although the science of animal behavior was still young in 1984, we applied what we knew and stayed true to nature's model by designing a zoo that enabled the expression of natural behavior. This is the formula that many other zoos have used to revitalize their futures. I've stressed the importance of naturalistic architecture in transforming a zoo, but it is important to emphasize that it is people who take a zoo from good to great. An important tactic in reforming a zoo is control of the hiring process. A reform administration must be able to set new standards for key staff, offer competitive salaries for talent and experience, and manage those accountable for leading the change. I had the good fortune of handpicking most of my top staff when I was director of Zoo Atlanta. This kind of quality control made a big difference. When new priorities demanded specialized expertise, I had the flexibility and the authority to fill the gaps.

PHILANTHROPY—THE KEY TO REFORM

My final retirement in 2011 forced me to reinvent myself. I made the announcement of my plans at the national conference of AZA hosted by Zoo Atlanta. My friends and associates helped me to celebrate this event by arranging a 65th birthday party. Never before had so many of my former employees and students and current collaborators, even former board members, met in one place to honor my work. On this occasion I stepped to the podium to tell them that I was not ending my zoo career but simply focusing on whatever bully pulpit I still enjoyed to advocate and promote the ideas we all shared about conservation and animal welfare. Given my age and experience, I knew that I could speak truth more forcefully when I wasn't protecting my job. At this point I was prepared to compete as a consultant to other nonprofits and government agencies. I would prioritize zoos, aquariums, and other animal facilities. I also foresaw that I would have plenty of time to continue writing. This was the principal way that I honored my promise to my Zoo Atlanta colleagues and students. I vowed that I would stay active by continuing to write research papers, commentary, and books on my own and by invitation from others. Free from the pressure of daily administration, my creative juices were flowing like never before. I was particularly committed to helping zoos to organize scientific programs and partnerships with colleges and universities. With help from someone with a union card from the academy, it ought to be possible for every accredited zoo to arrange a serious partnership with local academics. I am always available to help with the implementation of such partnerships, and I get a special thrill whenever a formal agreement is finalized.

In 2011 I began a consulting engagement for the San Francisco Zoo. This was my first opportunity to implement a wellness program since I first experimented with the construct at the Palm Beach Zoo in 2008. My experience teaching wellness to others convinced me that this idea could be implemented almost anywhere. Even though I regarded my expertise as primarily in the domain of leadership, I found the application of wellness a closer fit with the history of my research on the effects of captivity. In San Francisco the best use of wellness was its impact on branding. To encourage a commitment to wellness-inspired design, I invited my former collaborators at CLR Design to take a look at upgrades to old exhibits. They deployed a wellness approach to create many new visionary exhibit concepts. As exhibits have evolved in San Francisco, the zoo has been successful in matching donors with government investments so that many of the newer exhibits are named.

During my lecture engagement in Brazil, I was told that public–private partnerships are not possible in this country; if this is so, it is a tragic loss of opportunity. Few communities throughout the world are capable of dramatic change with government funding alone. My colleagues at the San Francisco Zoo comfortably accepted wellness as their new brand and accepted dynamic change in all areas of the organization. There can be no doubt that the San Francisco Zoo is the epicenter of wellness in the West. They have successfully paired wellness with conservation, and this makes perfect sense. Each time a new exhibit is funded by combining private and public funds, it offers encouragement to other institutions with the same aspirations. To meet wellness standards, new exhibits require a major fundraising campaign. Exhibits at this level of quality don't happen on demand; it takes time to build a zoo of consequence. With so much progress at the nearby Oakland Zoo, it is intriguing to think of Northern California as a locus of animal welfare science and services for western zoos. There is good reason for these two institutions to enter into a creative partnership. Both of them have been successful in tapping government and private support for dynamic reform.

When I worked in San Francisco, we discovered what could be done with a relatively understudied mammal when we put together surveys about the management and exhibition of Nile hippopotamuses in North American zoos (Tennant et al., 2018) and published our findings. Kim Denninger-Snyder, a graduate student at UC Davis, took an interest in hippos and contacted me to see if we could collaborate. With the zoos' support, we decided to survey North American zoos to better understand whether zoo hippos were thriving or suffering. We conducted the first survey from our base in San Francisco and then moved on to Jacksonville to complete the project. The data indicated that hippos were faring poorly in North American zoos with only DAK exhibiting hippos in a naturalistic setting. It was clear from our survey that zoos could achieve excellence in hippo exhibits if they made simple changes in their management protocols. The most important change was to encourage hippos to use their outdoor exhibits at night. Seeing hippos in a naturalistic exhibit open at night reminds me of many wonderful experiences in African safari camps surrounding riverine hippo pools alive with a vocal population of this unique species. They are among a zoo's most interesting mammals when they are exhibited properly, but San Francisco exhibits only one male hippo in a substandard facility. A naturalistic hippo exhibit designed for a herd of these animals would add immeasurably to the visitor experience in San Francisco.

MENTORS AT WORK

I discovered the wellness construct during my second period of service as a zoo director in West Palm Beach, Florida, but I only came to understand its full potential by sharing it with others during my third career as a consultant to zoos and aquariums. The fundamental challenge to those who adopt wellness as an animal welfare strategy is its high-level aspirations for virtually all factors that contribute to thriving. Social aspirations require that we enable the formation of appropriate group sizes for many species that have heretofore been housed in smaller units. Elephants now require herds to function as cohesive social groups as they do in the wild. We learned many years ago that gorillas needed to live in groups if we hoped to breed them; pairs of gorillas did not work (Maple & Hoff, 1982). Worse yet, many zoos kept adult males as singletons. AZA regulations no longer permit the isolation of group-living animals. Similarly, our growing understanding of orangutan behavior leads me to believe that this semi-solitary primate needs more space to separate from potential mates. An element of this conclusion is the requirement that orangutans are able to move about vertically. As we have discussed in this book, the hippopotamus has rarely been presented with ideal living conditions in zoos. We know how to deliver wellness with hippos; we just need to find a way to do it. To reach the goals of wellness, zoos are getting larger, more complex, and more expensive to build. One likely consequence of this trend is that guests will pay more to visit in the future. Zoos already offer many purchase points for food and gifts in order to capture more revenue. They have also spent a lot of money to hire experienced marketing and development officers with fund-raising goals that rival those of colleges and universities. What we don't have, compared to academia, are loyal alumni, but brand loyalty is a goal that is concerning to every zoo chief financial officer. For this reason, we are working with industry consultants to better understand shifts in attitudes toward zoos. Recent studies indicate that millennials and their successors do not like zoos as much as previous generations. Too many of them regard captivity as a negative, almost immoral condition. Modern zoos are far from prisons for animals, but antizoo activists have created this impression. In spite of the continuous drumbeat of criticism, public expectations are high for zoos and aquariums in North America, and these high standards are beginning to be important to other nations. In my travel to other parts of the world, Australia has impressed me as the region that competes most favorably with the elite zoos of North America. The advances made by Australian zoos in conservation and animal welfare represent the best ideas of scientists in academia and the zoo profession.

In conversations with donors and sponsors for more than four decades, I have a pretty good idea about how to persuade a donor to make a significant gift. The many million-dollar gifts I have obtained and the powerful sponsors who have stepped up to lift the zoo with their marketing and philanthropic dollars clearly demonstrate that people take pride in making a difference. For that reason, we were happy to name exhibits for individuals, foundations, and corporations. I believe that fund-raising for wellness will actually improve our chances of getting large gifts, since donors and sponsors can help us to truly optimize the lives of zoo and aquarium animals. Not long ago, a colleague asked me the following question: "Given the terrible forces acting against wildlife in nature, is it possible that zoo animals may one day be seen as living better than their counterparts in the wild?" I have no doubt that we are on the verge of building naturalistic exhibits for many species that do in fact deliver a superior quality of life when compared with the diminishing and very dangerous conditions faced by wildlife in the natural world. The positive trajectory of our creative exhibits and programs should continue to attract the support and participation of communities wherever great zoos are in place.

I am satisfied with the progress we have made in promoting a wellness approach to zoo design and zoo management, and I expect more and more zoos to turn to wellness as a promising way to reach our aspirations for superior standards and practices in the zoo. The design master plan developed by CLR Design for the Jacksonville Zoo and Gardens was wellness inspired, and I think many other master plans will take this approach. I've written this book to help others understand the broad scope of the wellness construct and why it is so useful in unifying our messages about conservation and wellness and for applications to both animal populations, captive and wild, and human communities throughout the world. It is a powerful idea. For those of us immersed in the advancement of wellness, we have an obligation to reach out to situations where animals are clearly suffering. So far, in the profession as a whole, we have failed in our efforts to discredit or close roadside attractions where the standards and practices are abysmally low. We can only hope that our communities will come to know the difference between the two options. Many good zoos are becoming great zoos, and this trend will only amplify the differences. We must also work with local and national media to help them tell the story of how great zoos are reimagined and rebuilt. If both media and visitors are patient and willing to support the reform, our accredited zoos will be all that we hoped they could be. Unfortunately, the universe of roadside attractions has resisted attempts to mentor and reform them.

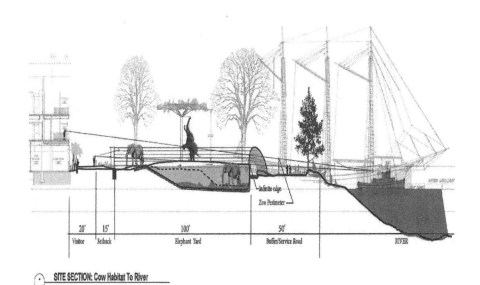

FIGURE 8.2. COMPLEXITY OF THE PROPOSED ELEPHANT HABITAT IN JACKSONVILLE. (N. LASH).

I am particularly concerned about zoos in South America and Asia where problems have become acute. The momentum in many developing nations including India, a relatively wealthy nation, is shifting to radical animal rights groups. When governments and communities are slow to change zoos, public opinion can be rallied to close them. Of course, the worst of them should be closed, but it is quite possible that we will see more zoos disappear from many countries in the near future. I am hopeful that Western governments will partner with accredited zoo associations and leading zoos with the resources to help others to offer new ideas and financial aid to rebuild zoos throughout the world. One very wealthy nation, China, could use mentoring from our best zoo experts as they are too focused on entertainment, and they have made many mistakes in the acquisition of animals for exhibition. For example, Chinese marine parks continue to be interested in exhibiting belugas and orcas and some large fish such as the whale shark, an immense species that does not do well in captivity. Whale rescues of a different kind may soon be necessary to release 11 orcas and 90 beluga whales currently confined by marine mammal dealers in ocean pens located on the east coast of Russia. International wildlife agents are investigating the possibility that these animals are being illegally held for sale to Chinese water parks and aquariums, transactions that violate laws on the capture of wild whales. According to Russian media, the company that captured these whales exported 13 of them to China between 2013 and 2016. This company is also suspected of renting whales as a diversionary tactic, and they have resorted to capturing calves, which is expressly forbidden. Ethical aquariums would never cooperate with such unscrupulous dealers, but there are many outlaw attractions that do not operate according to the best professional standards of accredited aquariums. It will be necessary to put legal and political pressure on the buyers and the sellers who have inflicted immense stress and pain and a life of uncertainty on these innocent victims. The world's accredited aquariums, through their associations, can also collectively censor the recipients and organize boycotts. As they have been captive for a short time, it may still be possible to release the whales back into the open ocean. While many injustices suffered by whales are unintended, illegal captures are as despicable as the anachronistic whaling industry that continues to butcher them for human consumption in Iceland, Norway, and Japan. After vociferous protests from the conservation, welfare, and scientific communities, Russia finally agreed to release the orcas and belugas back into the ocean. Likely as not there will be some losses in this transition, but the animals should not have been gathered and hoarded in the first place. As we advance wellness as our operating standard, we must continue to be vigilant wherever we see a need to educate our peers. Zoos and aquariums should organize globally to encourage our governments to influence maritime commerce and military vessels to help contain the discharge of plastics and other technology by-products that are injuring and often killing large marine mammals. This is an effort that can be made in the name of humane wildlife wellness. Collectively, the ability of accredited zoos and aquariums to share our expertise with others may ensure our survival as institutions dedicated to protection. On conservation, education, and animal welfare standards, we must gather a critical mass of collaborators, and we absolutely have to become leaders, not followers. We should look to our institutions that exhibit marine organisms, SeaWorld and the Monterey Bay Aquarium, for example, to lead the way in cleaning up our oceans. Virtually every institution that has performing marine mammals in their collection can give back by dedicating human and financial resources for recycling, reusing, and removing plastics from the world's water systems. Of course, SeaWorld has demonstrated time and time again their good citizenship as the world's foremost rescue and rehabilitation facility for injured marine mammals.

Chapter 9

THE CASE FOR
WELL BUILDING CERTIFICATION

The most important project under my direction at the Palm Beach Zoo was the LEED-certified Melvin J. and Claire Levine Animal Care Complex, which was dedicated on Earth Day, April 22, 2009. This unique facility was the first LEED-certified zoo veterinary hospital in North America. LEED Gold, the U.S. $4.8 million, 10,000-square-foot building opened just a few months earlier than a similar facility at the Hogle Zoo in Salt Lake City, Utah. At the time we planned the facility, we thought it would also contain the zoo world's first wellness center, but our budget for the complex was insufficient to include a contiguous building for wellness. The LEED green building rating system certification is the nationally accepted benchmark for the design, construction, and operation of high-performance green buildings. The Palm Beach Zoo in 2008 was on record as committed to a sustainable future. The building itself had a spectacular array of sustainable features, but it also offered an operating philosophy to serve the goals of sustainability while providing leadership for the community. To make sure the educational value of the building was paramount, I promoted Kristen Cytacki, our curator of education, to include "sustainability" in her title. She was instrumental in documenting all aspects of our complicated LEED application. The building is more than an animal health center; it is also a teaching facility.

Site Planning	• At least 50% of the site was restored with native plants.
	• At least 20% of the site was devoted to open space.
Water Management	• Drought-tolerant plants were favored.
	• Efficient irrigation reduced water needs by 50%.
	• Water-efficient fixtures reduced water use by 33.8%.
	• Reduced impervious cover, captured and treated storm water runoff from 90% of the average annual rainfall.
Microclimate	• Paving/roofing materials with high solar reflectance; automatic control of interior lighting; photovoltaic roof panels providing 12.8% renewable energy; no CFC (chlorofluorocarbon)-based refrigerants; efficient air-conditioning system; contract with green power company to offset 35% of the building's electric energy consumption.
Construction Process	• Controlled soil erosion, waterway sedimentation, and airborne dust generation; 75% construction waste was recycled; 20% of building materials were regionally extracted, processed, and manufactured; 50% of the wood products were certified by the Forest Stewardship Council; low-emitting carpets, composite wood products, adhesives, sealants, paints, and coatings to reduce volatile organic compounds.
Prompts	• Designated storage areas for recycling paper, cardboard, glass, plastics, and metals; low-emitting and fuel-efficient vehicles are offered preferred parking; secure bicycle storage and shower facilities; outdoor views for 90% of workspaces; educational materials explaining LEED process available in the lobby.

LEED buildings reflect a whole-building approach to sustainability by recognizing performance in five key areas of human and environmental health: site planning, water management, energy management, material use, indoor air quality, and innovation in design. Because LEED-certified buildings offer environmental benefits; economic, community, health, and safety benefits; reduce impact on natural resources consumption; enhance occupant comfort and health; and minimize strain on local infrastructure, LEED reflects many of the noble goals of wellness. The chart on page 176 reviews the major performance features of the animal care complex.

Many of these LEED features can be applied to human health and complement the goals of a WELL-certified building. For example, providing outdoor views from the workspace for most employees contributes to human health and wellness. There are many other examples. Because LEED certification has a head start in zoos, the fact that LEED and WELL are synergistic in many ways makes it more likely that zoos will find it useful to apply for WELL certification in the future. Zoos and aquariums that commit to wellness ought to commit to certification by both LEED and WELL standards. While LEED is about sustainability, WELL focuses on the people who use buildings, with a focus on health and wellness, nourishment, fitness, comfort, and mentality. Each approach builds on the other. Currently there are 5,223 members of the WELL community in 72 countries and 872 ongoing WELL projects comprising 165 million square feet in 34 countries. Certification is obtained through Green Building Certification Inc., the organization that reviews applications. Like LEED, WELL certification, once obtained, is rated Platinum (80–100 points), Gold (60–79), or Silver (50–59).

The Levine Animal Care Complex influenced decisions at the zoo for many years to come. Our relationship with Florida Power & Light gave us our first taste of solar energy in 2008. A few years later, Florida Power & Light helped the zoo to install additional solar panels in the zoo parking lot. The Palm Beach Zoo is modest in size, just 20 acres. It will be relatively easy if the zoo chooses to equip its existing buildings with both LEED and WELL features. A small zoo can more easily convert to green operations, and there are many companies in South Florida that are eager to help. Although our country is now energy independent, it is still important for nonprofits committed to conservation to do all they can to conserve energy and provide moral support for sustainable energy sources. The past 10 years have been a national highlight reel for renewable energy in zoos and aquariums. From what has been visible in the media, the nation's greenest zoos are the Cincinnati Zoo and Denver Zoo, but many others are catching up fast. In many cases, zoos are ahead of their local, regional, and state governments. Detroit Zoo announced recently that they will meet the goal of 100% renewable energy by 2020. As part of its "Greenprint" strategic plan, the zoo will source the renewable energy from three new wind parks in the region.

WELL: THE NEXT FRONTIER OF WELLNESS?

In a recent publication (Maple & Segura, 2018), we stated that wellness is the next frontier of animal welfare. Indeed, compared to the history of animal welfare science, wellness is relatively new and unexplored. As *Beyond Animal Welfare* enters circulation, I expect it to generate more research and more interest among animal welfare scientists and practitioners. Given the tremendous success of green building education, I anticipate that WELL certification is off to a similarly promising start. However, zoo and aquarium wellness (and welfare for that matter) have been primarily concerned with the animals in our midst, not the people. As I have argued in this book, wellness is a much broader topic, and it complements the WELL paradigm quite nicely. By certifying buildings in zoos and aquariums, they will meet the needs of the animals, the people who care for them, and those who visit to learn and gain inspiration about the natural world. For human beings, certainly, an important aspect of our world is the built environment. Zoo professionals have learned that animals live inside and outside zoo buildings constructed for their safety and their comfort. Particularly in Europe, where cold climates prevail much of the year, designers spend time and money finding new ways to enrich the lives of animals when they are confined inside. Massive elephant buildings in cities such as Cologne, Germany, are one solution to giving these large animals sufficient space to move about. The respected zoo biologist Jeremy Mallinson once observed that zoo gorillas spend two-thirds of their lives in the night house. At the famed zoo in Jersey, Channel Islands, United Kingdom, primate care staff found a way to soften the night house for apes. The WELL certification approach to design will surely result in significant upgrades to both health and wellness. A useful example of WELL certification is a building associated with a botanical garden. Until we have examples in zoos and aquariums, this one will be the most appropriate model of how we might proceed in Jacksonville and elsewhere.

PHIPPS CONSERVATORY AND BOTANICAL GARDENS, PITTSBURGH, PENNSYLVANIA

Unlike zoos and aquariums, the focus of botanical gardens is always on a visitor's response to plants. Compared to living animals, plants are passive and serve as context in an active educational setting. The 24,250-square-foot Center for Sustainable Landscapes encompasses space for education, research, and administration and opened at Phipps in 2012 with WELL building certification at the Platinum level. The centerpiece of the Phipps Conservatory and Gardens in Pittsburgh, this unique building generates more energy than it uses each year and treats all storm and sanitary water caught on site. It is the world's first and only building to meet four of the highest green certifications: The Living Building Challenge; LEED Platinum; Sustainable SITES Initiative four-star rating (the first of its kind); and WELL Platinum (the first of its kind). The Center for Sustainable Landscapes focuses on the interface between the built and natural environments, demonstrating that human and environmental health are inextricably connected. By attracting 500,000 annual visitors, it fosters a broader public understanding of sustainable design, technology, and strategy through interpretation, docent-led tours, and public education. The WELL building standards comprise seven categories: (a) The air category covers air-quality testing, direct source ventilation, a healthy entrance, volatile organic compounds reduction, smoke elimination, cleaning and Indoor Air Quality protocol, humidity control, and a healthy heating, ventilating, and air-conditioning system. (b) The water category covers treated nonpotable water being cleaner than municipal water, impurity reduction, and chlorine and fluoride reduction. (c) For the nourishment category, it is notable that Café Phipps uses local and organic foods grown from its own display gardens. This category covers 100% organic produce, vegetarian-fed meat and dairy that is free of growth hormones and antibiotics, and filtered water being made available to all staff and visitors. (d) The light category covers natural light illuminating the space 80% of the time, window performance and design, activity-based lighting levels, the color spectrum, interior sun and glare control, automated lighting controls, and Circadian lighting emulation. (e) For the fitness category, the Center for Sustainable Landscapes promotes the use of stairs. This category covers the building being situated within a park to encourage walking, dedicated interior exercise space, and a professional fitness program. (e) The comfort category covers humidifiers, personal fans, and adjustable desks and chairs being provided; electromagnetic field protection; ergonomics; healthy surfaces; thermal optimization; and biophilic sounds. (f) For the mind category, biophilic design principles have been incorporated throughout the center including nature-inspired artwork, tall ceilings, and expansive views. This category covers wellness literacy, an environmental display, a water feature, a wellness concierge, and knowledge transfer.

I am unaware of any examples of WELL building certification in North American zoos or aquariums, but the time is right for WELL standards to be paired with LEED and with the aspirations associated with the wellness construct. I have had the experience of working in sick buildings; it would be an absolute joy to work in a WELL-certified building. As we plan our wellness center building in Jacksonville, we will also look at WELL certification and the possibility that both LEED and WELL can be achieved in one synergistic building. Because we see so much opportunity to teach about wellness in a dedicated center, a WELL building makes the messages stand out. This bold step will also make it more evident that there is unity in health and wellness. Carried out properly in Jacksonville, the WELL-certified buildings on a wellness- oriented campus will be a model for business, governments, and nonprofits throughout Florida. By teaching others how to achieve LEED and WELL certification, we satisfy one of the principal goals of both programs.

As we examine our opportunity to build healthy buildings for animals and people in Jacksonville, we should welcome the responsibilities of leadership in green building design. My staff greatly enjoyed the moment when we opened the LEED Gold-certified Levine Animal Care Complex in West Palm Beach, and our Jacksonville team looks forward to our opportunity at the podium to take credit for building the first WELL-certified building in a North American zoological park. Programming such a noble building will bring us together in a group task that few zoos have experienced. Because conservation and education have become such high priorities for all accredited zoos and aquariums, WELL buildings provide the setting to teach far beyond the biological context of the zoo itself. In particular, the One Health Initiative looms large when zoo buildings reflect the combined relevance of LEED and WELL. There is great unrealized potential in the entire spectrum of wellness services, but the WELL building certification process may be the most promising new innovation available to zoos and aquariums today. I was tutored in WELL certification by Pete Choquette, an architect with the Epsten Group in Atlanta and Nevin Lash whose company, Ursa International, endorses the certification strategy. With their assistance I learned how WELL fits the wellness operating philosophy that I espouse. I feel comfortable suggesting to other zoo leaders that the WELL path is a good way to provide holistic environmental leadership for the zoo profession. However, just as with LEED, this is not something you can accomplish on your own. Firms such as the Epsten Group, with expertise on WELL certification, are prepared to guide us through the complex qualification process. Zoo planners will probably certify their buildings one at a time, but I would love to see entire new zoos built and WELL certified from day one. As a hypothetical I will examine the opportunity we have to certify a wellness center in Jacksonville. An early decision will be the location of the center. If we follow the laws of learning I reviewed in Chapter 6, we would locate the wellness center at the entrance to the zoo. The new entrance will be moved according to the master plan, but it won't move too far from its current location. In this position we can generate a vision for wellness that will be noticed by visitors going in and going out. In terms of WELL elements, this location serves an important function, but it might be better if it was located along the Trout River at the western boundary of the zoo. This location would have the advantage of the lengthy river view, a stimulating naturalistic perspective for employees and visitors who use the building. To optimize the view, plenty of glass on the river side would be desirable. In either location, air circulation and light will be important for workers in the building. At the river site, a nature walking trail for staff and visitors could be a feature of this location. Following WELL guidelines, we could also grow food in contiguous gardens and on the top of the building in a living-roof feature. Inside the building or next to it, we would position a natural food café available to visitors and for staff where much of the food would be grown on the zoo campus. Our vendor partners (e.g., rain-forestcoffeecompany.com) for coffee and tea would be carefully selected to reflect our commitment to supporting rain forest enterprise. Coffee made in Rwanda, for example, supports gorilla conservation, and this would be one of our featured items. The Rainforest Coffee Company refuses to use harmful chemicals and plants three trees for every bag of their organic, shade-grown coffee that is purchased.

During the construction of our wellness center, we will be careful about the selection of building materials to avoid toxic chemicals that might affect the workplace environment. Following what we have learned in this book, in preparing for construction at the entry or at the river, we will be careful to protect wildlife and wildlife habitat that might be displaced. A biological survey will be conducted prior to construction so we know what is there before breaking ground. Owls, for example, need large trees, so trees will be a high priority for protection. The grounds will also protect indigenous tree and plant species, taking special care not to harm lizard, tortoise and bird habitat. During construction, zoo staff will be responsible and ac-countable for the morbidity and mortality of indigenous wildlife. The care we take will doubtless slow the pace of construction, but a WELL-certified building requires that we be extremely careful. To include enough room for our think tank, audiovisual presentations, and student/faculty/staff labs, our wellness center will be three stories high. Inside, a stairway with handrails will encourage staff and visitors to exercise their way to the top. Perhaps we can add simulated lianas so athletic staff can brachiate up the ropes! Elevators will be available for handicapped individuals. Throughout the building, perhaps reflecting nature with a curvilinear shape, wildlife art will be presented with powerful images of animals and plants. A theme of this building will be expressed in the art and science of wellness. The Jacksonville Zoo and Garden's wellness center will be a unique blend of the natural and the technical as it uses advanced computer and audiovisual technology throughout the building. In locating this building on a zoo campus it is also synergistic with medical buildings and nutrition laboratories. A health and wellness complex would include all of this and more.

These ideas and many more will be part of the innovation displayed in our WELL-certified wellness center. If we reach the Platinum level of certification, our wellness center will be a model for the City of Jacksonville and for all zoos in North America and beyond. To reach this standard, the wellness center will test our fund-raising abilities, but I am confident that donors will like this unique building and find a way to help us reach our goal. The most important thing I have learned in my career as a fund-raising CEO is simply this: big donors don't like small ideas! Our LEED- and WELL-certified wellness center is a very big idea, indeed, and a compelling fund-raising opportunity.

BIOPHILIC DESIGN

If biophilia is in fact vital to human health and well-being, as Kellert believed, it will be important to encourage biophilic influence on the built environment in every way we can. This emphasis is needed because of our human history of resisting this connection to nature. Indeed, too many of us consider nature to be an obstacle in the way of progress that must be overcome or dominated by builders. Kellert was willing to put this to the empirical test when he wrote the following: "To advance the objectives of biophilic design we must demonstrate that nature substantially enhances human physical and mental health, performance, and wellbeing." Biophilic design should be an essential component of a WELL-certified building and a key feature of our wellness operating philosophy. In fact, biophilic design is a fascinating device for teaching about wellness in the zoo and in our personal lives.

Kellert defined biophilic design as "biophilia applied to the design and development of the human built environment." Another way to put this is to acknowledge that humankind's inherent ability to affiliate with nature contributes to human health, fitness, and well-being. We evolved to be a part of nature and not stand apart from it. Designers who are aware of this principle cater to our connectivity to the natural world. The following are the basic principles of biophilic design according to Kellert:

1. A focus on human adaptations to nature that advance physical and mental health, performance, and well-being.

2. Interrelated and integrated settings where the ecological whole is experienced more than its individual parts.

3. Engagement and immersion in natural features and processes.

4. Satisfies a wide range of values that people inherently hold about the natural world.

5. Emotional attachments to structures, landscapes, and places.

6. Fosters feelings of membership in a community that includes both people and the nonhuman environment.

7. Occurs in a multiplicity of settings, including interior, exterior, and transitional spaces and landscapes.

8. An authentic experience of nature, rather than one that is artificial or contrived.

9. Enhances the human relationship to natural systems and avoids adverse environmental impacts.

These nine principles fit perfectly with the wellness philosophy we have explored in this book. Thus, it seems reasonable to conclude that wellness-inspired design is functionally equivalent to Kellert's interpretation of biophilic design. One transitional element that brings the two approaches together is the wellness garden. Any zoo with a botanical component should be able to incorporate a wellness garden into the fabric of the zoo's plan for botanicals.

WELLNESS GARDENS

The architect Jon Coe has agreed to be a consultant to the Jacksonville Zoo's wellness-inspired design projects including the wellness center and the expanded African elephant habitat. Coe has expertise and history in the design and implementation of what he calls "wellness gardens." Depicted below is a wellness garden he designed for the Healesville Hospital in Australia. Jon was also involved in the early planning of the Phipps Conservancy, so he has the breadth of experience to advance our ideas. As an important feature of our wellness center concept, we intend to create public events to showcase the garden and the impact of such gardens. Our wellness speaker series, developed in partnership with UNF, will periodically feature garden gurus such as Shawna Coronado, a well-known garden wellness advocate and public speaker. Because our zoo is also a botanical garden, the introduction of a wellness garden will provide an opportunity to acknowledge the impact of gardens on health and wellness and to expand our botanicals devoted to the wellness philosophy. We intend to continue our experimentation with wellness within the naturalistic infrastructure that has been evolving in Jacksonville. Because wellness itself is evolving rapidly in many locations in North America and globally, we will soon learn if we have advanced the prospects of animals living in zoos and aquariums. Are we creative enough to provide people and wildlife with the tools to thrive? A thriving zoological park is the next best thing to protecting and growing the natural world around us. Of course, as zoo professionals we are actively involved in both. By engaging in the process of WELL certification, we can be certain that all of the many features of wellness will be explored and implemented at some level. There is so much going on in the world of wellness enterprise that there are no limits to what our entrepreneurial and wellness-inspired zoos and aquariums will do in the future. I look forward to future zoos and aquariums created in such a way that we cannot imagine their powerful impact on the world. It seems clear that by virtue of the breadth and depth of this emerging wellness culture, the world we create together will be better and more livable for all creatures big and small.

FIGURE 9.1. COE'S WELLNESS GARDEN, HEALESVILLE HOSPITAL.

BIBLIOGRAPHY

Akers, J. S., & Schildkraut, D. S. (1985). Regurgitation/reingestion and coprophagy in captive gorillas. *Zoo Biology, 4*(2), 99–109. doi:10.1002/zoo.1430040203

Allen, K. (2003). Are pets a healthy pleasure? The influence of pets on blood pressure. *Current Directions in Psychological Science, 12*(6), 236–239. doi:10.1046/j.0963-7214.2003.01269.x

Anderson, U. S., Kelling, A. S., & Maple, T. L. (2008). Twenty-five years of zoo biology: A publication analysis. In T. L. Maple & D. G. Lindburg (Eds.) [Special issue]. *Zoo Biology, 27*(6), 1–14. doi:10.1002/zoo.20177

Ardell, D. B. (1977). *High level wellness*. Emmaus, PA: Rodale Press.

Baker, K. C., & Easley, S. P. (1996). An analysis of regurgitation and reingestion in captive chimpanzees. *Applied Animal Behaviour Science, 49*, 403–415. doi:10.1016/0168-1591(96)01061-1

Ballantyne, R., Packer, J., Hughes, K., & Dierking, L. (2007). Conservation learning in wildlife tourism settings: Lessons from research in zoos and aquariums. *Environmental Education Research, 13*(3), 367–383. doi:10.1080/13504620701430604

Baotic, A., Sicks, F., & Stoeger, A. S. (2015). Nocturnal "humming" vocalizations: Adding a piece to the puzzle of giraffe vocal communication. *BMC Research Notes, 8*, 425. doi:10.1186/s13104-015-1394-3

Bashaw, M., & Allard, S. (2019, May 11). Modern zoos aren't just for entertainment. *Scientific American Blog Network.*

Bashaw, M. J., Kelling, A. S., Bloomsmith, M. A., & Maple, T. L. (2007). Environmental effects on the behavior of zoo-housed lions and tigers with a case study of the effects of a visual barrier on pacing. *Journal of Applied Animal Welfare Science, 10*(2), 95–109. doi:10.1080/10888700701313116

Bashaw, M. J., & Maple, T. L. (2001). Signs fail to increase zoo visitors' ability to see tigers. *Curator: The Museum Journal, 44*(3), 297–304. doi:10.1111/j.2151-6952.2001.tb01167.x

Beck, B. E., Stoinski, T., Maple, T. L., Norton, B., Hutchins, M., Stevens, B., & Arlott, M. (Eds.). (2001). *Great apes and humans: The ethics of coexistence.* Washington, DC: Smithsonian.

Bekoff, M. (2000). Animal emotions exploring passionate natures: Current interdisciplinary research provides compelling evidence that many animals experience such emotions as joy, fear, love, despair, and grief—we are not alone. *Bioscience, 50*(10), 861–870. doi:10.1641/00063568(2000)050 [0861: AEEPN]2.0.CO;2

Bekoff, M. (2016, March 26). Is "a life worth living" a "good life" for other animals? *Psychology Today.*

Birch, T. H. (1993). Moral considerability and universal consideration. *Environmental Ethics, 15*, 313–332. doi:10.5840/enviroethics19931544

Bittel, J. (2016, September 9). The plan to save the humpback whales and how it succeeded. *National Geographic Magazine.*

Block, K. (2019, February 22). Iceland says it may kill 2,000 whales over next five years. *A Human World.*

Bloomsmith, M. A., Marr. M. J., & Maple, T. L. (2007). Addressing nonhuman primate behavioral problems through the use of operant conditioning: Is the human treatment approach a useful model? *Journal of Applied Animal Behaviour Science, 102,* 205–222. doi:10.1016/j.applanim.2006.05.028

Bonnie, K. E., Bernstein-Kurtyccz, L. M., Shender, M. A., Ross, S. R., & Hopper, L. M. (2019). Foraging in a social setting: A comparative analysis of captive gorillas and chimpanzees. *Primates, 60,* 125–131. doi:10.1007/s10329-018-00712-x

Bradshaw, G. A., Schore, A. N., Brown, J. L., Poole, J. H., & Moss, C. J. (2005). Elephant breakdown: Social trauma, early disruption of attachment can affect the physiology, behavior and culture of animals and humans over generations. *Nature, 433,* 807. doi:10.1038/433807a

Braithwaite, V. (2010). *Do fish feel pain?.* Oxford, England: Oxford University Press.

Brambell, R. (1965). *Report of the technical committee to enquire into the welfare of animals kept under intensive livestock husbandry systems.* Cmd. (Great Britain Parliament), H. M. Stationery Office, 1–84.

Brando, S. I. C. A., & Burghardt, G. M. (2019). Studying play in zoos and aquariums. In A. Kaufman, M. Bashaw, & T. L. Maple. (Eds.). *Scientific Foundations of Zoos and Aquariums,* 558–585.

Brennan, Z. (2008, June 13). *Jurassic Park* comes true: How scientists are bringing dinosaurs back to life with the help of the humble chicken. *Daily Mail.*

Brockett, R., Stoinski, T., Black, J., Markowitz, T., & Maple, T. L. (1999). Nocturnal behavior in a group of unchained African elephants. *Zoo Biology, 18*(20), 101–109. doi:10.1002/(SICI)1098-2361(1999)18:2<101::AID-ZOO2>3.0.CO;2-4

Browning, H., & Maple, T. L. (2019). Developing a metric of usable space for zoo exhibits. *Frontiers in Psychology—Comparative Psychology, 10,* 1–11. doi:10.3389/fpsyg.2019.00791

Buckley, K. W. (1989). *Mechanical man: John Broadus Watson and the beginnings of behaviorism.* New York, NY: Guilford Press.

Burks, K., Bloomsmith, M. A., Forthman, D. L., & Maple, T. L. (2001). Managing the socialization of an adult male gorilla (*Gorilla gorilla gorilla*) with a history of social deprivation. *Zoo Biology, 20*(5), 347–358. doi:10.1002/zoo.1033

Casey, S. (2019, September). Freeing the whales. *Coastal Living Magazine.*

Chang, T. R., Forthman, D. L., & Maple, T. L. (1999). Comparison of captive mandrills in traditional and ecologically representative exhibits. *Zoo Biology, 18*(3), 163–176. doi:10.1002/(SICI)1098-2361(1999)18:3<163::AID-ZOO1>3.0.CO;2-T

Clarke, A. S., Juno, C. J., & Maple, T. L. (1982). Behavioral effects of a change in the physical environment: A pilot study of captive chimpanzees. *Zoo Biology, 1*(4), 371–380. doi:10.1002/zoo.1430010411

Clayton, S., & Myers, G. (2009). *Conservation psychology: Understanding and promoting human care for nature.* New York, NY: Wiley/Blackwell.

Clegg, I. L. K., Rodel, H. G., Boivin, X., & Delfour, F. (2018). Looking forward to interacting with their caretakers: Dolphin's anticipatory behavior indicates motivation to participate in specific events. *Applied Animal Behaviour Science, 202*, 85–93. doi:10.1016/j.applanim.2018.01.015

Coe, J. (1985). Design and perception: Making the zoo experience real. *Zoo Biology, 4*(2), 197–208. doi:10.1002/zoo.1430040211

Dierenfeld, E. S. (1996). Nutritional wisdom: Adding science to the art. *Zoo Biology, 15*, 447–448. doi:10.1002/(SICI)1098-2361(1996)15:5<447::AID-ZOO1>3.0.CO;2-B

Dodd, N. L., Gagnon, J. W., & Schweinsburg, R. E. (2010). *Evaluation of an animal-activated animal crosswalk integrated with retrofit fencing applications.* International Conference on Ecology and Transportation.

Dunphy, S. (2018, September 28). Whale populations are still under threat from PCB pollution. *European Scientist.*

Dunn, H. L. (1959). What high-level wellness means. *Canadian Journal of Public Health, 50*(11), 447–457. doi:41981469

Dunn, H. L. (1961). *High-level wellness.* Arlington VA: Beatty Press.

Erwin, J., Maple, T. L., & Mitchell, G. (Eds.). (1979). *Captivity and behavior: Primates in breeding colonies, laboratories and zoos.* New York, NY: Van Nostrand Reinhold.

Finlay, T. W., James, L. R., & Maple, T. L. (1988). Zoo environments influence people's perceptions of animals. *Environment and Behavior, 20*(4), 508–528. doi:10.1177/0013916588204008

Finlay, T. W., & Maple, T. L. (1986). A survey of research in American zoos and aquariums. *Zoo Biology, 5*(3), 261–268. doi:10.1002/zoo.1430050304

Finn, H. (2017). Land clearing isn't just about trees—it's an animal welfare issue too. *The Conversation.*

Fleming, G. J., & Skurski, M. L. (2012). In *Fowler's Zoo and Wild Animal Medicine.*

Forthman, D. L., Kane, L. F., Hancocks, D., & Waldau, P. F. (Eds.). (2009). *An elephant in the room: The science and well-being of elephants in captivity.* North Grafton, MA: Tufts University Cummings School of Veterinary Medicine/Center for Animals and Public Policy.

Foster, L. C., & Keller, C. P. (2007). *The British Columbia atlas of wellness* (1st ed.). Victoria, Canada: Western Geographical Press.

Fravel, L. (2003). Critics question zoos' commitment to conservation. *National Geographic News, 13.*

Fredrickson B.L., Cohn M. A. (2008). Positive emotions. In: Lewis M, Haviland-Jones JM, Barrett LF, (Eds.). *Handbook of Emotions.* Vol. 3. New York: Guilford Press, 777–796

Friedmann, E., & Thomas, S. A. (1995). Pet ownership, social support, and one-year survival after acute myocardial infarction in the cardiac arrhythmia suppression trial (CAST). *American Journal of Cardiology, 76*, 1213–1217. doi:10.1016/S0002-9149(99)80343-9

Furguson, D. (2016, May 18). Paws for thought: Why allowing dogs in the office is a good idea. *The Guardian.*

Gagnon, J. W., Dodd, N. L., Sprague, S. C., Ogren, K. S., Loberger, C. D., & Schweinsburg, R. E. (2019). Animal-activated highway crosswalk: Long-term impact on elk-vehicle collisions, vehicle speeds, and motorist braking response. *Human Dimensions of Wildlife, 24*(2), 132–147. doi:10.1080/10871209.2019.1551586

Garnefeld, I., & Steinhoff, L. (2013). Primacy vs. recency effects in extended service encounters. *Journal of Service Management, 24*(1), 64–81. doi:10.1108/09564231311304198

Gold, K. G., & Maple, T. L. (1994). Personality assessment in the gorilla and its utility as a management tool. *Zoo Biology, 13*(5), 509–522. doi:10.1002/zoo.1430130513

Gosling, S. T., & John, O. P. (1999). Personality dimensions in non-human animals: A cross-species review. *Current Directions in Psychological Science, 8*(3), 68–75. doi:10.1111/1467-8721.00017

Gould, E., & Bres, M. (1986). Regurgitation and reingestion in captive gorillas: Description and intervention. *Zoo Biology, 5*, 241–250. doi:10.1002/zoo.1430050302

Gove, E. (2018, November 8). More than 100 animals trapped in "whale jail" off Russian's coast. *CBS News* online.

Grant, A. M., & Schwartz, B. (2011). Too much of a good thing: The challenge and opportunity of the inverted U. *Perspectives on Psychological Science, 6*(1), 61–76. doi:10.1177/1745691610393523

Hancocks, D. (2001). *A different nature: The paradoxical world of zoos and their uncertain future.* Berkeley: University of California Press.

Harlow, H. F. (1971). *Learning to love.* Chicago, IL: Aldine.

Harlow, H. F., & Mears, C. E. (1979). *The human model: Primate perspectives.* Washington, DC: V. H. Winston & Sons.

Harlow, H. F., Uehling, H., & Maslow, A. H. (1932). Comparative behavior of primates. I. Delayed reaction tests on primates from the lemur to the orang-outan. *Journal of Comparative Psychology, 13*(3), 313–343. doi:10.1037/h0072093

Hediger, H. (1955). *Studies of the Psychology and Behaviour of Animals in Zoos and Circuses.* London, England: Butterworths Scientific Publications.

Herzog, H. A., Jr., Betchart, N. S., & Pittman, R. B. (1991). Gender, sex role orientation, and attitudes toward animals. *Anthrozoös, 4*(3), 184–191. doi:10.2752/089279391787057170

Hesselmar, B., Hicke-Roberts, A., Lundell, A.-C., Adlerberth, I., Rudin, A., Saalman, R., Wennergren, G., & Wold, A. E. (2018). Pet-keeping in early life reduces the risk of allergy in a dose-dependent fashion. *PLoS ONE, 13*(12), e0208472. doi:10.1371/journal.pone.028472.

Hill, H. M., & Nollens, H. (2019). Providing belugas (Delphinapterus leucas) in controlled environments opportunities to thrive: Health, self-maintenance, species-specific behavior, and choice and control. *Frontiers in Psychology, 10*, 1776. Doi:10.3389/fpsyg.2019.01776

Hoff, M. P., Forthman, D., & Maple, T. L. (1994). Dyadic interactions of infant lowland gorillas in an outdoor exhibit compared to an indoor holding area. *Zoo Biology, 13*(3), 245–256. doi:10.1002/zoo.1430130306

Hoff, M. P., & Maple, T. L. (1995). Post-occupancy modification of a lowland gorilla enclosure at Zoo Atlanta. *International Zoo Yearbook, 34,* 153–160. doi:10.1111/j.1748-1090.1995.tb00674.x

Hoff, M. P., Powell, D., Lukas, K. E., & Maple, T. L. (1997). Social and individual behaviour of adult gorillas in indoor conditions compared to outdoor conditions. *Journal of Applied Animal Behaviour Science, 54,* 359–370. doi:10.1016/S0168-1591(97)00002-6

Hopper, L. M., Lambeth, S. P., & Schapiro, S. J. (2012). An evaluation of the efficacy of video displays for use with chimpanzees (*Pan troglodytes*). *American Journal of Primatology, 74*(5), 442–44. doi:10.1002/ajp.22001

Huey, R. B., Losos, J. B., & Moritz, C. (2010). Are lizards toast? *Science, 238,* 832–833. doi:10.1126/science.1190374

Jones, G., Coe, J. C., & Paulson, D. (1976). *Long range plan for Woodland Park Zoological Gardens.* Seattle, WA: Seattle Department of Parks and Recreation.

Junge, R. E., Williams, C. V., & Campbell, J. (2009). Nutrition and behavior of lemurs. *Veterinary Clinics of North America: Exotic Animal Practice, 12*(2), 339–348. doi:10.1016/j.cvex.2009.01.011

Kagan, R., Carter, S., & Allard, S. (2015). A universal animal welfare framework for zoos. *Journal of Applied Animal Welfare Science, 18,* S1–S10. doi:10.1080/10888705.2015.1075830

Kaufman, A., Bashaw, M., & Maple, T. L. (Eds.). (2019). *Scientific foundations of zoos and aquariums: Their role in conservation and research.* New York, NY: Cambridge University Press.

Kellert, S. R. (1993). The biological basis for human values of nature. In S. R. Kellert, & E. O. Wilson (Eds.), *The biophilia hypothesis* (pp. 42–69). Washington, DC: Island Press.

Kelling, A. S., Dampier, S. M. A., Kelling, N. J., Sandhaus, E. A., & Maple, T. L. (2012). Lion, ungulate, and visitor reactions to playbacks of lion roars at Zoo Atlanta. *Journal of Applied Animal Welfare Science, 15*, 1–16. doi:10.1080/10888705.2012.709116

Kelling, A. S., Snyder, R. J., Gardner, W., Marr, M. J., Bloomsmith, M. A., & Maple, T. L. (2006). Color vision in the giant panda, *Ailuropoda melanoleuca. Learning and Behavior, 34*(2), 154–161. doi:10.3758/BF03193191

Kerlin, K. (2018, November 7). Learning from gorillas to save killer whales: A wild approach to personalized health care. *UC Davis News*.

King, J. E., & Figueredo, A. J. (1997). The five-factor model plus dominance in chimpanzee personality. *Journal of Research in Personality, 31*, 257–271. doi:10.1006/jrpe.1997.2179

Kisling, V. N. (Ed.). (2000). *Zoo and aquarium history: Ancient animal collections to zoological gardens.* Boca Raton, FL: CRC Press.

Kuhar, C. W. (2008). Demographic differences in captive gorillas' reaction to large crowds. *Applied Animal Behaviour Science, 110*, 377–385. doi:10.1016/j.applanim.2007.04.011

Love, K. (2019). Federal auction sells leasing rights on thousands of acres of prime sage-grouse habitat. *Washington Post*.

Lukas, K. E., Hamor, G., Bloomsmith, M. A., Horton, C. L., & Maple, T. L. (1999). Removing milk from captive gorilla diets: The impact on regurgitation and reingestion (R&R) and

other behavior. *Zoo Biology, 18*, 6, 515–528. doi:10.1002/
(SICI)1098-2361(1999)18:6<515::AID-ZOO6>3.0.CO;2-T

Lukas, K. E., Hoff, M. P., & Maple, T. L. (2003). Gorilla behav-
ior in response to systematic alternation between zoo enclosures.
Applied Animal Behaviour Science, 81(4), 367–386. doi:10.1016/
S0168-1591(02)00237-X

Lukas, K. E., Marr, M. J., & Maple, T. L. (1998). Teaching operant
conditioning at the zoo. *Teaching of Psychology, 25*(2), 112–116.
doi:10.1207/s15328023top2502_7

Lund, F. H. (1925). The psychology of belief IV: The law of primacy in
persuasion. Journal of Abnormal and Social Psychology, 20, 183–91.

Lyengar, S. S., & Lepper, M. R. (2000). When choice is demotivating:
Can one desire too much of a good thing? *Journal of Personality and
Social Psychology, 79*(6), 995.

MacKinnon, J. B. (2018, July 30). It's tough being a right whale these
days. *The Atlantic.*

Mallavarapu, S., Bloomsmith, M. A., Kuhar, C. W., & Maple, T. L.
(2013). Using multiple-joystick systems in computerized-assisted
enrichment for captive orangutans. *Animal Welfare, 22*(3), 401–409.
doi:10.7120/09627286.22.3.401

Maple, T. L. (1979). Primate psychology in historical perspective. In J.
Erwin, T. L. Maple, & Mitchell (Eds.), *Captivity and Behavior* (pp.
29–58). New York, NY: Van Nostrand Reinhold.

Maple, T. L. (1980). *Chimpanzee reproduction, rearing, and rehabilitation
in captivity.* Report presented to the Ad Hoc Task Force, National

Chimpanzee Breeding Program, Tanglewood, N.C. Atlanta: Georgia Institute of Technology Technical Report, 1–93.

Maple, T. L. (1996). The art and science of enrichment. In G. M. Burghardt, J. T. Bielitzki, J. R. Boyce, & D. D. Schaeffer (Eds.), *The well-being of animals in zoo and aquarium sponsored research* (pp. 79–84). Greenbelt, MD: Scientists Center for Animal Welfare.

Maple, T. L. (1999). Zoo Atlanta's scientific vision. *Georgia Journal of Science, 101,* 159–179.

Maple, T. L. (2001). The power of one. In G. Rabb (Ed.), *The apes: Challenges for the 21st century: Conference proceedings* (pp. 208–209). Chicago, IL: Chicago Zoological Society.

Maple, T. L. (2012, April). A zoo where the animals come first. *APS Observer,* 39–41.

Maple, T. L. (2014). Commentary: Elevating the priority of zoo animal welfare—the chief executive as an agent of reform. *Zoo Biology, 33*(1), 1–7. doi:10.1002/zoo.21117

Maple, T. L. (2014, April 12). Copenhagen Zoo's giraffe killing was wrong and disturbing. Op-Ed. *San Francisco Chronicle.*

Maple, T. L. (2015). Four decades of psychological research on zoo animal welfare. *Magazine of the World Association of Zoos and Aquariums,* 41–44.

Maple, T. L. (2016). *Professor in the zoo.* Fernandina Beach, FL: Red Leaf Press.

Maple, T. L., & Bashaw, M. J. (2010). Trends in zoo research. In D. G. Kleiman, K. V. Thompson, & C. K. Baer (Eds.), *Wild mammals in captivity* (Vol. 2, pp. 288–298). Chicago, IL: University of Chicago Press.

Maple, T. L., & Bloomsmith, M. A., Eds. (2018). Optimal animal welfare [Special issue]. *Behavioural Processes, 156*, 1–96.

Maple, T. L., Bloomsmith, M. A., & Martin, A. (2009). Primates and pachyderms: A primate model of zoo elephant welfare. In D. L. Forthman, L. F. Kane, D. Hancocks, & P. Waldau (Eds), *An elephant in the room: The science and well-being of elephants in captivity* (pp. 129–153). North Grafton, MA: Tufts University Cummings School of Veterinary Medicine/Center for Animals and Public Policy.

Maple, T. L., & Bloomstrand, M. (1988). Feeding, foraging and mental health. In T. P. Meehan & M. E. Allen (Eds.), *Proceedings of the Dr. Scholl Conference on the Nutrition of Wild Animals* (pp. 1–8). Chicago, IL: Lincoln Park Zoo Publication.

Maple, T. L., & Bocian, D. (2013). Wellness as welfare. *Zoo Biology, 32*(4), 363–365.

Maple, T. L., Erwin, J., & Mitchell, G. (1973). Age of sexual maturity in laboratory-born pairs of rhesus monkeys (*Macaca mulatta*). *Primates, 14*(4), 427–428. doi:10.1007/BF01731364

Maple, T. L., & Finlay, T. W. (1986). Evaluating the environments of captive nonhuman primates. In K. Benirschke (Ed.), *Primates: The road to self-sustaining populations* (pp. 480–488). New York, NY: Springer-Verlag. doi:10.1007/978-1-4612-4918-4_38

Maple, T. L., & Finlay, T. W. (1987). Post-occupancy evaluation in the zoo. *Applied Animal Behavior Science, 18*, 5–18. doi:10.1016/0168-1591(87)90250-4

Maple, T. L., & Kuhar, C. W. (2006). The comparative psychology of Duane Rumbaugh and his impact on zoo biology. In D. A. Washburn (Ed.), *Primate perspectives on behavior and cognition* (pp. 7–16). Washington, DC: American Psychological Association.

Maple, T. L., & Lindburg, D. G. (Eds.). (2008). Empirical zoo: Opportunities and challenges to research in zoos and aquariums. *Zoo Biology, 27*(6), 431–504. doi:10.1002/zoo.20214

Maple, T. L., & Morris, M. (2018). Behavioral impact of naturalistic and wilderness settings. In A. Devlin (Ed.), *The environment and human behavior: The effects of built and natural settings on wellbeing* (pp. 253–279). New York, NY: Academic Press. doi:10.1016/B978-0-12-811481-0.00010-X

Maple, T. L., & Perdue, B. M. (2013). *Zoo animal welfare.* Berlin/Heidelberg, Germany: Springer/Verlag.

Maple, T. L., & Segura, V. (2015). Advancing behavior analysis in zoos and aquariums. *The Behavior Analyst, 38*(1), 77–91. doi:10.1007/s40614-014-0018-x.

Maple, T. L., & Segura. V. (2017). Comparative psychopathology: Connecting comparative and clinical psychology. In Exploring the Intersection of Comparative and Clinical Psychology [Special issue]. *International Journal of Comparative Psychology, 30*, 1–11.

Maple, T. L., & Segura, V. (2018). Wildlife wellness: The next ethical frontier for zoos and aquariums. In B. Minteer, J. Maienschein, & J. P. Collins (Eds.). *The ark and beyond: The evolution of zoo and aquarium conservation* (pp. 226–237). Chicago, IL: University of Chicago Press.

Maple, T. L., & Sherwen, S. (2019). Does research have a place in the zoological garden? In A. Kaufman, M. Bashaw, & T. L. Maple (Eds.), *Scientific foundations of zoos and aquariums: Their role in conservation and research.* New York, NY: Cambridge University Press.

Maple, T. L., & Warren-Leubecker, A. (1983). Variability in the parental conduct of captive great apes. In M. D. Reite & N. G. Caine (Eds.), *Child abuse: The nonhuman primate data* (pp. 119–137). New York, NY: Alan R. Liss.

Markowitz, H. (1982). *Behavioral enrichment in the zoo.* New York, NY: Van Nostrand Reinhold.

Marston, D., & Maple, T. L. (2016). *Comparative psychology for clinical psychologists and therapists: What animal behaviour can tell us about human psychology* (p. 254). London, England: Jessica Kingsley.

Martin, A. L., Bloomsmith, M. A., Kelley, M. E., Marr, M., & Maple, T. L. (2011). Functional analysis and treatment of human-directed undesirable behaviors in a captive chimpanzee. *Journal of Applied Behavior Analysis, 1*(44), 139–143.

Maslow, A. H. (1936). The role of dominance in the social and sexual behavior of infra-human primates. I. Observations at Vilas Park Zoo. *Journal of Genetic Psychology, 48*, 261–277.

Maslow, A. H. (1962). *Toward a psychology of being.* New York, NY: Van Nostrand Reinhold.

Mason, G., & Clubb, R. (2003). Captivity effects on wide-ranging carnivores. *Nature, 425*, 473–474, doi:10.1038/425473a.

Mason, W. A., & Kenney, M. D. (1974). Redirection of filial attachments in rhesus monkeys: Dogs as mother surrogates. *Science, 183*, 1209–1211. doi:10.1126/science.183.4130.1209

McGlashen, A. (2019, February 28). The greater sage grouse's most important habitat is on the auction block. *Audubon.*

Mellen, J. (2019, June 27). Animal Welfare: An Organizational Priority. Retrieved from http://www.zooadvisors.com/editorial/2019/6/26/animal-welfare-an-organizational-priority

Mellor, D. J., Hunt, S., & Gusset, M. (2015). *Caring for wildlife: The world zoo and aquarium animal welfare strategy.* Gland, Switzerland: WAZA Executive Publication.

Minteer, B., Maienschein, J., Collins, J. P. (Eds.). (2018). *The ark and beyond: The evolution of zoo and aquarium conservation* (pp. 226–237). Chicago, IL: University of Chicago Press.

Minteer, B. A., & Collins, J. P. (2005). Why we need an "ecological ethics." *Frontiers in Ecology and the Environment, 3*, 332–337. doi:10.1890/1540-9295(2005)003[0332:WWNAEE]2.0.CO;2

Mitchell, G. D. & Clark, D.L. (1968). Long-term effects of social isolation in nonsocially adapted rhesus monkeys. *Journal of Genetic Psychology* 113, 117-128.

Mitchell, G. D. (1970). Abnormal behavior in primates. In Rosenblum, L.A. (Ed). Primate Behavior: Developments in field and laboratory research. New York: Academic press, 195-249.

Murray, H. B., Thomas, J. J., Hinds, A., & Hilbert, A. (2018). Prevalence in primary school youth of pica and rumination behavior: The understudied feeding disorders. *International Journal of Eating Disorders, 71*(5). doi:10.1002/eat.22898.

Myers, D. G., & Diener, E. (2018). The scientific pursuit of happiness. *Perspectives on Psychological Science, 13*(2), 218–225. doi:10.1177/1745691618765171

Myers, O. E., Jr., Saunders, C. D., & Birjulin, A. A. (2004). Emotional dimensions of watching zoo animals: An experience sampling study building on insights from psychology. *Curator: The Museum Journal, 47*(3), 299–321. doi:10.1111/j.2151-6952.2004.tb00127.x

Nieuwenhuijsen, K., & de Waal, F. (1982). Effects of spatial crowding on social behavior in a chimpanzee colony. *Zoo Biology, 1*(12), 5–28. doi:10.1002/zoo.1430010103

Norton, B. G., Hutchins, M., Stevens, E., & Maple, T. L. (Eds.). (1995*). Ethics on the ark: Zoos, animal welfare and wildlife conservation.* Washington, DC: Smithsonian.

Novak, M., & Suomi, S. (1988). Psychological well-being of primates in captivity. *American Psychologist, 43*(10), 765–773. doi:10.1037/0003-066X.43.10.765

Ogden, J. J., Finlay, T. W. and Maple, T. L. (1990). Gorilla adaptations to naturalistic environments. *Zoo Biology, 9*(2), 107–121. doi:10.1002/zoo.1430090205

Ogden, J. J., Lindburg, D. G., & Maple, T. L. (1993a). Preferences for structural environmental features in captive lowland gorillas. *Zoo Biology, 12*(4), 381–396. doi:10.1002/zoo.1430120408

Ogden, J. J., Lindburg, D. G., & Maple, T. L. (1993b). The effects of ecologically-relevant sounds on the cognitive and affective behavior of zoo visitors. *Curator, 36*(2), 147–156.

Paquet, P. C., & Carbyn, L. N. (2003). Wolf, *Canis lupus*, and allies. In G. A. Feldhamer, C. B. Thompson, & J. A. Chapman (Eds.), *Wild mammals of North America: Biology, management, and conservation* (pp. 482–510). Baltimore, MD: Johns Hopkins University Press.

Paquet, P. C., & Darimont, C. T. (2010). Wildlife conservation and animal welfare: Two sides of the same coin? *Animal Welfare, 19*, 177–190.

Petersen, C. (2006). *A primer in positive psychology*. New York, NY: Oxford University Press.

Piff, P. K., Dietze, P., Feinberg, M., Stancato, D. M., & Keltner, D. (2015). Awe, the small self, and prosocial behavior. *Journal of Personality and Social Psychology, 108*(6), 883–889. doi:10.1037/pspi0000018.

Powell, D., & Bullock, E. (2014). Evaluation of factors affecting emotional responses in zoo visitors and the impact of emotion on conservation mindedness. *Anthrozoos, 21*(3), 389–405. doi:10.2752/175303714X13903827488042

Reade, L. S., & Waran, N. K. (1996). The modern zoo: How do people perceive zoo animals?. *Applied Animal Behaviour Science, 47*(1–2), 109–118. doi:10.1016/0168-1591(95)01014-9

Rogers, C. (1980). *A way of being*. New York, NY: Mariner Books.

Ryan, R.M. & Deci, E.L. (2001). On happiness and human potentials: A review of research on hedonic and eudaimonic wellbeing. *Annual Review of Psychology* 52, 141-166.

Ryff, C. D. (2018). Well-being with soul: Science in pursuit of human potential. *Perspectives in Psychological Science, 13*(2), 242–248. doi:10.1177/1745691617699836

Saunders, C. D. (2003). The emerging field of conservation psychology. *Human Ecology Review*, 137–149. doi:24706965

Schlegel, J., & Rupf, R. (2010). Attitudes towards potential animal flagship species in nature conservation: A survey among students of different educational institutions. *Journal for Nature Conservation, 18*(4), 278–290. doi:10.1016/j.jnc.2009.12.002

Schweitzer, A. (1946). *Civilization and ethics: The philosophy of civilization II* (3rd ed.). London, England: Adam and Charles Black.

Seligman, M. E. P. (1975). *Helplessness. On depression, development, and death.* San Francisco, Freeman.

Seligman, M. E. P. (2011). *Flourish: A visionary new understanding of happiness and well-being.* New York, NY: Free Press.

Seligman, M. E. P., & Csikszentmihalyi, M. (2014). *Positive psychology: An introduction.* Netherlands: Springer.

Serpell, J. (1996). *In the company of animals: A study of human-animal relationships.* Cambridge University Press.

Smith, K. N., & Kuhar, C. W. (2010). Siamangs (*Hylobates syndactylus*) and white-cheeked gibbons (*Hylobates leucogenys*). *Journal of Applied Animal Welfare Science, 13*, 154–163. doi:10.1080/10888700903579895.

Sneddon. L. U. (2011). Pain perception in fish: Evidence and implications for the use of fish. *Journal of Consciousness Studies, 18*(9), 209–229.

Snyder, R. J., Bloomsmith, M. A., Zhang, A. J., Zhang, Z. H., & Maple, T. L. (2006). Consequences of early rearing on socialization and social competence of giant pandas. In D. E. Wildt, A. J. Zhang, Z H. Zhang, D. Janssen, & S. Ellis (Eds.), *Giant pandas: Biology, veterinary medicine and management* (pp. 334–352). New York, NY: Cambridge University Press.

Snyder, R. J., Zhang, A., Zhang, Z., Li, G., Tian, Y., Huang, X., Luo, L., Bloomsmith, M. A., Forthman, D. L., & Maple, T. L. (2003). Behavioral and developmental consequences of early rearing experience for captive giant pandas (Ailuropoda melanoleuca). *Journal of Comparative Psychology, 117*, 235–245. doi:10.1037/0735-7036.117.3.235

Sommer, R. (1925). *Tierpsychologie.* Leipzig: Verlag von Quelle & Meyer.

Sommer, R. (2008). Development of the zoological garden and mental hospital. *American Journal of Orthopsychiatry, 78*(3), 378–382. doi:10.1037/a0014200

Staples, A. (2019, February 4). Why Geoff Collins' Georgia Tech rebound starts with a rebrand. *Sports Illustrated.*

Stoinski, T. S., Allen, M. T., Bloomsmith, M. A., Forthman, D. L., & Maple, T. L. (2002). Educating zoo visitors about complex environmental issues: Should we do it and how? *Curator, 45*(2), 129–143. doi:10.1111/j.2151-6952.2002.tb01187.x

Stoinski, T. S., Hoff, M. P., & Maple, T. L. (2001). Habitat use and structural preferences of captive lowland gorillas: The effect of environmental and social variables. *International Journal of Primatology, 22*, 431–447. doi:10.1023/A:1010707712728

Stoinski, T. S., Hoff, M. P., & Maple, T. L. (2002). The effect of structural preferences, temperature, and social factors on visibility in western lowland gorillas. *Environment and Behavior, 34*(4), 493–507. doi:10.1177%2F00116502034004005

Swaisgood, R. R., & Sheppard, J. K. (2010). The culture of conservation biologists: "Show me the hope!" *BioScience, 60*(8), 626–630. doi:10.1525/bio.2010.60.8.8

Tennant, K., Morris, M., Segura, V., Denninger-Snyder, K., Bocian, D., Lee, G. H., & Maple, T. L. (2018). Achieving optimal welfare for the Nile hippopotamus (*H. amphibius*) in North American zoos and aquariums [Special issue]. *Behavioural Processes, 156*, 51–57. doi:10.1016/j.beproc.2017.07.00

Thame, M., Burton, K. A., & Forrester, T. (2000). The human ruminant. *West Indian Medical Journal, 49*(2), 172–174.

Tutin, C. E. G., & Fernandez, M. (1993). Composition of the diet of chimpanzees and comparisons with that of sympatric lowland gorillas in the Lope Reserve, Gabon. *American Journal of Primatology, 30*, 195–211. doi:10.1002/ajp.1350300305

Ullrey, D. E. (1996). Skepticism and science: Responsibilities of the comparative nutritionist. *Zoo Biology, 15*, 449–453. doi:10.1002/(SICI)1098-2361(1996)15:5%3C449::AID-ZOO2%3E3.0.CO;2-B

U.S. Department of Commerce, NOAA Fisheries. (2018). *North Atlantic Right Whale*. Species Directory.

Van Hooff, J. A. R. A. M. (1973). The Arnhem Zoo chimpanzee consortium: An attempt to create an ecologically and socially acceptable habitat. *International Zoo Yearbook, 13*, 195–203. doi:10.1111/j.1748-1090.1973.tb02148.x

Veasey, J. S. (2017). In pursuit of peak animal welfare: The need to prioritize the meaningful over the measurable. *Zoo Biology, 36*, 413–425. doi:10.1002/zoo.21390

Victor, D. (2019, March 19). Dead whale found with 88 pounds of plastic inside body in the Philippines. *The New York Times*, A10.

Wagman, J. D., Lukas, K. E., Dennis, P. M., Willis, M. A., Carroscia, J., Gindlesperger, C., & Schook, M. W. (2018). *Zoo Biology, 37*, 3–15. doi:10.1002/zoo.21391.

Warwick, C., Arena, P. & Steedman, C. (2019). Spatial considerations for captive snakes. *Journal of Veterinary Behavior*, 30, 37-48. doi: 10.1016/j.jveb.2018.12.006

Washburn, D. A. (2015). The four c's of psychological well-being: Lessons from three decades of computer-based environmental enrichment. *Animal Behavior and Cognition, 2*(3), 218–232. doi:10.12966/abc.08.02.2015

Webster, J. (2016). Animal welfare: Freedoms, dominions and "a life worth living." *Animals, 6*(6), 2–11. doi:10.3390/ani6060035.

Wilson, M., Kelling, A., Poline, L., Bloomsmith, M. A., & Maple, T. L. (2003). Post occupancy evaluation of Zoo Atlanta's giant panda conservation center: Staff and visitor reactions. *Zoo Biology, 22*(4), 365–382. doi:10.1002/zoo.10102

Wilson, M. L., Bashaw, M. J., Fountain, K., Kieschnick, S., & Maple, T. L. (2006). Nocturnal behavior in a group of female African elephants. *Zoo Biology, 25*(3), 173–186. doi:10.1002/(SICI)1098-2361(1999)18:2%3C101::AID-ZOO2%3E3.0.CO;2-4

Wilson M. L., Perdue, B. M., Bloomsmith, M. A., & Maple, T. L. (2015). Rates of reinforcement and measures of compliance in free and protected contact management systems. *Zoo Biology, 34*, 431–437. doi:10.1002/zoo.21229

Wineman, J., & Choi, Y.K. (1991). Spatial/visual properties of zoo exhibition. *Curator: The Museum Journal, 34*(4), 304–315. doi:10.1111/j.2151-6952.1991.tb01475.x

Wineman, J., Piper, C., & Maple, T. L. (1996). Zoos in transition: Enriching conservation education for a new generation. *Curator: The Museum Journal, 39*(2), 94–102. doi:10.1111/j.2151-6952.1996.tb01082.x

Wobber, V., & Hare, B. (2011). Psychological health of orphan bonobos and chimpanzees in African sanctuaries. *PLoS ONE, 6*, 1–10. doi:10.1371/journal.pone.0017147

Worland, J. (2017, February 16). The future of zoos: Challenges force zoos to change in big ways. *Time Magazine.*

Yerkes, R. M. (1927). The mind of a gorilla. *Gen Psychology Monographs, 2*, 1–193.

INDEX

A

A Primer on Positive Psychology 48

Abraham Maslow 9

Adam Rosenblat 34, 64

Aeronautics and Space Administration 23

Africa 28, 36, 40, 86, 94, 104, 111, 112, 117, 133, 154, 156, 160, 182, 195

Alan Campbell 22

American alligator 64

American Association of Humanistic Psychology 46

American Humane, Center for Disease Control 36

American Psychological Association 46, 88, 246

Anacondas 66, 152, 153

Andrew Rowan 128

Andrew Young 13, 80, 150

Animal Behavior Society 23

Animal Behavior Society's Certified Applied Animal Behaviorists 23

Animal Care and Conservation Committee 97

Animal Wellness Campus 53

Animal Wellness Plaza 53

Anne-Marie Campbell 13

Anthropomorphism 174, 176

Apenheul Primate Park 190

Applied behavior analysis 21, 22, 29, 196

Arctic Ring of Life 72

Arianna Huffington69
Association of Zoos and Aquariums14, 84, 110, 184, 245
Atlanta Journal-Constitution80
Atlanta Zoo31
Atlanta Zoological Society31, 134, 208
Atlanta-Fulton County Stadium208
Audubon Zoo31, 36, 205, 207
Australian Wildlife Health Centre192

B
Barcelona dolphinarium184
Barcelona Zoo184, 185, 191
Bean Award136, 210
Bear Taxon Advisory Group150
Bears19, 66, 72, 122, 133, 148, 150, 151, 159, 173, 178, 202
Beluga whales118, 217
Berkeley Wellness Letter44
Bernstein-Kurtycz63
*Beyond Animal Welfare*1, 2, 6, 7, 10, 11, 12, 14, 183, 188, 223
Big Cat Society69
Bill Hetler44
Biophilia56, 230, 242
Birds66, 72, 103, 114, 132, 159, 173, 194, 195, 199, 202
Birmingham Zoo36, 74
Boa constrictors152
Bonnie Perdue7, 152
Bonobos91, 117, 141, 176, 255
Boomer Ball149
Born Free Foundation125, 126
Brevard Zoo54, 95, 99
Bronx Zoo86, 168
Brookfield20, 73, 147, 169
Buckhead Elephant Park131
Bureau of Land Management115

Burgers' Zoo102, 190
Bushmeat103

C
California condor126
California National Primate Research Center7
Carl Rogers46, 52
Carolyn Boyd Hatcher167
Case Western Reserve University33
Center for Great Apes117
Center for Sustainable Landscapes224
Center for the Science of Animal Care and Welfare73
Center for Zoo and Aquarium Animal Welfare and Ethics127, 193
Cetacean118
Charles Smithgall36
Chester Zoo145
Chimp Haven117
Chimpanzees61, 64, 67, 102, 117, 120, 136, 177, 190, 234, 236, 237, 241, 253, 255
China Daily198
Chiropractors48
Chris Kuhar13
Christopher Peterson48
Chuck Gillespie128
Cincinnati Zoo53, 99, 223
Cleveland Metroparks Zoo33, 36, 178, 198
CLR Design41, 82, 138, 157, 160, 211, 216
Cognitive science92
College of Veterinary Medicine at Washington State University51
Conservation Action Resource Center178
Copenhagen Zoo120, 245
Coyotes122

D

Dalton State College36, 136, 137
Dan Maloney13, 18
Dave Stanton20
David Bocian37, 75
Denver Zoo96, 98, 99, 223
Detroit Zoo36, 54, 72, 73, 76, 82, 149, 193, 195
Detroit Zoological Society's Universal Animal Welfare Framework127
Dian Fossey Gorilla Fund International36, 111, 125
Dietrich Schaff40
Disney's Animal Kingdom30, 36,645, 83, 84, 155, 170, 213
dogs43, 49, 56, 57, 59, 60, 116, 168, 169, 174, 194, 239
Dolphins23, 108, 146, 148, 156, 162
Dr. Scholl61, 246
Duane Jackson28, 38
Duane Rumbaugh30, 246
Duckie57

E

Earth and Life Studies of the U.S. National Academies200
Earth Day82, 220
Ed Lyman108
Elephants22, 39, 40, 41,43, 52, 61, 70, 90, 104, 116, 117, 126, 131, 133, 140, 148, 151, 156, 168, 178, 182, 185, 193, 196, 209, 236, 239, 245, 255
Emory University9, 21, 28, 35, 134, 136, 181, 209
Enzo60
Epcot Center in Walt Disney World53
Epsten Group,227
Evan Zucker142
Everglades114, 199

F

Fatima Ramis13, 25

Fewer species, living large204
Fish19, 66, 107, 109, 149, 153, 159, 166, 173, 199, 202, 217, 236, 252
Five dimensions of wellness45
Five Freedoms of animal welfare122
Florida Atlantic University52
Florida Institute of Technology95
Florida panther114
Ford African Rain Forest41, 167, 209
Ford Motor Company100
Forks Over Knives and The China Study170
Franklin & Marshall College36
Frans de Waal26, 32, 190
Fred King134
Fresno Chafee Zoo24
Frontiers in Psychology38, 88, 237

G
Gail Eaton82
Gary D. Mitchell7, 13
Gary Lee82, 138, 157
Genetic management84
Geoffrey Bourne30
George Rainbolt12
Georgia Aquarium109
Georgia State University30, 36, 136, 177
Georgia Institute of Technology9, 28, 33, 35, 37, 41, 84, 87, 93, 130, 136, 166, 181, 205, 208, 209, 252
Giannini Foundation77
Giant Panda Species Survival Plan85
Giraffes27, 40, 70, 186, 193, 209
Global Wellness Institute45, 56
Gordon Burghardt66
Gorilla Doctors111, 112
Gorilla Foundation36

Gorillas33, 40, 52, 61, 62, 63, 67, 91, 100, 111, 112, 133, 134, 136, 137, 138, 141, 156, 167, 172, 178, 198, 209, 213, 224, 234, 236, 240, 241, 243, 250, 253

Green Building Certification222

Greenpeace110

Gregory Kohn 34

H

Habitat encroachment137

Hagenbeck72, 189

Halbert Dunn43

Hans Kummer32

Happiness-inspired design175

Harmonious development124

Harry F. Harlow7, 13, 30, 47

Hawaiian Islands Humpback Whale National Marine Sanctuary108

Healesville Sanctuary192, 233

Hearst Grizzly Gulch exhibit19

Heather Browning87

Hediger9, 42, 93, 127, 131, 180, 189, 241

Heini Hediger9, 13, 32, 93, 127

High-Level Wellness51, 71

Hippos70, 212, 213, 214

Howard Hunt65

Humane Society International128

Humane Society of the United States110

humanistic psychology9, 46, 52

Humanistic psychology48

Humpback whale104

I

Indian gharials65

Indianapolis Zoo74, 141, 144

International Whaling Commission104, 108, 111
invasive species200

J
J. B. MacKinnon105
Jack Hanna174, 209
Jack Horner132
Jack Marr37
Jacksonville Zoo and Gardens12, 17, 21, 23,35, 37, 53, 64,91, 92, 95, 97, 99, 139, 176, 216,229,231
Jacques Cousteau86
Jakarta Zoo138
Jardim Zoológico de Brasilia187
Jason Watters20
Jay Crouse134
Jean Wineman38, 130
Jenny Gray191
Jeremy Mallinson224
Jill Mellen15
Joe Erwin8
Joe Mendelson136
John Travis 44
John B. Watson94
Jon Coe6, 13, 117, 138, 143, 156, 157, 193, 205, 231, 233
Jonathan Balcombe160
Journal of Veterinary Behavior152, 254

K
Kaiser Permanente79
Kaylin Tennant33
Ken Gould134
Kennesaw State University36, 136
Kim Bard37
Kim Denninger-Snyder,212

Kindle Direct12
Komodo National Park113
Kristen Cytacki82, 220
Kristen Lukas33

L
La Trobe University49
Lance Miller147
Leadership in Energy and Environmental Design81
LEED81, 220, 222, 223, 225, 226, 229
Lessie Smithgall, Carolyn Boyd Hatcher13
Lev Gasparov13
Levine Animal Care Complex82, 220, 223, 226
Lincoln Park Zoo15, 36, 61, 73, 117, 155, 194, 246
Lion Country Safari Parks156
Lions29, 43, 70, 120, 138, 148, 194, 204, 209, 235
Loyola University New Orleans36
Lynn College of Nursing52
Lynx122

M
Maisie57, 58, 59, 60
Manatees95, 156, 197
Mandrills39, 40, 141, 237
Maria Fernanda188
Marisa Spain34, 64
Markowitz39, 40, 75, 76, 77, 176, 236, 248
Marlin Perkins205
Martin Seligman48
Martin T. Gipson13
Mary Beth Dennon142
Megan Morris13, 24, 34
Melbourne Zoo192
Melvin and Claire Levine13, 81

Michale E. Keeling Center for Comparative Medicine and Research36
Michigan State University195
Mike Hoff135
Minnesota Zoo155
Monkeys7, 27, 43, 49, 52, 91, 103, 138, 190, 246, 248
Monterey Bay Aquarium110, 219
Morehouse College28
Mystic Aquarium119

N
National Geographic86, 235, 239
National Institute of Mental Health23
National Wellness Institute128
National Zoo39, 74, 86, 139
Nature by Design56
Nestle Company59
Nevin Lash41, 151, 157, 182, 227
New England Aquarium110
New Orleans's Loyola University142
New York Zoological Society85
New York's Bronx Zoo74
Night safaris71
Nocturnal species154
North Carolina Zoo54, 166

O
Oakland Zoo204, 212
Ohio State University College of Veterinary Medicine50
Oklahoma City Zoo36, 136
One Health125, 227
Orangutan26, 39, 102, 117, 132, 142, 143, 194, 214
Orcas16, 90, 112, 147, 156, 162, 196, 198, 217
Organized husbandry84

P

Palm Beach Zoo16, 30, 31, 52, 54, 69, 76, 81, 99, 172, 211, 220, 223
Palmetto Publishing12
Pat Conroy197
Paul Piff164
Pauleen Bennett49
PETA126, 150
Pete Choquette41, 227
Philadelphia Zoo5, 91, 140, 190
Pinnipeds119, 178, 198
Poaching103, 104, 113, 137
Polar bears149
Polk Penguin Conservation Center72
Porpoises108
Portable cognitive workstations141
Positive Psychology48, 49
Precision Behavior29
Professor in the Zoo12, 21
Psychological well-being17, 23, 55, 67, 75, 92, 118, 146, 155, 254
Pythons66, 152, 199

R

Rainforest Coffee Company228
Rebecca Snyder27
Regurgitation and reingestion62, 234, 243
Reptiles64, 65, 104, 114, 132, 136, 152, 153, 154, 173, 199
Rhinos70, 193, 197
Richard K. Davenport13, 26, 130, 141
Richard Reynolds30
Ringling Brothers Circus30
Rita McManamon171
Robert Baird77
Robert C. Petty13
Robert M. Holder209

Robert M. Sapolsky104
Robert Sommer9, 13
Robert Yerkes30
Rollo May46
Ron Forman13, 204, 205
Ron Kagan72, 127, 195
Ron Swaisgood116

S
Sacramento Zoo31
San Diego International Airport166
San Diego State College30
San Diego Zoo27, 30, 36, 86, 116, 164
San Francisco Zoo18, 19, 20, 21, 31, 46, 54, 66, 75, 76, 77, 78, 79, 95,
    97, 99, 120, 150, 173, 211, 212, 213, 245
San Francisco State University75
Santa Barbara Zoo36
Science magazine107
SeaDocs112
SeaWorld16, 90, 147, 162, 198, 219
Shedd Aquarium110
Shender, Ross63
Simon Skjodt International Orangutan Center144
Singapore Zoo36, 70, 194
Snake husbandry153
Social marketing86, 100
SSP182
St. Louis Zoo141
Stephanie Allard82, 127,128
Steven Kellert56
Sustainability180, 220, 222
Sydney Zoo193

T

Tanya Peterson76
Ted Finlay100
Thad Lacinak29
iger69, 75, 91, 132, 139
Tight Spaces9
Tom Butynski40
Tony Vecchio12, 17, 37
Trump administration110

U

U.S. Department of Agriculture87, 150
UC Berkeley School of Public Health44
UC Davis medical school77
UC Irvine164
UNF32, 33, 35, 37, 53, 64, 231
United States Navy23
University of California (UC), Davis7
University of Georgia181, 209
University of North Florida12, 33, 54
University of Oxford148
University of the Pacific21, 77
University of Utrecht190
University of Wisconsin9, 30, 47
University of Zurich9, 93
Urban Design Award209
Ursa International41, 151, 157, 227

V

Valerie Segura13, 21-23, 37
Van Hooff32, 190
Van Nostrand Reinhold143, 238, 244, 248
Venomous snakes154
Vertical space91, 144

Victor Frankl46
Virginia Zoo53, 54, 97, 99
Virtual and augmented reality technologies165
Virtual Center for Conservation and Behavior87

W
Walt Disney Company53, 83
WCS85, 86
WELL certification222, 223, 226, 227, 232
Wellness brand76, 95, 96
Wellness Resource Center44
Wellness tree91, 141
Wellness-inspired design19, 89, 91, 98, 137, 140, 156, 161, 163, 190, 203, 211, 231
Wellness-inspired exhibit153
WellPet Foundation50
Werribee Open Range Zoo192
What a Fish Knows160
Wildlands Adventure Zoo Emmen189
Wildlife Conservation Society85
William B. Hartsfield133
Willie B97, 133, 135, 136, 171, 209
Wolverines12
Woodland Park Zoo74, 131,133,242
World Organization for Animal Health15
World Wildlife Fund86
Y
Yale University30
Yerkes National Primate Research Center30,36, 134, 136

Z
Zebras104, 193
Zoo Atlanta10, 17, 22, 27, 28, 30, 36, 40, 41, 61, 65, 70, 80, 86, 93, 100, 131, 133, 136, 150, 166, 178, 181, 188, 197, 207, 208, 209, 210

*Zoo Biology*16, 20,34-35, 75, 93,143, 178
Zoos Victoria183, 191, 192
Zurich Zoo32

Made in the
USA
Columbia, SC